THE PSYCHOLOGY OF
THE LEARNING GROUP

Psychology

Editor
GEORGE WESTBY
Professor of Psychology
University College Cardiff
University of Wales

THE PSYCHOLOGY OF
THE LEARNING GROUP

John McLeish
Professor of Psychology
University of Alberta

&

Wayne Matheson
Royal Alexandra Hospital,
Edmonton, Alberta

&

James Park
Professor of Psychology
McGill University

HUTCHINSON UNIVERSITY LIBRARY
LONDON

HUTCHINSON & CO (*Publishers*) LTD
3 Fitzroy Square, London W1

London Melbourne Sydney Auckland
Wellington Johannesburg Cape Town
and agencies throughout the world

First published 1973

© John McLeish, Wayne Matheson and James Park 1973

*This book has been set in Times type, printed in Great Britain
on smooth wove paper by Anchor Press, and
bound by Wm. Brendon, both of Tiptree, Essex*

ISBN 0 09 114010 2 (cased)
0 09 114011 0 (paper)

CONTENTS

PREFACE

This book crystallises the work of many individuals who helped, and some who hindered, the attempt to discover what actually happens in small learning groups, and to relate this to a body of theoretical principles. It reports a considerable amount of research which was carried on over a number of years in various locations. This was developed as a team effort which involved a great number of collaborators, running into the hundreds, participating in the groups and discussions in a variety of roles. The senior author has normally taken the responsibility for designing a series of interrelated experimental studies centred on the outcomes of different teaching methods. These studies culminated in the definitive experiment on two kinds of learning group (structured and unstructured) reported in this book. Here they are used as a kind of peg on which to hang a number of relevant points about teaching learning groups of other kinds.

Without the financial support of the Canada Council (grant no. 570–1039) this experiment could not have been attempted. The other work on learning groups was carried out at the Cambridge Institute of Education when the senior author was Research Fellow there. We would like to acknowledge also the assistance and support of many individuals. Vena Nastajus and Emma Collins provided essential material resources, as well as psychological support, at critical points in our research. The Division of Audio-visual Services of the Faculty of Education (Andy Lamothe and Larry Le Clair) gave unstinting technical help and advice at all points. The Division of Clinical Services (Harvey Zingle) allowed us the use of their one-way screen rooms for observation of group processes. Larry Eberlein played a crucial role in our experimental work. Several other colleagues gave us their support in a number of ways, but our major debt in the theoretical field is to two people, both in their different ways 'prime movers' in their work on groups. I refer to Pierre Turquet of the Tavistock Institute of Human Relations, who encouraged the work in its earliest stages by providing opportunities for observation of his groups and an initial training in 'group dynamics'. Robert Freed Bales of the Harvard Department of Human Relations, through his writings and academic 'life-style' has been the other main source of inspiration to all of us. We hope that the former will be able to accept perhaps twenty per cent of what follows, and that the latter will agree with about eighty per cent. Lastly, we have to thank Bob Bedecki who served in many ways to facilitate the research project and also wrote the first draft of pp. 67–77 with the help of Terri Davis.

Edmonton
June 1972   J. McL.
                                                              W. M.
                                                              J. P.

GLOSSARY

CONDITIONING is a process by which an old-established response is attached to a new stimulus ('classical conditioning'—Pavlov) or by which an emitted form of behaviour, an 'operant', is associated with some reward ('operant conditioning'—Skinner). In either event, the result is that the operant, or response, will be more likely to repeat itself. This is put forward as an explanation of learned behaviour.

If the reward or 'reinforcement' is withheld over a period, the response or operant will be likely to disappear, that is, it will be 'extinguished'. It is usual for the response, in the early stages of classical conditioning, to be elicited to stimuli *similar* to the one being used in training—this is known as 'generalisation'. If the responses to these similar stimuli are not associated with the reward they will die out: in this way 'discrimination learning' takes place. If the operants are reinforced as the behaviour changes in a specific direction, and not reinforced if they diverge from this developing path, the behaviour-pattern will change in accordance with the principle of 'shaping'. In this way extremely complex patterns of behaviour can be built up, including, of course, verbal behaviour.

CYBERNETIC MECHANISMS, or 'governors', are particular devices, or processes, which monitor changes which may arise in a system initially in equilibrium. They set in motion mechanisms or processes opposing the change the function of which is to return the system to its initial 'steady state'.

DIRECT COMMUNICATIONS TRAINING is a programme of activities, usually including role-play, case studies, demonstration by an expert with 'modelling' by students, designed to develop interpersonal skills which will enable the trainees better to handle human relations problems. Robert Carkhuff has developed one such programme for training counsellors and therapists in skills such as empathic ('warm') response, respect, genuineness, self-disclosure, concreteness, confrontation, immediacy and self-exploration.

DEFENCE MECHANISMS are unconscious modes of reaction to psychological threats of one kind or another. They are said to develop from an early stage in the life of the individual and to become habitual to him. Particular over-developed responses (for example, projection, rationalisation, denial) are thought to be at the basis of particular kinds of neuroses or psychoses. But it must be stressed that the ego-defence mechanisms are associated with *normal* development, shielding the developing individual from the worst effects of growing up in a civilised, that is, human environment.

DEPENDENCE includes forms of behaviour and response characterising the individual member's feelings towards the authority and power of the leader. The individual may respond in a submissive or deferential manner to an extreme degree ('over-dependent') or he may react by various assaults on the external manifestations of power and control ('counter-dependent').

DESENSITISATION is a process of 'deconditioning' extreme types of response to certain objects, persons or situations normally of a threatening, disturbing or punishing kind. Wolpe has developed a method of desensitisation by means of 'reciprocal inhibition'. Here, a feared or wounding situation is set up, in reality or in thought, and associated with a relaxed or pleasurable state of mind. The concerned individual goes through a systematic and graduated programme of experiments through which his original response (anxiety, fear, anger, horror, etc.) is changed to a neutral or pleasurable one. The same process is at work in the spontaneous or deliberate 'hardening' processes of war, gangsterism and extermination training provided for administrators of concentration camps.

DYSFUNCTIONAL reactions or processes are forms of behaviour which subvert the normal operation of a system and change the outcome, or output, in an unexpected and unwanted manner. If they persist they will eventually disrupt and even destroy the system itself. However, in most cases the system develops particular compensatory devices or mechanisms which mitigate or even negate the worst consequences of the malfunctioning by giving rise to a new, or altered, system which retains the capacity to survive. Therefore, what is dysfunctional from one point of view may be quite functional from another. Neurotic forms of behaviour constitute a good example.

EMPATHY is the psychological process (or skill) which enables us to understand the emotion being experienced by another person. It is a matter of reflecting, and, to some extent, experiencing, whatever emotion the other person is feeling. It is not the same as *sympathy* which implies a concern for, and an expression of this concern for the other individual who is reacting to some traumatic experience. In empathic communication we may be reflecting any kind of emotion—anger, fear, hostility, pleasure, love, etc., etc.

EQUILIBRIUM HYPOTHESIS, as appertaining to social groups, states that there is a condition of homeostatic balance which is established as a precondition of the continuance of the group. Change is the result of some disturbance of this balance, the disturbance creating a tension which calls into play certain built-in mechanisms (see CYBERNETIC MECHANISMS) which act to correct the imbalance and to restore the group to its normal condition of equilibrium. Thus, the theory does not hold that change is impossible or undesirable: it merely seeks to discover how it takes place. The normal condition posited by the theory is that of an *unstable* equilibrium. Social groups are thus conceptualised as 'steady-state systems'.

FUNCTION implies that any aggregation of matter, be it an atom, an amoeba, a mammal, or a social group, has some kind of organisation ('structure') by which it is adapted to the surrounding environment on which it operates in reciprocal interaction. The actual change produced in the relations of matter and forces in the environment, conceived of as some *integral* product or outcome of this section of organised matter and capable of being defined, is the function. Stating this otherwise, function is the relationship between an organised or structured portion of reality, recognised as having some kind of unitary quality, and the surrounding environment.

GROUPS consist of a relatively small number of subjects, normally about twelve, who come together on a regular basis with some kind of task, implicit or explicit, in mind. It is a basic assumption of this book that there are certain fundamental constraints which function to limit the behaviour of the subjects in these groups. Indeed, the purpose of research on groups is to attempt to discover the nature of these constraints and the various ways in which they operate. This is the area sometimes called 'group dynamics', implying that there are causal processes which generate particular kinds of behavioural outcomes.

PHASE MOVEMENT in groups is the appearance of qualitatively different activities within a total continuous period of interaction. These phases are believed to be generated by virtue of the fact that the groups necessarily confront certain kinds of problem which arise *seriatim*. For example, most authorities recognise that the group alternates between 'task-confronting behaviour' and behaviour in the 'expressive, social–emotional' area. Bales believes that the group moves in *'nested'* phases in which successive paired categories of behaviour achieve prominence in the group in a pre-determined order, from the middle of his category system out towards the extremities. Another explanation of phase movements takes them to be *'repetitive'*, that is, the group returns again and again to the same kind of activities. Still another theory attributes a *'circular'* movement to the dynamic process in the group, that is, the group returns to its original starting point. Bales has developed still another explanation of task-oriented groups, that they move in a pre-determined fashion from a fixed point in three-dimensional, social–psychological space as they attempt to solve the various problems of *'communication'*, *'evaluation'*, *'control'*, *'tension reduction'*, *'reintegration'*. This is his overall phase movement hypothesis.

ROLE-DIFFERENTIATION is a theory that the individual in a group situation makes his contribution to the interaction in one of a number of socially acceptable, learned and recognisable behaviour-patterns which shapes his contribution. These roles are assumed and cast aside through the reception and de-coding of cues which are sent out, and received, largely unawares by the group members. Two basic leadership roles, for example, which seem to be essential for the continuing functioning of the group, are those of the *'affective'* leader whose concern is primarily with promoting the social–emotional interaction of the group participants and the *'instrumental'* leader whose basic function is to promote the effective work of the group in relation to its assigned or accepted task. As the group develops, the various phases produce certain specific and relatively stereotyped patterns (another word for which is 'roles'). These signal to the group that the individual assuming a particular role will 'tackle' the current problem on the basis of some integrated set of basic assumptions and procedures which belong to the role—for example, by joking, by an excessive display of emotion, by an appearance of thoughtfulness, by confronting individuals, or by some other method. These roles are developed out of the two initial and essential leadership roles.

SENSITIVITY TRAINING, so called, is the attempt by various exercises to develop the ability to understand, to react in an accepting manner, and to help a particular individual who has, or claims to have, 'a problem' in the area of interpersonal relations. There are very numerous varieties of group training which claim to do this for trainees: there is little available evidence, apart from personal declarations by interested parties, that the training 'works'.

SET, or anticipatory set, is an attitude of selective attention or direction taken towards a particular object, situation, or problem which pre-sensitises the individual to perceive, to feel an emotional response, and to act in a specific manner towards the source of stimulation. It is a matter of developing certain expectations of the object, situation, or problem which may or may not be based on the objective reality.

A SYSTEM is an organised whole made up of particular parts or elements which interact on the basis of definite relations to each other and to the organisation of these as a whole. Systems may be *'open'*, in which case they accept inputs from an external source; they deliver outputs to the surrounding environment. Or they may be 'closed' systems, which are independent and self-sufficient. Nature, human personality, society are examples of open systems. Systems may also be expanding, contracting or steady-state in character. As regards the social system, a noticeable characteristic is that it is subject to change: this is thought to take place according to certain laws or rules.

TAVISTOCK METHOD is a form of group psychoanalysis where the behaviour generated in the group is interpreted by the 'trainer' in terms of the myth of the 'primal horde', Oedipal conflicts and Freudian constructs in general. The latent content of behaviour should become clear to the participants as a result of the insights gained into their *own* emotional response to the trainer and his interpretations. There are two similar techniques, one consisting of a training in group dynamics intended for those professionally occupied with people (teachers, managers, psychiatric workers, etc.); the other consisting of therapy offered to behavioural deviants of one kind or another—delinquents, neurotics, homosexuals, etc.

VICARIOUS LEARNING is a process by which an individual (or organism) is placed in a learning situation involving some other individual (or organism) who is rewarded for performance. Although the subject has not received any practice in the skill or performance of the act, nor any reward for success, the behaviour of the individual changes in the desired behaviour. If this happens, we have a case of vicarious learning.

For items starred, but not defined in Glossary, consult the Index to find the page on which the term is introduced.

INTRODUCTION: THE SCOPE OF THE PROBLEM

Psychologists and psychiatrists, sociologists and other workers in the domain of behavioural science are increasingly concerning themselves with the phenomena of *group dynamics. Courses on 'human relations training' proliferate. As scientists we have an obligation to examine the dynamics and processes involved in such groups. This cannot be said of all those involved in 'human relations training', 'group dynamics' or 'sensitivity training'. Traditionally, in the fields of psychotherapy there is a strong disinclination to seek to uncover the therapeutic effectiveness of treatment. In discussing the functions of groups we will attempt to elicit the helping or maturational effects of membership in such groups, if such there be.

More recently, many educators have come to see 'the group' as a potentially powerful new medium for learning when viewed as a largely self-teaching unit, especially for learning about human relationships. Certain kinds of group experience might have valuable transfer value for teachers, and students. In each instance we care to look at, however, the burgeoning interest is expressed in an increasingly vague and inchoate demand for 'sensitivity training', 'encounter groups', 'T-groups', 'group dynamics', or 'human relations training'. Practice has outrun not only theory but outcome research and validation as well. The majority of practitioners who seek to satisfy the demand seem oblivious of the need to discover what actually happens in groups. They blindly leap on the 'bandwagon' in case they are left behind, in an alleged morass of 'inhuman', 'impersonal' and 'insensitive' scientific procedures. They 'know' intuitively that the method works—or at least that 'it is doing some good'. As a consequence, they become increasingly averse to understanding,

* Starred items are defined in the Glossary, p. 9.

through research, what is happening in this area: vested interests develop—the research worker might end by taking the bread and butter (or is it caviar and pheasant?) out of their children's mouths. 'Sensitivity training' appeals to them intuitively as a self-evidently 'humane' approach to the understanding of behaviour, to changing 'people'—psychology allegedly basing its learning theory on 'manipulation' of rats.

Certainly, to many people, it is more interesting than learning from books and lectures about these things. There is a historical parallel between the proliferation of groups these days and the phrenological 'movement', and more recently with the 'existentialist–psychoanalytic movement'. There is a strong, unsatisfied need to discover something about human behaviour, some intuitively divined 'magic' that 'works'. This book poses two simple questions: (i) 'Do groups work, and (ii) if so, how?' Some consequential questions are: What really goes on in groups? What exactly do members learn by participating in them? Are groups of general value as a teaching method? What are the preconditions of their use in an educational setting?

These are the questions which are examined in this book, the product of several years of experimentation, critical observation and experience in small groups varied in size, in composition, and in their assigned task. Several methods of analysis are described which can be used as an aid to understanding the forces, patterns and processes which operate.

Experience has taught us that there is, in fact, little knowledge based on experimental evidence on human behaviour in small group settings; there is much speculation indeed, hunches, assertion and dogmatism but a dearth of hard fact. At best, the present state of 'group psychology' must be described as primitive. We are encouraged, however, by the work of several twentieth-century authors (e.g. Freud, Bion, Bales) whose theories and techniques provide a basis for increasing our understanding in this field. Skinner, while not actually working with groups, has developed concepts which seem also to be relevant and applicable. Working more and more in the classroom settings and other applied fields his disciples have developed theoretical and practical resources which seem powerfully applicable in human affairs outside the laboratory.

WHAT HAPPENS? THE RAW DATA OF GROUP PROCESSES

Consider the following excerpt from the transcript of a group discussion. It is drawn from the fifth session of a *self-analytic group.

The group was composed of twelve members and the trainer (J. McL.).

Fred Bob and Carol and Ted and Alice.

Ann What was that again? Did you see it?

Cecil Why?

Ann I don't know, I found it very amusing.

Fred Do you know Paul Field? . . . everybody in the theatre was quiet . . .

Ann I noticed that too.

Fred . . . except Paul and myself. We laughed so much we got everybody thoroughly embarrassed around us. I thought it was so funny, especially the sensitivity sessions.

Ann I really identified the first time with the table. I've gone through that.

Ellen Say something. It's a sign of tension.

Cecil How I've learned to relax in love groups . . .

Fred Learning to live in a non-structured environment and sort of have anything.

Cecil I think the first four sessions, whether they've been meant to result in that, I think they have been.

Fred No, no, but so far that's been the act.

Cecil I'm kind of curious to know if anybody has written anything meaningful in the diary, anything that could help the group. The reason I say this is whenever I attempt to write something, I usually come up with two things and two things only. I can say them about ninety-seven different ways, in shades of mood actually. The two things are—what do we want to do, what is a group like this capable of doing without work, and what do I do?

Bill Yes, that's right, basically the same kind of questions that's true. I don't think I've written anything important or momentous about interaction.

Cecil Okay, is it because there's an inhibiting influence, is it because we are by nature non-curious, or not creative, or sort of *laissez-faire*?

Ann It's certainly not being facilitated . . .

Cecil Okay, then my question is what do you do about it, and not being able to facilitate something, whatever it is. As I tried to frame the question today, I said: what can a group like this be used for? What can we do, what can come out? Have we given up an hour a week in bondage or, you know, as a contribution to charity?

Bill Perhaps you've hit the nail on the head.

Cecil Here we are. In that sense, we're prisoners.

Bill That's almost like line for line from a play. It sounds so corny to me. So it's just . . .

Dr McLeish The group is saying it is not prepared to learn anything
it doesn't already know, and on its own terms.
Cecil Well, that's killed *that* subject!

A naive observer might be content to believe that the members of
this group were simply engaging in 'social conversation', or chit-
chat. The disjointed character of ordinary speech will, no doubt,
come as a revelation to such a person. Of course, there may be some
danger involved in assuming that anything more than social chit-chat
is taking place. Perhaps the participants were fully aware of the
meanings which could be attached to their remarks. Having observed
such groups for some hundreds of hours, seeking to make sense of
what happens repeatedly, the 'social chit-chat' interpretation comes
over as somewhat shallow. In the light of experience, it seems more
likely that group members act according to definite rules of behaviour, of most of which they were not consciously aware. The presence
and the nature of the fantasy statements, various covert sexual
gestures and overtures, unconscious and conscious messages to certain members (the trainer in particular), the degree of anxiety
expressed, the 'shaping' of the behaviour of certain members by the
group, quasi-neurotic and psychotic modes of thinking—these can
all be noted in the transcripts of small learning groups over a period
of time. A familiarity with the works of Freud, Bion, Skinner, Bales
and other key psychologists is particularly helpful in attempts to
clarify whatever rules, themes, and patterns of behaviour prevail, and
which often block any movement towards the solution of the group
task. A review of basic contributions considered to be fundamental
to understanding groups in action is included later.

As psychologists, working in an educational setting, it has become
an engrossing task to attempt to establish whether and to what
degree unspoken and often unconscious rules govern group interaction; what conditions govern the development of group activities
such as fantasy 'flights'; what conflicts arise to prevent or partially
block learning in small groups. In an effort to obtain definitive
answers to these questions, a systematic analysis of human relations
groups was undertaken. As a result, we now have serious reservations
about the claims made for certain kinds of groups which pass themselves off under the heading of 'human relations training', but which
are more akin to communal emotional baths. We intend to consider
certain specific kinds of groups in depth (and certain other kinds
more superficially). The groups which have been chosen for study are
those where it is claimed an understanding of human behaviour is
learned, where a clearly defined technique is followed and which

would be acceptable as a learning group in even a conservative educational institution without questions being raised about the moral issues which might be involved.

These include groups based on a modified *Tavistock model (Bion, 1961), *case-study groups, and *direct communication groups (Carkhuff, 1969). The members of these groups receive a combination of didactic and experiential training in various kinds of communication skills. Most of the groups are composed either of postgraduate or undergraduate student-teachers and trainee counsellors. Two groups consisted of psychiatric nurses. The size of the groups studied ranged between nine and fourteen members; the normal size was twelve. As it was our intention to develop first-hand knowledge of group behaviour through systematic study, a definitive investigation was launched where the groups were conducted in a suitably sized room equipped with audio- and video-recorders and a *one-way screen. In general, the group sessions lasted an hour and were offered once a week over a period of ten weeks. One of the authors acted as 'trainer' whilst the other two observed, usually in company with groups of students.

We recognised, of course, that the one-way screen might interfere with group interaction. The presence of unseen observers would also affect group processes, or so it would appear. But in addition to a need to observe first-hand, there were at least two other reasons in favour of using an observation room provided with essential facilities. Firstly, it enabled 'live' scoring of the ongoing behaviour of the groups, using Bales', Flanders' and Mann's systems of interaction analysis. The use of Bales' techniques was found to be particularly fruitful. The use of his analytical categories sharpened our awareness of group coalitions and of the movements of the various camps which formed during the group sessions. Secondly, it seemed to be of considerable value to follow his procedure of allowing two or three group participants the opportunity in particular sessions of observing the rest of the group interact in their absence. Indeed, we came to believe that there may be more value in learning about group dynamics by *observing* a group instead of participating in it as a member. With that 'hunch' in mind, we altered our original research plan to include an evaluation of the effects of observing human relations groups over an extended period of time as compared with actually participating in these groups.

The results of the several hundred hours of our observation of learning groups are outlined later. At this point it is perhaps best to explain why it is necessary to devote so much effort to the study of small groups.

THE PRESENT VOGUE OF GROUP METHODS

In recent years there has been a marked increase in the use of various types of small group activities to develop human relations skills, interpersonal competence and so on (Schein and Bennis, 1965). Typically, such groups involve ten to fifteen people in a 'face-to-face' setting: The amount of structure provided seems to vary, depending upon the trainer and the objectives involved. We would suggest the following classification descriptive of the various types of different kinds of teaching methods in common use (see Figure 1).

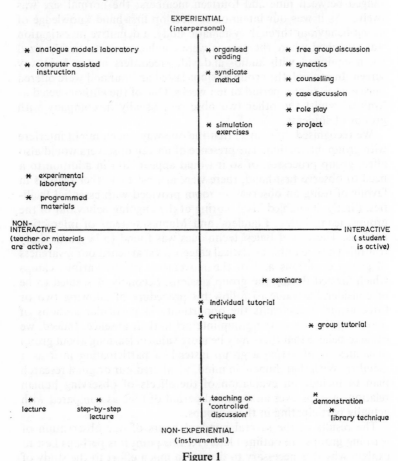

EXPERIENTIAL
(interpersonal)

* analogue models laboratory

* computer assisted
  instruction

* organised
  reading

* syndicate
  method

* simulation
  exercises

* free group discussion

* synectics

* counselling

* case discussion

* role play

* project

* experimental
  laboratory

* programmed
  materials

NON-
INTERACTIVE ───────────────────────────────────── INTERACTIVE
(teacher or materials   (student
are active)   is active)

* seminars

* individual tutorial

* critique

* group tutorial

* lecture   * step-by-step
             lecture

* teaching or
  'controlled
  discussion'

* demonstration

* library technique

NON-EXPERIENTIAL
(instrumental)

Figure 1

A classification of learning groups (McLeish)

It will be observed that group methods tend to be in an antipodal relation to the lecture method—this indeed is one reason for their popularity with certain kinds of student who prefer methods high in the interactive and experiential dimensions. This same enthusiasm has been shown by psychologists, therapists, and educators for groups which favour 'maximal' involvement of the learner. Included in this category are a bewildering variety of supposed 'growth' groups which proceed under a myriad of titles—encounter groups, self-directed groups, sensitivity groups, workshop, marathon, T-groups, and so on. Other more direct methods of developing inter-personal competence, such as the case-study method, which have a 'tighter' structure and which usually give group members less freedom 'to play around', seem to have declined in popularity in comparison with the affectivity-oriented group.

The question remains: Why are human relation groups gaining in popularity? Why is it that in some quarters group experience has achieved a quasi-religious status? Several explanations have been given for the sudden spread of interest in such groups. Some psycho-logists point to the increase in technology and urbanisation which allegedly creates a 'philosophical neurosis' in many individuals (Schofield, 1964). This is supposed to show itself in a feeling of a lack of any 'real meaning' in life. People complain of a feeling of hollow-ness, an unsatisfied need to relate to others; a need to share inner feelings with others and to be accepted by them. There is no doubt that groups satisfy such expressed needs as there is no doubt that they increasingly generate the expression of such needs. Another explanation of the increase in group activities is that they permit members to engage in forms of behaviour which are socially un-acceptable in other settings. For instance, some trainers not only allow, but encourage, members to do whatever they feel like doing. This may lead to grown men crying in public, hugging and petting involving couples of different marriages, and so on. Undoubtedly, some groups are primarily dominated by the urge many people have for socially approved public sexuality. Therapists and educators, of course, present these reasons in slightly different ways.

It is true that groups for discussion of personal problems have made therapeutic help available to clients who otherwise would be unable to obtain such services. The man-in-the-street now has access to 'therapy' which some years ago was available only to the wealthy: the 'group' is a substitute for the prohibitively expensive individual psychoanalysis. Experimental groups exemplify an aspect of the democratisation of conspicuous consumption so characteristic of our times. Some educators are convinced that human relations groups provide an economical, as well as an experiential means of developing the communications skills of administrators, business managers and teachers-in-training.

However, it is crystal-clear that the greatest impetus behind the enormous proliferation of groups are the promises made by their sponsors. For example, an advertisement from a centre which supposedly focuses on the study of human interaction and potential promised the following experiences:

LIFE SPACE WORKSHOPS
The focus of these weekend workshops will be primarily upon exploring intrapersonal and interpersonal alienation by utilising encounter experience, gestalt, fantasy, and sensory exploration.

COUPLES WORKSHOPS
Participating couples will be invited to become aware of the significance of issues in their relationships relating to manipulation and control, dependency, expectation, confrontation, trust and intimacy. The workshops will focus upon the 'fight styles' and patterns of interaction used in dealing with these issues.

INTERCULTURAL ENCOUNTER WORKSHOPS
In these workshops, participants will be able to explore cultural differences and examine their interpersonal impact. The workshop is to be seen as a search for ways and means of alleviating alienation. These workshops will be arranged in response to specific requests by interested persons and groups.

SPECIAL WORKSHOPS

PERSONAL GROWTH
A five-day residential laboratory experience involving the use of gestalt, fantasy and other encounter group methods to facilitate personal growth and human understanding. In addition, the residential experience allows the establishment of a unique community in which participants can explore their own creative human potential.

Other group experts have made similar promises. In their comprehensive review of the effectiveness of *T-groups, Campbell and Dunnette (1968) listed the following outcomes commonly claimed by advocates:

(1) Increased self-insight or self-awareness concerning one's own behaviour and its meaning in a social context . . .
(2) Increased sensitivity to the behaviour of others . . .

(3) Increased awareness and understanding of the types of group functioning and the interactions between different groups . . .

(4) Heightened diagnostic skill in social, interpersonal, and inter-group situations . . .

(5) Increased action skill . . .

(6) Learning how to learn . . .

An interesting variety of outcomes, indeed! It is little wonder that innovators in education think of incorporating human relations group training into their curricula. The sceptical research worker must, of course, doubt the promises made by the academic as much as by the commercial sponsors of groups. Is there any evidence that groups do really alleviate alienation and increase sensitivity to others? Or are we witnessing a simple illustration of the law of demand, where one section of society expresses a need and a body of self-styled experts proceeds to nominate itself as competent to satisfy this need?

The answer must be that there is very limited evidence that group training actually induces the behavioural changes suggested by its adherents (Egan, 1970). Golembiewski (1970) found few studies which suggested that transfer of learnings from groups to other settings took place. Many other evaluative studies draw a similar blank.

Our interest in group research is founded on an initial scepticism of the value of groups. We begin from the null hypothesis and the legal dictum: 'He who asserts, must prove.' After reviewing the literature on groups, we conclude that practice and promotion have out-distanced understanding. As a result, practitioners govern their activities by faith in what they are doing. If one asks why group activities work, or what conditions must prevail to ensure that certain outcomes will occur, it is likely that any answer forthcoming will be based on ideology, mythology or a certain kind of religious faith in groups.

Commonly, attempts to separate myth from reality are met with resistance. We are told that we must accept the testimony of group advocates as gospel for, we are told, there are no valid criteria for evaluating groups anyway. The net result of the mythology of the group movement has been to polarise educators: for or against. Those who favour group training are not very explicit about the 'whats' and the 'whys' of their activities. On the other hand, those who doubt the value of group training either do not want to investigate the phenomenon for fear of dabbling in the unknown; many are put off by over-zealous 'groupies'. A sober evaluation of group activities, applying standard research techniques, seems to be called for.

SMALL GROUPS IN EDUCATIONAL CONTEXT

Advocates of sensitivity training, sometimes described as human relations training, are pretty well unanimous that all participants increase in self-understanding as a result of being in a sensitivity group. This understanding is supposed to develop primarily on the basis of constructive 'feedback' from others in the group. It is claimed that there is a kind of *cybernetic 'governor' effect. A person who interacts gives out information about himself to the group. Members interpret and comment on this. In this way the participant receives 'feedback' on his characteristic ways of interacting. Free comment is normally one of the basic rules of group membership. As a result of this feedback, it is presumed that the behaviour of the group member will alter. He is free to accept or reject the information given by other participants and adapt his future behaviour accordingly. Whether his behaviour actually does change or not, he is still exposed to information. This is information about himself that he will not normally get in such a concentrated form. As a result of this continual process, behaviour followed by immediate feedback, the group member should come to understand more about the discrepancy between his own view of his performance with other people, and the views of other group members.

Within an educational institution, there is little opportunity for this cybernetic process of performance and feedback in relation to personal style of communication. The feedback an individual normally receives in this setting relates *only* to his intellectual performance, or to a particular skill. But this is just one aspect, perhaps a minor aspect of an overall, personal performance. Education is often directed to the head instead of to the whole person. Education frequently has little experiential emphasis. The learning environment is often deliberately structured; more often, unawares, the teacher's procedures act to minimise participation and the open expression of negative feeling. The provision of a certain amount of feedback on other aspects of behaviour besides intellectual performance seems an acceptable and desirable improvement in educational emphasis. The small group situation, if used in an educational sphere could be the vehicle for such feedback. This is the rationale for adopting 'group' methods.

Another commonly accepted objective of human relations training is that those who have undergone group training become more sensitive to others, as well as to their own behaviour. As a result of engaging in this cybernetic behaviour–feedback process, and of learning something about their own behaviour, the individual also becomes part of the feedback process directed towards other participants. The group member provides his own interpretation of the impact the behaviour of others is having on him. He is able to compare the different behaviours he can observe around him as well as their positive and negative effects. Supposedly, he comes to understand more clearly, with the help of other participants and a qualified trainer, the behavioural 'cues' that are available. He notices nonverbal behaviour as well as verbal: he learns to discriminate these cues in terms of their impact on him, and on other members.

As an extension of these learnings, the group participant is encouraged to become aware of the group processes themselves. In this way the participant is asked to escape temporarily from the member-to-member interaction so as to be free to examine the overall dynamics of the group process. For example, the member can focus on the power relationships existing between the trainer and other members. He can follow the progress of the various cliques which are established over the life of the group. He can review the themes and myths that develop. He can seek to identify the various phases the group has successfully passed through, where it became fixed, and so on. This is a cognitive exercise, different from the previous types of learning the group participant is invited to engage in. Rather than be engrossed in affective interaction with other important group members, the participant must 'cool' it a little, so as to return to a more focused exercise designed to improve the 'quality of his cognition' rather than the 'clarity of his identity' (Hampden-Turner, 1970). This type of cognitive exercise should have considerable appeal in an educational framework. It would be relatively easy to justify workshops designed around understanding the overall group dynamics. This is but one step removed from the very involving interpersonal interactions, which result in characteristic emotional upheavals which occur frequently in human relations groups. The educator would feel much more at home in operating groups with goals such as these in place of 'sensitivity training'. But the question remains: Do people *really* learn? Do they really *change*?

The long-term value to the educator of orienting his group-work around such goals as understanding group processes, is that group members are encouraged to develop skills closely related to important educational aims. The members of groups with these objectives would learn diagnostic skills, and be provided with a repertoire of helpful concepts. These skills and concepts could then be put to work in classroom situations to facilitate group functioning to maximise intended instructional outcomes. The members of groups oriented towards understanding the dynamics of group process would then carry away with them some valuable learnings which had direct applicability to future learning situations. It is not easy to see how the learnings about oneself resulting from sensitivity training can be transferred so readily. It is indeed possible that the individual continues to *behave* stupidly, but with insight into his stupidity! Admittedly, it is important to engage in this kind of interpersonal learning. But from an educational standpoint it could be considered more advantageous to engage in cognitive, as well as highly affective exercises.

From the educator's point of view, perhaps the most meaningful goal outlined by the advocates of *sensitivity training is that of 'learning how to learn' (Campbell and Dunnette, 1968). This has been described by Schein and Bennis (1965) as

. . . the development of concepts and theoretical insights which will serve as tools in linking personal values, goals, and intentions to actions consistent with these inner factors and with the requirements of the situation. (p. 17)

This involves the integration of interpersonal learning and process learning. The members must be concerned with applying what they have learned about themselves and about others, as well as what they have learned about groups. They must be able to take what they have learned from these interpersonal and process aspects and *apply it to a new situation*. This implies that whatever has been learned by the members of the group must be capable of being transferred to a new situation. The participant must be able to leave the old group experience with new knowledge about himself, or certain new skills, which he can then apply outside the old group setting in such a way as to improve his social performance. Little evidence exists that such transfer of learning occurs.

I

THE PRESENT APPROACHES TO
SMALL GROUP RESEARCH

The most important shift in emphasis in the studies made on small groups in the past ten years is from a preoccupation with the effect of groups on individual participants to a concern with the effects that individuals have on the group. The emphasis in group-work has moved from experiments where attitude and ability measures were taken before and after the experience to discover group changes and learning, if this happened, to the use of measures which were concerned with the 'here and now' experiences of the group members. This meant that the focus of research became the internal dynamics and internal composition of the group.

This change in the approach to groups is the result of questions which must be posed increasingly sharply in view of theoretical differences that exist: 'what *is* the reality of the group experience; how do the participants actually behave; what do they learn?' Answers to these questions depend in large part on where you received your initial orientation and training. A number of 'schools' exist in group psychology: these attempt to provide their own explanation of the processes involved. Each 'school' has its own particular and distinctive emphasis; each has considerable support within that area of psychology which is concerned with therapy. But these different schools do not value research and analysis of process equally, nor do they equally understand the need for validation. Some schools are more research-oriented than others. Some are concerned more with the application of their principles for the benefit of clients or trainees. Their attitude is that it is better to do something which looks good, lacking full understanding of its effects, than to do nothing until we are sure of what we are doing.

The three most influential 'schools' in small group research are the psychoanalytic, behaviouristic and interactionist. If we consider each of these theoretical systems in turn, expanding on the distinctions and differences between them, we obtain a clear picture of the current state of the most important small group research and where it has its present applications.

<h3 style="text-align:center">PSYCHOANALYTIC SCHOOL—RATIONALE</h3>

Using the principles derived from the writings of Sigmund Freud, the psychoanalytic school places a great deal of emphasis on the influence of unconscious mechanisms in the functioning of the individual. The individual personality is basically complete after the first few years of life. During these early years the influence of parents and family is crucial. There is a process similar to 'imprinting' by which critical learnings take place. The remainder of future behaviour is the resultant of a relatively closed system of libidinal (psychic) forces which act to conserve energy, to preserve the system and to maintain it in equilibrium. The state of equilibrium in the personality system is maintained basically by means of certain transformations of libido produced by inbuilt psychic mechanisms. Thus symbolic language is a means through which sexual and aggressive impulses are expressed by being cathected (attached) to socially acceptable stimuli. In later life there is a transference of feelings which are learned in early life to other significant individuals. Fantasy, which represents the attempt to deny certain aspects of present social reality, is the other predominant method (defence mechanism) through which the individual discharges his socially unacceptable impulses. These are all unconscious processes which go on without awareness or reflection. Through *insight* the individual may become aware of his defensive mechanisms. Insight is arrived at with the help of an extremely knowledgeable individual (the trainer or therapist) who uses the techniques of free association and interpretation to understand each individual's defensive structure as well as the defences erected by the group against reality. With insight the individual and the group can begin to cope with the irrational impulses and so behave more rationally in future situations. This insight can be arrived at either through individual psychoanalysis, or in group sessions, with the assistance of the therapist or trainer.

Among the analytically-oriented group workers special mention should be made of the Tavistock Institute of Human Relations and the Tavistock Clinic. Here the group psychoanalytic approach, invented by Bion, continues to receive attention and generates some research. Among the early practitioners are, in addition to Bion, Foulkes and Anthony. Foulkes and Anthony (1957) explain their method as dealing with the group as though it were a super-individual, and adapting the classical psychoanalytic techniques and interpretations to the group so conceptualised. The analyst, or trainer, confines himself to the transference phenomenon as it presents itself in the here-and-now. The therapist is not a participant in any usual sense of the word, but remains passive; his role is that of non-directive and non-interactant observer (except when offering an interpretation of the present state of group to the group-as-a-whole). Otherwise stated, the trainer or therapist becomes a blank screen upon which are projected the authority images of the participants. The essential difference between individual and group analysis lies in the greater variety of interpretations in the group situation. The basic principles of group analysis are closely allied to the methodology of individual psychoanalysis. The characteristics of the therapist's group interpretations consist of: (1) breaking down the latent symbolic unconscious messages of the participants, (2) discovering, and (3) interpreting the mechanisms of defence being used by the individuals in their interaction with other members, (4) allowing the participants to grapple with his assigned role of transference figure, and (5) allowing this engagement to become a focus of concern and analysis in the same way as any other material emerging in the group session might be. These symbols, defences and transference relationships are translated in the best way possible, being offered to the participants as 'insights' in a neutral way and as close to their occurrence as possible. Thus the participant can, according to Foulkes and Anthony (1957),

. . . freely voice his innermost thoughts towards himself, towards any other person, and towards the analyst. He can be confident that he is not being judged, and that he is fully accepted, whatever he may be or whatever he may disclose. . . . Further, by the particular attitude and role which the psychoanalyst takes up, the analysis of the all important transference situation is made possible. (p. 40)

A considerable amount of research is published on the Tavistock method. This is made available through the *Human Relations Journal* and the *International Journal of Group Psychotherapy*. A modified version of the Tavistock method, adapted to an educational rather than a therapeutic milieu, has been in use for a number of years at the University of Alberta.

Heavily influenced by Freud, Bion (1961), who devised the psychoanalytic technique of group therapy, emphasises the existence of unconscious forces which dominate the life of groups. Using the model provided by Freud in *Group Psychology and the Analysis of the Ego*, the small group is regarded as an analogue of the family which in turn is related to such institutions as the church and the army. The overwhelming influence of the authoritarian leader in church or army is identified with that of the trainer or leader in the small group. One of the major concerns of the members of the small group is to overcome their difficulties with this leader or trainer who, according to Freud's theory, represents childhood authority figures, reviving images of past control and resurrecting infantile attitudes to such images. In the church, or in the army—as in the family—repressive and disciplinary controls are provided and maintained to keep members in line, to prevent any disobedience to authority. In the small group the participant is given the opportunity freely to act out his feelings and attitudes towards authority.

These activities are not discouraged, nor are they specially encouraged. But eventually, sooner rather than later, they become the focus of concern. Thus the members of the group respond to the trainer's leadership in fixed and stereotyped ways. These represent the techniques they have learned for coping with authority. The whole group adopts a characteristic 'culture' which enables it to function. That is to say, implicit approval is given to particular members of the group to deal with the issue of authority in a certain fashion which has become habitual with them. Individuals act on behalf of the group up to the point when the group withdraws its mandate from them. Bion (1948) must be credited with first expressing the theme of 'basic assumptions' as exemplifying these very cultures which groups characteristically adopt. The culture of the group is a sort of group mentality. The group, represented for the moment by a particular individual's overwhelming concern with authority, is caught up in a vortex of fantasy which expresses unconscious and symbolic associations and impulses. These 'basic assumptions' take such forms as dependency, fight-flight and pairing, depending on the stage the group has reached. Individuals adopt corresponding conflicted or unconflicted postures with respect to the prevailing mentality of the group as it is caught up in one or other of these 'cultures'.

Redl (1942) in his essay 'Group emotion and leadership' examined this aspect of leadership as representing images of parental or early authoritarian control. He used the classroom situation to provide examples of different teacher personalities. These specific teacher personalities provided the pupils with different 'identifications' with authority. In each instance the result of a distinct, although different, identification with these teachers provided opportunity for a different 'culture' to occur in the classroom. Although Redl did not use the term 'culture' there is a remarkable similarity between the theoretical positions of Bion and Redl. Redl provides a portrait of various kinds of what he calls 'conflicted' individuals and their characteristic behaviour when seeking to deal with their different pictures of authority. The conflicted individual is the pupil who has difficulty coping with the unconscious images and emotions which are stirred up by a particular teacher. The pupil reacts, not in terms of the reality of the teacher in the here-and-now, but rather to significant other individuals in the pupil's past experience. There is an overt acting out by the pupil which reflects his basic needs. Maybe it is a need for attention, or for affection, or an urge to be aggressive. What-ever the basic need may be it finds expression when this particular teacher model is provided. Others in the class who can deal success-fully with their emotions, but who may have residual desires or urges with respect to this teacher, give approval to the conflicted pupil to act out, as their representative, his conflicted desires. In this way a classroom 'culture' is established. Redl describes it as 'the influence the unconflicted exercises on the conflicted personality in the group'.

Research workers who have taken up the psychoanalytic model presented by Freud, Bion and Redl, tend to develop explanatory models of group dynamics which are variations on a single theme. This is to the effect that groups go through discernible *phases* in their lifetime; these phases can be recognised from the various roles which are adopted by members at different stages of the life of the group. These roles may aid or hinder the group in achieving its assigned task. There is a kind of group growth towards maturity, similar to individual development.

With respect to the so-called *self-analytic group, Dunphy (1964) suggests that the roles played by members and the phases of the group are synonymous. Indeed, he claims that the phases are simply periods of time when apparently rational 'role-specialists' enunciate and work through certain pre-established fantasies or myths about the trainer. As the emotional state of the group changes, so does the image of authority. These changes are reflected in the phase move-ments of the group. Other research workers, using the self-analytic or some other group technique, provide different explanations for what seem to be similar phenomena to those described by Dunphy. Bennis and Shephard (1956), for example, cite the major concerns of groups as being the problem of dealing with *authority* and the prob-lem of *intimacy*. A series of phases is generated by the attempts which the group makes to overcome these two hurdles. Various 'role-specialists' are again located within the group. They are useful to the group since they force it towards the resolution of certain focal conflicts. For example, in an initial phase of dependence, that individual who has the greatest need for structure, guidance and dependency, volunteers (unconsciously), and is at the same time 'chosen' (unconsciously) by the group, to present the desires of the dependent faction. He, or she, 'satisfies their needs'. The group relinquishes its hold on this most dependent individual only when the members have exhausted their dependency stratagems, or when other conflicts overcome or suppress the dependency needs. They then choose someone else to represent the emergent need as the group tackles the next phase. All the time, the group continues to move within these two focal concerns of authority and intimacy. It is an essential presupposition of this theory that the group itself remains totally unaware of these dynamics.

In a fashion similar to Bion and Redl, Bennis and Shephard (1956) also describe individuals as 'conflicted' because they cannot handle the anxiety and frustration of disappointed needs by themselves. In our view, other members give them their 'vote' to confront the authority figure—they are at once 'drafted' by the group and at the same time 'volunteer' for the job. The position adopted by Bennis and Shephard is that it is the unconflicted members who are *really* responsible for moving the group along. They remain inactive in the background, 'grey eminences'. This view corresponds, to some extent, with the earlier principles outlined by Redl. As we have seen, he speaks of the 'influence of the unconflicted on the conflicted personality'.

Bennis and Shephard elaborate on these earlier conceptions of group development provided by Freud, Bion and Redl. They provide a more elaborate description of the subgroups or factions which appear within the total 'basic assumption' cultures. These factions or subgroups take up their position on a two-dimensional continuum of authority and intimacy, as shown in the diagram (Figure 2).

The important subgroups may be 'conflicted' on the issue of authority and exist as *over-dependent (A) or *counter-dependent (B) individuals or cliques. Over-dependence is an infantile attachment to the 'leader'; counter-dependence is an infantile, aggressive rejection of him. Alternatively or as well, they may be conflicted on the issue of intimacy and behave in the group as *over-personal(C) or *counter-personal (D) individuals, or cliques. They may operate as unconflicted individuals (shaded area) who, although not demonstrating their cultural preference overtly, are responsible for giving tacit approval or a 'vote of confidence' to the conflicted individuals. The conflicted individuals may then behave overtly towards the authority in the preferred cultural area of that group of unconflicted individuals who have given them tacit approval.

During the phase movement in the life of the group, it is claimed that the various subgroups clash and vie for power and influence over other members. They are also contesting with each other for

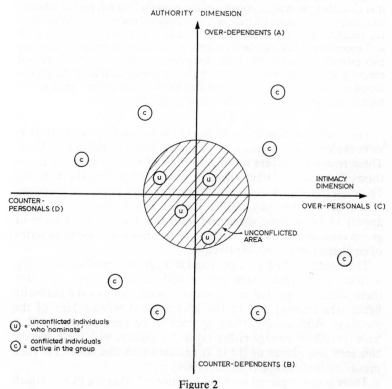

Figure 2

Bennis and Shephard's Model of group dynamics

attention and approval in the eyes of the trainer. With respect to these elaborations on group affiliation, Bennis and Shephard (1956) have provided a very interesting extension of the earlier principles stated by Bion and Redl.

Mann (1966) agrees basically with the statements of Bennis and Shephard. But he offers some minor modifications. He points to a distinction between the unconflicted and what he calls the 'independent enactors'.

B

Bennis and Shephard's (1956) discussion of group development notes
the early split between dependent and counter-dependent members, with
each dominating a subphase of the group. Similarly, the group later
polarises around the intimacy issue and the most conspicuous members in
this phase are the 'over-personals' and 'counter-personals'. Although the
authors do not trace the subgroup affiliations of these members over time,
it is clear that the central polarity in the group is between two 'conflicted'
subgroups who cannot tolerate one another's efforts to find a solution to
the problem. It is the 'unconflicted' members who emerge at each stage
and encourage other members to forge a viable compromise between the
two extreme positions. We have described the role of the 'independent
enactors' during the internalisation phase as similar to that of the unconflicted members but we have found that their careers are far more varied
than Bennis and Shephard have suggested. (p. 260)

The writings of Stock and Thelen (1958) are replete with corrobor-
ative evidence on the group development model postulated by Bion.
These research workers use the writings of Bion to generate hypotheses for testing. Other theories which fall within the basically
Freudian framework delineated in the previous pages are available.
Bales, Bennis, Dunphy, Mills, Kaplan and Roman, and Schutz
appear to be in basic agreement with this kind of description of
group development. These writers, where they differ, do so in terms
of emphasis rather than of principle.

There seems to be basic agreement amongst this psychoanalytically
oriented group that phases appear with some regularity, and that
these phases are related to the group's perceptions of the authority
figure (the trainer) and to the interpersonal relationships of the
members. Additionally, there appears to be basic agreement that
'role-specialists' emerge either (a) in association with these specific
concerns and phases or (b) in connection with the emotional state
prevailing in the group (Dunphy, 1964).

There is some quarrel over the question whether the phases which
groups go through are *nested (Bales, 1951), *repetitive (Bion), or
*circular (Schutz, 1966). There is also disagreement over whether
such role developments as do occur are a function of group influence,
or of the personality of the individual and his private value structure
(Bales). There is conjecture over whether individuals are 'conflicted'
or 'unconflicted' with respect to certain issues. These questions
will be taken up later and looked at in the light of our empirical
evidence.

BEHAVIOURIST APPROACH—RATIONALE

Advocates of behaviourist principles take exception to psycho-analytic theory on the grounds that the internal mechanisms and forces associated with personality structures cannot be observed, and therefore cannot become the object of scientific study. The behaviourist approaches the study of behaviour with the belief that what is 'real' is that which is manifest and observable. Influenced by Pavlov and Skinner, present-day behaviourists interpret behaviour in terms of the principles of *classical and *operant *conditioning. The difference between these two techniques lies in the relationship between the stimulus (S) and response (R). In classical conditioning (Pavlov) the unconditioned stimulus (UCS) *precedes and elicits the response.* Once learning is established, the same response will follow the UCS. The simultaneous occurrence of stimuli which are not associated initially with the response elicits the same response as did the UCS. This is how learning occurs. This paradigm refers to involuntary learning but it can be extended to verbal and voluntary learning. With *operant conditioning (Skinner) the *response is emitted, then some environmental event becomes associated with the emitted behaviour.* Either it reinforces the response or it suppresses it. In this way learning is established based upon the environmental *contingencies which happen to be present at the time of the response. With operant conditioning, the learner can be selective in his response and in certain ways can be said to be *responsible for what he learns.* Positive and negative environmental stimuli then become extremely important in what is learned.

For learning theorists the early life of the individual is extremely important. But it is not crucial, as it is for the psychoanalyst. It is in his early life that the child learns his first responses. It is then too that the child begins to make his first discriminations between what is rewarding and what is not; what is socially acceptable and what is not; what is attention-getting and what is not; what is affection-inducing and what is not. These responses become part of his behavioural repertoire, or response hierarchy; they are carried with him into future interactions. The child learns to expect certain types of encounters, and he is prepared to respond in terms of his hierarchy of available responses. It is crucial to note, however, that these responses, although learned in childhood, serve only as building blocks for future interaction. If childhood responses continue to be rewarded, they will be retained: if not rewarded they will be extinguished. In this way the behaviourist approach makes a sharp break with the psychoanalytic. As Ullman and Krasner (1965) point out:

If the goal of treatment is the emission of new behaviour that will be positively reinforced, it is difficult to see why insight into what occurred in early childhood is either sufficient or necessary for bringing about such a change, even if the behaviour that is to be changed was first manifested in childhood. An adult is not a child, and his childish behaviour is not childlike. (1969, p. 164)

Psychologists who accept these learning principles view 'personality' as a complex of stimuli, responses and *mediating variables. Personality may act as a social stimulus to other people, or as a response to other people. It may be otherwise viewed as a mediating variable leading to individually different responses to identical stimuli. Personality is not a relatively 'closed system' as in the psychoanalytic tradition, but an 'open system' capable of being influenced and of changing.

It is possible to alter behaviour directly. This does not involve treating the symptoms of some underlying unconscious malady. For the learning theorist symptoms *are* the malady. The actual observable behaviour is what constitutes the reality of the problem. Where the emphasis for therapy within the psychoanalytic tradition is upon 'insight', the emphasis for the behaviourist school is on the 'development of new responses to stimuli'. Where the analyst considers 'symptom-substitution' an ever-present hazard in treatment, the behaviourist regards the concept of symptom-substitution as a misnomer. Unless all the stimuli associated with a given response are dealt with the response might well occur again. This gradual extinction of response hierarchies is an aspect of treatment which must be regarded as essential rather than considered to be dangerous. Behavioural change consists in providing adaptive responses for the present environment. It may also require a change of environment itself because present responses (a) may be acceptable in a new environment or (b) newly acquired responses may not be acceptable in the old environment. The previous experiences of the group members will very likely dictate the early behaviour of the members in the new group. This is not because of unconscious conflicts stemming from psychosexual development but because these group members have *learned to respond* to new social situations in characteristic ways. Past experience has taught each individual to go through a certain repertoire of responses. Each response in the hierarchy is designed to elicit a rewarding consequence. Past situations enable group members to 'generalise' from selected environmental cues. This often brings out idiosyncratic responses, for no two individuals can be expected to behave exactly the same in this new group situation as

their previous experience will be different. The differences in characteristic responses occur because the person in the group may respond

... in a manner considered inappropriate (deviant) by others—because he
has identified the situation inaccurately—because he has been conditioned
aversively to particular cues that are part of the situation but not necessarily
crucial to defining it—because he does not have the appropriate responses
—or because he has previously been extinguished for making these
expected responses. (Ullman and Krasner, 1969, p. 70)

Within the group situation, speech is treated as behaviour, and it
is subject to the same laws of behaviour as is any other *operant,
(Skinner, 1957; Ullman and Krasner, 1965). The trainer, and other
group members, may respond positively or negatively to what is
said. If the person providing the positive or negative reinforcement
to the act of speaking, or to what is actually said, is an important
person in the eyes of the initiator, then the power of his reinforcement
increases. In the case of the trainer, who has considerable personal
power within most groups, his positive or negative verbal reinforcement is very influential. It operates as a source of group control.
Words generate power, especially if selectively used. Apply these
verbal operant conditioning principles, where intelligent use is made
of paying attention, using affective terms, applying negative sanctions
to undesirable behaviour; the results can be very influential in
determining the future behaviour of the group.

If we examine group dynamics from a behaviouristic standpoint
we obtain many new and different insights distinct from those given
by the analytic approach. Looking at the problem of the authority
'hang-up' (which many new group members face, especially in the
early life of the group), the learning theorist must call upon the
previous social experience of the involved member to find an explanation of behaviour. These previous social experiences, together with
present contingencies, dictate his response in this new social situation.
But the explanation is not in terms of unconscious conflicts stemming
from his psychosexual development (psychoanalytic interpretation)
but rather that past experiences have taught the new member to
respond with a repertoire of learned responses. Each succeeding
response in the hierarchy is calculated to elicit a rewarding consequence. The reward takes the form of praise, approval or consideration from the leading authority figure, the trainer. Previous
social situations have provided members of the group with a variety
of environmental cues or 'anchorages': these supply a framework for
present behaviour towards the trainer and towards others in the
group. Suppose, for example, that the trainer communicates similar

verbal commands as did some significant individual in the previous experience of the member. The participant can be expected to react in a fashion similar to that in which he responded in the previous situation.

For the learning theorist this is generalisation of the response: the same response is attached to a similar stimulus. In a very superficial sense it shows similarities with the transference phenomenon discussed previously. This is especially the case if the initial response was directed toward a parent, or some significant person in the early childhood experience of the member. In any case, the generalising of old responses to new situations by virtue of some environmental cue gives us an alternative explanation for the behaviours focused on by the analytic school. No two individuals can be expected to respond in the same way to the group situation or to the trainer's behaviour. At least, the behaviourist theory would suggest this since, as already noted, no two individuals will have such similar backgrounds that they would be likely to choose the same behavioural cues to respond to in the group situation. The idiosyncratic or individual responses of each member towards the trainer's remarks might be accounted for, as follows: (1) the individual may perceive and identify the situation inaccurately and thus interpret the behaviour of the group or of the trainer quite differently from what was intended; (2) the individual may not have any response available in his repertoire; (3) in previous situations of a similar kind, where the individual did respond in an appropriate way, he may not have been given reinforcement, or perhaps even punished, in which case the response may have been *extinguished (dropped from his repertoire).

Regardless of the particular response the member makes in this new group situation, according to behaviourist assumptions, it will either be a previously 'learned' response, or it will be a 'spontaneous' reaction to a novel stimulus shaped up and brought to full expression by group influences and cues. In most cases everyone involved will remain totally unaware of the source of the response and the nature of the reinforcers. In no sense, however, can the response be interpreted as a function of some unconscious blocking of repressed impulses striving to come into awareness and to find expression.

Thus the 'basic assumption' cultures described by Bion are explained somewhat differently from the behaviourist point of view. Suppose two or more individuals are involved in similar behaviours. There is agreement about a particular desired response from the trainer (say it is seeking praise, approval or consideration from the trainer). The group selectively rewards the member who emits the verbal operant by nodding or smiling towards the initiating member.

They may use less obvious reinforcing behaviour such as eye contact, or by indicating their interest in what is being said by not interrupting the business being transacted 'on the floor'. It is in such ways that a particular 'culture' is established. In this specific case it would be a dependency culture centred on the trainer.

In the same way the phase hypothesis of Bennis and Shephard, or of other analytic authors, could be described in learning theory terms. The basic distinction between learning theory and psychoanalysis is that there is no place for the 'unconscious' in the explanations of the learning theorist. It is clear, however, that the establishment of a 'culture' in the group, elucidated in the previous example, is an unconscious process, if only in the sense that it goes on outside of the awareness of the participants. Behaviourism and psychoanalysis are in agreement on this point. Similarly, the question whether the initiating member is aware of the rewards being made available to him by his peers or not has hardly any bearing on this question. In many cases the total context suggests that members continue to 'have the floor' without really knowing why they appear to be such a success! And, more obviously, when the rug is pulled from under his feet by the group, it is clear that the dismissed leader has no understanding of the group dynamics involved. We fall back on the behaviourist theory that many signals and cues which initiate and sustain particular behaviour patterns in the group are of a subliminal and non-verbal character. Rarely are they centrally focused in attention.

In similar fashion particular roles are established. Along with their particular *hierarchies of response, individuals bring into the group a propensity to adopt particular positions on fundamental group issues. The 'authority' issue is one which has already been referred to, briefly. Because of the rewards available to participants, whether these rewards are very obvious or not, members of the group will vie with each other for position, using these fundamental issues as the arena in which the struggle is conducted. The available rewards —power, prestige, favour, intimacy, and so on—will divide various members and unite others. Characteristic postures will be adopted with respect to these issues: these could be said to constitute the group roles.

Suppose we extend the 'dependency culture' example by considering in more detail those individuals who attempt to elicit praise, approval or consideration from the trainer. We already have seen that the dependent individual is selectively reinforced by other members of the group for behaving in this way. As this behaviour continues, and since it is being selectively reinforced by other members, particular types of soliciting postures are being* shaped (Skinner, 1953) by the group to the point where a specific role emerges. Thus, the dependent member finds himself to be the leader of the most dependent faction: he is their spokesman. Because of his (temporary) popularity with the group, an index of which is the amount of reinforcement he is receiving from other members, he is temporarily located very high in relation to intimacy, the other basic group issue. It may even surprise him somewhat to be chosen so frequently as director of group tasks, and spokesman for group concerns which relate to the demand for structure from the trainer. Thus the behaviourist theory explains how individuals are 'moulded', how they are singled out for leadership, how they become very influential and also how they are eventually dropped and become of no importance to the group.

It is when the past experience of members is varied and extensive that they develop expectations about their performance, and that of others. They are 'set' to encounter reinforcing experiences. It would appear from our observations that, no matter how much they may be told about what to expect in the group, or the nature of the task in the group, participants just will not give up these prior expectations. This has the result that invariably the 'keyed-up' participants appear to misinterpret, or selectively misperceive, important cues. They also invariably appear selectively to forget certain important statements. In all the groups we have observed, it is clear that the participants come with certain expectations; when these are disappointed this affects the whole group process in the most radical way. The group can make no progress in the task until it works through its self-generated 'set' and relinquishes its unrealistic expectations. In one case, members of the group failed to remember for the full term of the life of the group (fifteen sessions) what the trainer had said about the group task. This misperceiving, or forgetting, occurred even though the task instructions constituted the first and most significant communication the trainer made to the group.

It would appear that as long as the expectations of participants are associated with positive emotions and feelings they will be retained, in spite of all evidence that they are unrealistic. It is only at the point when the negative consequences of refusing to face reality outweigh the positive affect associated with retaining the group fantasies that the participants finally accept that there is no prospect of their expectations being realised. The first effect of even a slight deviation from the expectations of the group about the performance of others, especially of the trainer, may be extremely upsetting. In the above case, the trainer was expected to introduce himself, and to lessen the initial anxiety by means of polite conversation. When he entered the group, and immediately defined the task, proceeding with group 'work' instead of pleasantries, the result was anxiety, doubt, shock, forgetting, discouragement. The magnitude of the reaction depends on the level of expectation and the resources available to the participants for dealing with trauma, disappointment and their own negative feelings.

We have mentioned such basic learning principles as stimulus—response, hierarchies, *generalisation of response, *extinction of response, selective reinforcement, phase and role developments, shaping behaviour, *anticipatory set, expectations. As a basic presupposition underlying all this discussion has been a cardinal principle of behaviourist thought. This can be stated as an axiom: what a person says, as well as what he does, is behaviour, and is subject to the same laws as any other type of response (Skinner, 1957). The group may respond positively or negatively to what is said. If the participant providing positive or negative reinforcement to the act of speaking, or to what is actually said, has high status in the eyes of the initiator then the power of this reinforcement increases (Patterson, 1970). The trainer, who by virtue of his role and of the group expectations has considerable personal power within most groups, is very influential. His remarks, whether perceived positively or negatively, are a source of group control. They reinforce, positively or negatively, particular behaviour patterns in the group. Other group members also act as reinforcers. In terms of verbal operant conditioning the techniques of reinforcement include such things as discriminating use of attention, using emotionally-toned terms as negative verbal sanctions applied to undesirable behaviour, etc. The results of these techniques, used with deliberation or relatively unawares, can be very influential in shaping the behaviour of the group.

The use of terms such as those mentioned above are associated with classical (Pavlov) and operant conditioning (Skinner) procedures. These approaches to learning are heavily attacked on the grounds that they have a mechanistic or 'dehumanising' effect on the study of human behaviour. They are also attacked on the grounds of their denial of the unconscious as an influential force in behaviour. However, as a theory descriptive of behaviour, the behaviouristic model is an extremely powerful one. It attempts to deal with what is, rather than with what ought to be. It seems to us to be an established fact that the group shapes the behaviour of the participants; that this is done by positive reinforcement of certain types of behaviour; that this process goes on largely unawares. The fact is that human beings

behave in this way: it is our function as scientists to describe what
we see, not to express regret or disappointment, nor yet to change
the picture of reality to make it more acceptable to the tender-minded.

Social learning theory
Another approach, closely connected with classical and operant
conditioning principles, but whose focus is on social interaction, is
social learning theory. This does not receive the same brickbats as
behaviourism does, perhaps because of the type of question to
which it addresses itself. These are: What kinds of learning occur in
typical forms of social interaction? How does the behaviour of one
person influence another? Addressing itself to such questions, and
applying behaviouristic principles to find the answers, the social
learning approach has become very influential, adding considerably
to our understanding of group situations. We have examined some
social learning principles previously. Such concepts as *shaping,
and *reinforcement are basic. But perhaps the most important principle is that the social environment is the overall learning situation
and, as a totality, is the deciding factor in the stability of any
learning which occurs. This means that we pay no regard to the
distinction between classical and operant conditioning. Regardless
of how learning first occurs or is subsequently altered, whether this
be by the physiological 'temporary connections' of classical conditioning, or by the selective reinforcement of a given response, as
in operant conditioning, it is the environment in which conditioning
takes place that is decisive.
    Let us suppose that a group of delinquents is provided with a
special treatment designed to discourage abusive language. The
trainer has a background in behaviour modification and normally
uses such techniques as: *conditioning, *counterconditioning,
*desensitisation (these will be elaborated on later). He decides on a
schedule designed for the progressive extinction of abusive language
in a group situation. The trainer withholds positive reinforcement
every time abusive language is used, having first defined specifically
what he considers abusive language. Treatment might consist of
withholding monetary rewards every time abusive language is used
in the group. As time progresses, the delinquents become more
inclined towards the monetary reward and less fond of using foul
language. By the time the group has ended, abusive language has
virtually disappeared. The trainer prepares to approach the school
system to have these pupils reinstated. The social learning principle
mentioned earlier now becomes relevant. The important question
which suggests itself to the teachers, and to the therapist as well, is:

will these reinstated students cease their abusive language when again confronted by the particular authorities who brought the delinquency charges in the first place and when monetary rewards are no longer available for 'good' behaviour?

There is considerable evidence to show that the social situation the juvenile group member returns to after the group therapy will play an extremely important part in deciding the answer to this question. For example, if the parents of the juveniles concerned, or the peer groups they associate with, provide a model which encourages these pupils to return to their previous ways they will do so. The results of the group treatment will then be abortive: it will have no effect in changing the behaviour of the involved individuals. It is the social system in which the involved member is embedded which must be influenced by the treatment. If the treatment of abusive language is to have any desired effect, it should focus on the entire social system of these juveniles. The treatment must be given *within* and not *apart from* the normal environment of the delinquent.

One of the most important aspects of this recent emphasis on the relationship between social milieu and learning is the idea that a crucial influence is exerted by key social agents who provide reinforcement for specific behaviours. Research consistently indicates the special influence which social agents such as teachers, peers, parents, group leaders exercise on the acceptable or unacceptable behaviour of the individuals in their charge (Patterson, 1970). With regard to deviant behaviour, the influence of adult social agents becomes less and less; at the same time the influence of peers becomes ever more powerful. Additionally, it is possible that *only* certain types of social agents, such as male authority figures, are able to provide behavioural controls for particular individuals. We must therefore speak not in a generalised way about certain types of social agents such as parents, but rather of certain classes of parents who may or may not be influential (Patterson, 1970).

These findings have obvious implications for groups. Although adult leaders provide a potential source of influence, it is clear that they are not influential to all members simply because of their adult status. Only certain types of leaders, male or female, authoritarian or permissive, can provide generalisable *cues for desired behaviour or expected learning on the part of group participants. It is also clear from these principles that there is an extensive influence exerted by peers. These are social agents with reinforcing properties far beyond the capacity of most leaders, trainers or therapists to counteract certain forms of behaviour.

Behaviour therapy is the application of the principles of learning in a therapeutic setting. Additionally, it is an acceptance of the importance of social environment and of influential social agents in learning. Amongst the various kinds of therapists, it is characterised particularly by a high regard for the experimental verification of results. The emphasis in behaviour therapy is on behavioural change which is achieved mainly: (1) by extinguishing undesirable behaviour patterns through the application of unrewarding consequences (aversive conditioning); (2) by building up new responses to replace those which were extinguished (reconditioning); (3) by building up new associations to compete with previous responses, although not necessarily extinguishing the previous responses in the process (counterconditioning and desensitisation).

Various group approaches to behaviour therapy are available. Each of these lays particular emphasis on a specific technique, based on one or other of the learning principles outlined above. Specifically focusing on these group techniques, it is possible to recognise certain distinctive features in each approach. Group techniques based on learning principles were initially derived from, although they were in competition with, group psychoanalysis. As a result, an early approach formulated explanations of faulty learning in terms of influences operating in early childhood. Specifically, this approach explained present behavioural problems as symptoms of some unconscious conflict. Present behaviour patterns represented learned responses adequate to deal with the anxiety associated with this supposed conflict. In a group situation, the verbal activity of participants provided the medium through which the therapist could arrive at an interpretation of the symptomatic behaviour of the clients. Each member provided reinforcement for the individual reporting on his problems in the group. But basically the therapy was conceived as a dyadic process going on between the therapist and the patient. The goal consisted in removal of symptomatic behaviour and its replacement by socially-acceptable behaviour. Kanfer and Phillips (1969) explain these rather rudimentary attempts to apply learning principles in explaining personal conflicts as representing a merger of psychotherapy and learning theory. The major figures who advocated this eclectic compromise were Dollard and Miller (1950) and Rotter (1954).

Group behavioural approaches proliferated when it was recognised that the learning approach was a viable method on its own, and that there was no necessity to neutralise the influence of psychoanalysis by assimilating its principles. An understanding of the importance of the social environment in generating maladaptive behaviour led to attempts to let the environment dictate the available change. A group method using this technique involved a family coming together with a behaviour therapist to control and remodel the maladaptive behaviour of some member. The family learns from the therapist to avoid specific reinforcements contingent on specified behaviours occurring in the home situation. In the group situation, the problem of the malfunctioning individual's behaviour is outlined by the family and by the individual involved. The therapist thus provides a limited amount of reinforcement and control, but to produce any large behavioural change attention is focused on the family situation itself. Progress, and eventual success, is measured by the change which takes place in the actual family environment, not within the therapy group. The therapist may act as a model (Bandura and Walters, 1963) for certain kinds of anticipated behavioural change. But the family is the responsible and crucial vehicle for producing long-term change. The major practitioner of group methods such as these is Goldiamond (1965a,b,c).

Another behavioural group approach attempts to bring the environment inside the group setting. The group is asked, for example, to provide a role-play situation, or a psychodrama of a real life situation of one of the members. The therapist is the programmer-reinforcer along with various other actors in the situation. It is hoped that old forms of unacceptable behaviour will be extinguished and new behaviour produced as a result of insight. It is also hoped that the eventual result will be that new behaviour patterns will generalise to the home environment. The work of Wolpe (1958) in reciprocal inhibition is based on these behaviour modification principles. The concerned individual, in the presence of the therapist and others, is asked to imagine an anxiety-provoking situation. Using this mental image and simultaneously associating the anxiety it produces with a state of relaxation it is possible to *desensitise, or countercondition, the anxious state produced by the real situation.

The logical extension of this kind of work is for the therapist to go to the group in the real life situation itself. The method involves carrying the behavioural modification techniques into homes, schools and other institutions. At the present time the institutional settings receive major consideration in this work. Primarily this is because the intervention techniques are used in cases of extreme deviancy, where considerable control can be exercised by the therapist over the involved individuals. In these cases, the individuals are passive recipients of treatment, and not active agents as in previous examples. It is claimed that therapist-patient rapport is not crucial to the method. But the therapist must be all-powerful in controlling available rewards and programming extinction rates. This technique is adaptable to the classroom and does not require extensive skills (Kanfer and Phillips, 1969, p. 453). It can focus on interpersonal behaviour; it can use verbal behaviour as the sole medium and it is applicable to large groups as well as in dyadic situations.

In summary, Krumboltz (1965) makes the claim that there are five distinct features in the group behavioural approaches. Firstly, each individual enters the group with explicitly stated behavioural goals; these are usually similar, but not necessarily identical for each member. An example is the desensitisation of phobias by Lazarus (1961). The group participants in this case all suffer from irrational fears of one kind or another; they all actively wish to change. The group may contain individuals with phobias about confined spaces, sexual phobias, phobias about cats, and various other mixed phobias. Lazarus claims a 'cure' for thirteen of the eighteen members treated by this method. The second point Krumboltz makes in favour of the behavioural group approach is that the nature and size of the group are based on a consideration of the composition most likely to achieve each member's goals efficiently. He cites evidence showing that group size and composition can be controlled in favour of the participants with particular kinds of goal (Goldstein, Heller and Sechrest, 1966). Thirdly, Krumboltz argues that in behavioural approaches to groups the trainer is clear and open in his purposes, his methods, and about his expectations for the members. There is no doubt, no unnecessary building up of anxiety, nor of false expectations. With other group methods, such as 'sensitivity training', there are a number of ethical considerations relating to how the participants are dealt with by the trainer (Lakin, 1969). Krumboltz shows that where ambiguous instructions about the task, or unclear directions about the member's expectations or obligations are given by the trainer, the results are, more often than not, unfavourable for the participants. The fourth advantage of the behaviourist group approach reiterates the concern with ethical considerations mentioned earlier. If ethics becomes a primary focus of the group, they can at least be evaluated by the trainer to see how far they were helpful in accomplishing the goals for the group. Fifthly, the success rate achieved by group therapy is frequently reviewed. As we have previously recorded, there are instances where the group approach can be said to have got out of hand. The technique can be used to excess, especially where there is no attempt at evaluation of outcome or follow-up of participants. It can be said in favour of behaviouristic techniques that they encourage practitioners continually to assess their approach and to apply scientific rigour to the whole enterprise.

INTERACTION THEORY—RATIONALE

In business and industry, secretaries are trained in special skills which enable them to cope with staff meetings, conferences and with quick-thinking executives. These may not be the skills that preserve them from the clutches of over-enthusiastic and opportunistic bosses, but they are the basic work-skills which keep them employed. The skills we have in mind are stenography and shorthand. Interaction analysis is analogous to these; it is the descriptive shorthand of interpersonal behaviour. Interaction analysis is made up of skills such as observing, recording and analysing the record of behaviour in such a way as to make sense out of what has happened. In most systems in use, it consists of taking very small 'bits' of the action, identifying them by means of a coding scheme and recording them in these special categories. The categories are designed to incorporate all possible types and forms of behaviour. The interaction analysis system should include: (1) the affective or emotional components of behaviour; (2) the cognitive or intellectual components; (3) the non-verbal or 'meta-language' components should be taken into account; (4) content or message components should be incorporated in the code; (5) it should include the sociological or personal network segments of behaviour. The great variety of behavioural systems and the claims for the inclusiveness of some or all of the above dimensions has generated a great deal of research within classroom, T-groups and other human relations groups, institutional settings, counselling and therapeutic settings. It is mainly small task groups and classroom settings that have received the most attention. The original purposes of interaction analysis were describing and categorising behaviour as it occurs in social situations, such as the classroom or small problem-solving groups. Initially enquiries were very empirical in character. The kind of questions investigated originally had to do with devising an economical and comprehensive system of categories. The teacher's role was the focus of early interest: interest was concentrated on developing 'models' for effective teaching, and contrasting teaching styles. Increasingly, the interaction systems themselves became a focus of interest as training rather than research tools. Analysis was used to provide 'feedback' for practising teachers, to supervise teacher trainees, and to check on teacher's actual behaviour in the classroom. The objectives of this training have been formulated as (1) to increase personal insight in student trainees through objective and non-evaluative feedback; (2) to provide opportunities to practise and test the effect of new behaviour with corresponding feedback; (3) to demonstrate individual differences between trainees, to separate opinions about behaviour from the reality; (4) to develop skills for use in future evaluative situations, and so on. In these and other ways, the systems of interaction analysis have become tools for research workers, supervisors, trainers, and participants in small groups.

At present, the best all-purpose system of interaction analysis in small group settings is Bales' *Interaction Process Analysis (IPA)*. Bales' system (1951) is founded on certain basic assumptions about human behaviour. These include the idea that everything that is said and done in a group is important and should be recorded. However trivial or unimportant the behaviour may seem to the observer, in principle it can be integrated and related to the overall development of the group. It is no small task to develop a category system which includes everything that occurs and can be observed. It is made an even more complicated task when the system has to be simple enough to remember and use in an ongoing, active group. Bales provides twelve categories to work with. He believes that these twelve categories are comprehensive, being capable of encompassing every kind of 'act' with the utmost economy of categories. No behaviour should be omitted from the record if it is observed. The twelve categories are shown in the analysis of Plato's dialogue 'Ion'— where Socrates and Ion are engaged in a discussion about poetry and the art of the rhapsodist.

The procedure consists in a trained observer recording the behaviour observed in these categories, by number, as they occur. The sequence consists of noting that a particular group member (say, Bob, who is given number 5) addresses another member (say, John given number 8) in terms which can be categorised as 'seven' (7) asking for information. A simple example of this might be: 5 says to 8, 'What time is it?' The definition of a scoreable act and the category to which it belongs is not left to the intuitive judgement of the observer, but is given in the comprehensive definition of categories and of acts provided by Bales in 1950 and again in 1970 (see Table 1). Once an observer is completely familiar with the categories and definitions, the system appears considerably more stable than it does at the outset. In addition to verbal behaviour, such as the example provided above, non-verbal acts are also coded. Any overt form of behaviour, such as facial expression, body posture, tone of voice, must be considered very relevant in deciding the category to which to assign a verbal contribution. The non-verbal behaviour, unaccompanied by words, may be directed towards any member of the group, or to the group as a whole, or even to the individual himself. When the systems of categories, the definition of acts, and the refer-

Table 1
The verbal analysis of behaviour: Bales' system (1970)

All behaviour, verbal or non-verbal, is observed and classified in *one* or other of twelve categories.

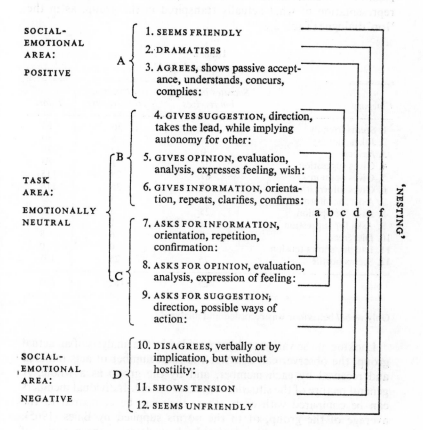

SOCIAL-EMOTIONAL AREA: POSITIVE

A
1. SEEMS FRIENDLY
2. DRAMATISES
3. AGREES, shows passive acceptance, understands, concurs, complies:

TASK AREA: EMOTIONALLY NEUTRAL

B
4. GIVES SUGGESTION, direction, takes the lead, while implying autonomy for other:
5. GIVES OPINION, evaluation, analysis, expresses feeling, wish:
6. GIVES INFORMATION, orientation, repeats, clarifies, confirms:

C
7. ASKS FOR INFORMATION, orientation, repetition, confirmation:
8. ASKS FOR OPINION, evaluation, analysis, expression of feeling:
9. ASKS FOR SUGGESTION, direction, possible ways of action:

SOCIAL-EMOTIONAL AREA: NEGATIVE

D
10. DISAGREES, verbally or by implication, but without hostility:
11. SHOWS TENSION
12. SEEMS UNFRIENDLY

a b c d e f

'NESTING'

Triads		*Key to problem areas*	
A	Positive reactions	a	Problems of communication
B	Attempted answers	b	Problems of evaluation
C	Questions	c	Problems of control
D	Negative reactions	d	Problems of decision
		e	Problems of tension reduction
		f	Problems of reintegration

ents for action become totally familiar to the observer, he or she has an instrument in the form of a viable system for recording on-going behaviour as it occurs in any small group. A scoring grid can be provided on which the group behaviour is recorded and tallied. The resulting tabulations can then be organised into a meaningful representation of what actually transpired in the group, as in the 'Ion' dialogue (Table 2).

Table 2
Analysis of Plato's 'Ion'

Category	Socrates initiates, Ion receives	Ion initiates, Socrates receives	Totals
1. Seems friendly	28	30	58
2. Jokes, fantasy	44	6	50
3. Agrees	0	39	39
4. Gives suggestion	62	1	63
5. Gives opinion	87	28	115
6. Gives information	82	36	118
7. Asks for information	19	3	22
8. Asks for opinion	25	5	30
9. Asks for suggestion	1	1	2
10. Disagrees	2	6	8
11. Laughs, shows tension	0	0	0
12. Seems hostile	75	26	101
Totals	425	181	606

Only *verbal* behaviour was recorded and analysed.

Looking at the various tables provided by the analysis of an actual group, the observer can discover the total number of acts initiated and received by each member, and by the group as a whole. A general picture of the situation begins to unfold. Individual members can be compared with each other; they can be compared to the average of the group, or to the norms supplied by Bales (1965). Different indices can be calculated which describe the position of each group member in relation to the overall group interaction. Such information as the position of individuals with respect to access to group resources such as information, opinions, and suggestions is provided by combining certain categories. His position in relation to group control, and information about his overall generalised status, can be arrived at from his rates of initiating and receiving certain kinds of acts. In addition, the individual's power position in the hierarchy can be understood from a count of his acts addressed to the whole group and to individual members. It is a fact of observation that persons in power positions tend to address the group more often than they address individuals.

It is also meaningful to look at the behaviour *patterns* generated by the group as this is shown by the categories. Bales' system is organised in such a way that the twelve categories constitute an organised system. It is symmetrical in a number of ways. The three initial categories are regarded as belonging to the positive socio-emotional area (A); correspondingly the last three categories are in the negative socio-emotional area (D). There is a further division in the classification such that particular pairs of categories are related to particular group concerns. Categories 4, 5 and 6 are in the task area as 'answers' (B), categories 7, 8, 9 are located in the task area as 'questions' (C). Categories 6–7 focus on problems of communication; 5–8 focus on evaluation; 4–9 focus on the issue of control; 3–10 are concerned with decision-making in the group; 2–11 are concerned with tension reduction and 1–12 focus on the issue of reintegration. These pairs, and their association with particular group problems or concerns, are considered to be 'nested', in that particular pairs are found within the total scheme at coordinate positions. 'Nesting' is also shown in reality by the fact that a group finds its first concern to be the issue of *communicating* the particular task to the various members. As a result, there is a predominance of acts recorded in categories 6 and 7 during initial phase of the group. Gradually the group moves out of this particular problem area into an *evaluation* of the task. In this phase categories 5 and 8 predominate. In time the group moves through the whole series of problem areas, in regular order. This is the *nesting* hypothesis: that each set of category pairs has special prominence in a predetermined order. The tendency is for the group to move from the central categories (6, 7) out to the extremities (1, 12). In other words, the group moves from an initial phase of communication to a final phase of reintegration where the emotional concerns are dealt with. This is the normal sequence in the groups we have studied.

Returning to the triads of categories described earlier: the extreme categories, labelled A and D, are concerned with the emotional side of the interaction process. The middle categories, classified as B and C, are instrumental or task components of the group interaction. It is clear from the description of the phase movements that the group's initial concern is cognitive in character, with subordinate emotional resources. The questions for the group are: what are we supposed to do? What is the task? The focus is such that acts can be scored in categories 6, 7 (areas B, C). As time goes on, the group moves out of the cognitive area into the affective one. Problems of tension reduction (categories 2, 11 and areas A, D), and reintegration of the group then predominate (categories 1, 12, areas A, D).

Theoretically, this is how it works. In practice events rarely follow this neat scheme exactly. The phase movement can be perceived as an overall movement, but the actual group interaction is an unstable, ever-changing process, subject to all sorts of influences. Forces operate which drive the group in opposite directions, for example, towards an adaptation to the external reality of the outside world. On the one hand, members clamour for structure, for goals and achievement (instrumental activity). In addition there are stresses and strains, feelings of frustration and anger, hostility builds up, petulant forms of behaviour appear (socioemotional activity). The group never seems to remain long in a stable state: there is a continuing turnover of decisions which alternate between the desire to achieve the task and giving way to feelings. But we believe that the law of causality continues to operate through this plethora of apparently random events. At present, we see this as through a glass, darkly.

Bales' assumption is that the solution to the functional problems imposed by the task, and the socioemotional concerns that arise invariably when people come in contact with one another, can be clarified by attempting to outline them as objectively as possible. His premise is that the best model we have for understanding what goes on inside the individual is that of what goes on between individuals in the group in the course of this problem-solving process. The individual in the group re-enacts the social gambits he found successful in other situations. By using this perspective we come to understand behaviour better than we could in any other way.

A cursory look at the analysis of small groups using Bales' original scheme indicates that until 1968 the system did not allow for a comprehensive description of individual personality. It provided an actuarial picture of small group processes rather than a depth analysis. With the publication of his recent book (1970) a change in emphasis can be observed. Bales has extended his IPA system in line with an increased concern for understanding particular role developments and the influence of individual personality on the problem-solving process within the group. Additionally he has developed questionnaires to serve as additional tools to supplement the IPA descriptions of individual personality.

The IPA system, studies in Bales' laboratory at Harvard involving *sociometric data, questionnaire materials and personality tests, have resulted in the concept of the systematic description of 'directions of social psychological movement' or 'personality types'. It is claimed that individuals in a group can be classified, by analysis of the patterns of group interaction, in terms of one or another of these social psychological directions (SPDs), in a three-dimensional psychological space (see Figure 3). These axes are described as: dominant–submissive (upward–downward); arousing pleasant or unpleasant feelings in others (positive–negative); accepting or rejecting the group

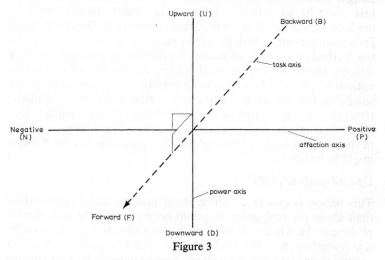

Figure 3

Three dimensions of individual personality and group movement

norms (forward–backward). To visualise the 'social psychological directions', the axes can be thought of as meeting at the central point in a cube made up of 27 blocks (the 27th block is at the centre, and signifies a 'direction' which is neutral in all respects). It is possible with this scheme to place each member of a group in one of these 27 locations, his location (or SPD) being symbolised by a unique combination of one, two or three letters indicating the axes along which he is 'moving'. The individual is 'located' by analysis of his scores in the 12 IPA categories. As a group continues to interact, roles and behaviour can be predicted on the basis of the SPDs indicated; these predictions can then be checked.

It should be emphasised that the detailed description of each 'direction' refers to individuals who are moving 'most strongly' in that direction. As an illustration, descriptions are given below of three adjacent 'upward' types (3): the upward–positive–forward (UPF) member; the upward–positive (UP) member, who is in psychologically neutral territory on the forward–backward axis; the upward–forward (UF) member who is psychologically neutral on the affective axis.

Upward–positive–forward (UPF)

This person advocates social solidarity and progress; identifies himself with a good image of authority; shows great interest in the task given by an authority figure; over-idealises positive feelings; tends to submerge, deny or transform negative feelings; will speak for equilitarianism (which he sees as meaning no dissent); speaks for the 'orthodox' content of whatever religious or political belief he adheres to; is the inspirational leader, but on behalf of existing authority; tends to fuse the group together in a monolithic group solidarity for the sake of 'progress' rather than of individuals; tends to use a deductive method in solving problems (values first) rather than an inductive one (facts first); is seen by others as interested in the group task. As an example of this 'type', the late Josef Stalin might be instanced.

Upward–positive (UP)

This person is concerned more about positive social relationships than about the realisation of group norms or specific task accomplishment; he wholly identifies with the group and has a powerful and rewarding place in it; individuals respond frequently to him and express their ideas to him; he tends to take a position of leadership; his outlook is benign; he has an over-expanded image of his own success and omni-competence; he is seen by others as personally involved, and valuable for a logical task; he provides stimulus and rewards complementary to other members' task efforts, but a great deal of the actual work comes from them though they do not always realise it; this is a personality which neither strongly accepts nor strongly rejects social norms or the achievement of group goals. The late Clement Attlee is a good example of this type.

Upward–forward (UF)

This person shows a main concern with cooperation towards task achievement and the preservation of group unity through loyalty; he apparently identifies himself with a larger, impersonal plan which transcends the group; he does not ignore individual differences, but calls them to attention and tries to bring them into line; the persuasion used by him is not individually tailored to the motives of each divergent member but consists in simply insisting that cooperation is necessary; he tries to avoid seeming either positive or negative in feeling, as a father may avoid taking sides in quarrels among his children; he makes others feel he regards them as individualistic; he believes that 'a group cannot get its job done without voluntary cooperation from everybody' (but the inclusion of everybody turns 'voluntary' into 'compulsory'); the opposition he arouses in others is frequently turned not against him, but against an external enemy or a deviant in the group; thus he may polarise the group—and even split it—through the very strength of his desire to effect cooperation. The late General de Gaulle is perhaps a good example of this type.

To summarise; it appears that various claims are made for IPA of the greatest interest to all students of human behaviour. These claims require verification or rebuttal by an independent investigation. The claims may be summarised as follows: (1) it is possible to infer personality traits from social interaction in groups recorded and analysed by IPA; (2) that predictions of subsequent behaviour can be made from an informed reading of the interaction recorded in earlier sessions of the group, this being especially the case with respect to leadership patterns; (3) that observers, completing Bales' specially devised Interpersonal Ratings Questionnaire for each member of the group, can check the resulting SPD against the analysis of IPA scores. It would be of the greatest relevance to ask whether the SPD from the IPA analysis and/or the questionnaire is recognisable as the person in question. In addition, we suspect that Bales' IPA system provides a valuable tool for understanding the various reinforcements unconsciously emitted by trainers and their sub-sequential effects on member learning. We know of no studies so far which have attempted to employ IPA in this way.

2

WHAT ARE THE DYNAMICS OF CHANGE IN

LEARNING GROUPS?

In the preceding chapter three basic approaches to the realities of
group functioning were outlined in a summary way. In this chapter a
more detailed theory of group process will be covered in some detail,
others will be dealt with in a more cursory fashion. The theories will
be confronted with empirical data to test their credibility and to set
out in a systematic way what we know of the inner life of the small
learning group.

The theory of group development which is most acceptable is based
on the *action theory of Talcott Parsons (1953) and developed in
detail by Robert Freed Bales at Harvard. As we have seen, Bales
was primarily responsible for elaborating the system of Interaction
Process Analysis (IPA) to describe and categorise social interaction.
His theoretical perspective is much more comprehensive than any of
his competitors: at the same time his views are expressed in such a
way that they are capable of empirical verification or falsification.

BALES' THEORY OF GROUP DEVELOPMENT

Bales' approach to the understanding of group dynamics starts from
the fundamental premise that group behaviour is a recapitulation, or
analogue, of what occurs within the human personality. Individuals
in problem-solving activities with others run through the same
procedures as have been found successful in previous social encounters. Moreover, an analysis of what goes on between individuals
in a learning group can provide a model of what goes on within the
individual learner, and vice versa (1951, p. 62).

When individuals are placed in a public situation various problems arise for them: Bales' contention is that two of these are particularly pressing. The primary problem is that of solving the presented 'task'. Additionally, the problem arises of constantly re-structuring affiliative ties in the group so that the interpersonal needs of the membership will be met. These are usually referred to as the 'task' and 'social–emotional' concerns. For Bales, group development is best understood as successive attempts to solve these problems as they arise over time and across persons. Changes, whether in the social structure or the membership 'culture', can be understood best as a reaction to the attempted solutions of these two crucial problems.

Related to the two areas of 'task' and 'social–emotional' development are to be found certain sources of variation which account for the distinctiveness of each group. One source of variation is the nature of the learning task and of the resources available in the present environment; another source of variation is the culture and values established through previous and present group experience; lastly, the social relationships and the roles elaborated by the members over time constitute another possible way of explaining differences between groups. The concerns of 'task' and 'interpersonal relations', and the four sources of variations specified cause unique happenings within any small group. Here too, we find the possibility of all necessary permutations to account for the special 'functional problems' which arise in the life of a given group. These problems are categorised in four groups, as follows:

(1) An *instrumental* problem is concerned with implementation of the needs and desires of the group membership;

(2) An *adaptive* problem is concerned with the fitting of activities to the social system external to the group;

(3) An *integrative* problem is concerned with those activities within the group social system which are directed towards unification and the preservation of the unity of the group.

(4) An *expressive* problem is concerned with the emotional tensions within personalities as a result of changes in the social system of the group.

This brings Bales' thinking about the small group (microsociology) into line with Parsons' 'action' theory about the great society (macrosociology), that is, the social system in general (McLeish, 1968).

For Bales, then, the group is a social system in miniature, with certain kinds and levels of inputs. The inputs derive from personality, culture, and the external environment, including the large systems of society and of nature. Given these inputs, the group is confronted with a task which demands not only understanding but the development of a group structure (the distribution of roles for the utilisation of available resources) necessary to achieve a solution. In attempting to solve the task, the group meets with particular functional problems, falling into the four categories just defined. The solutions put forward are in the first place institutionalised and commonplace, since the group attempts to solve the problem through the primitive social structure and from habitual responses. Normally, this won't do— changes of some kind are necessary to solve the problem. But any divergence from the institutionalised solution brings about changes in all parts of the system. Group dynamics is the study of some of these changes, their antecedents and consequents.

In grappling with the functional problems which necessarily arise, the group must work through a definitive framework of social interaction. Bales, and Strodtbeck (1951), have developed a 'phase hypothesis' to describe how groups move to a decision, or resolution, of fully fledged, functional problems. A phase is defined as a 'qualitatively different sub-period within a total continuous period of interaction in which a group proceeds from initiation to completion of a problem, involving group decision' (ibid., p. 485). The phase hypothesis describes the group as moving from an initial period where the emphasis is upon *orientation to other members and to the task, to the problem of *evaluation, finally to problems of *decision and *control. Concurrently, as the life of the group continues, the relative frequencies of both *negative reactions* and *positive reactions* tend to increase (p. 485).

The phase hypothesis is expected to hold true under certain specified conditions (Bales, 1951). The task should be such that

... with regard to *orientation* members have some degree of ignorance and uncertainty about the relevant facts . . . with regard to the problems of *evaluation* . . . the problem not be an 'open and shut case' . . . and with regard to *control* . . . there be both pressure for a group decision and the expectation of further joint action . . . When problems lack or greatly minimise any of these three characteristics, we speak of them as being 'truncated'. When the three characteristics are present, we speak of the problem as being 'full-fledged'. (p. 487)

The phase hypothesis refers to a circular process wherein the initial focus is the task dimension. This focusing on task leads to a build-up of emotion which is released through both positive and negative behaviour. This leads back to the task and so the cycle begins anew (see Figure 4).

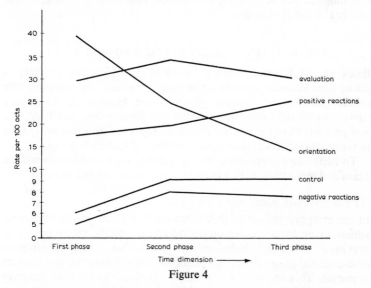

Figure 4

Relative frequency of acts by type and phase based upon 22 sessions
(Bales, 1951 b)

This is an over-simplification of the *equilibrium model of group development postulated by Bales in 1951. This model states that any disturbance or change, or imbalance in the social system of the group, creates a state of tension which is followed by an attempt to correct the imbalance and restore the system to its previous condition of 'equilibrium'. The group is in uneasy balance, poised between task and social–emotional concerns.

When the equilibrium is disturbed, members of the social system are subject to insecurity. They proceed to *act* to remove the resultant tensions by adaptive–instrumental activity in the task area. This focusing on the task is aimed at attempting to adapt to the reality existing outside the miniature social system, now in disequilibrium. If attempts to alleviate the disequilibrium are not successful, insecurity persists; there is a rise in expressive–malintegrative behaviour within the social system. This equation of failure to solve the task-adaptive crisis with the onset of *malintegrative behaviour is true in each sequence of the phase movement. In other words, if the group cannot successfully cope with any of the orientation, evaluation or control phases, the output of expressive and malintegrative behaviour will rise. This is shown by fantasy, withdrawal, aggression and more pathological ways of coping with affect. This behaviour is anti-task and backward in character.

THE REALITIES OF LEARNING GROUPS: DATA

Bales' theory has now been outlined in general terms. In fact, he states four distinct hypotheses relating to phase, equilibrium, role differentiation, and overall group phase movement. These are variations on the same theme which has already been declared. We will proceed to report on the four hypotheses of group development in terms of our observations and analyses of learning groups.

To facilitate the reporting of the results, each hypothesis will be examined separately, with a brief general discussion to follow.

(1) The *'nested' phase hypothesis

In the category system of IPA there are particular paired categories which, taken together, are indicative of the specific group problems previously discussed. Bales' contention is that in any learning or task-oriented group the group problems are encountered in a definite sequence. This sequence is directly related to the *nested category system. In other words, the problem indicated by the paired categories in the 'task' area of the IPA system demand solution before those in the extreme categories of the affective domain.

This is merely to reiterate the phase hypothesis—that the problems of *orientation, evaluation* and *control* (indicated by paired categories 6+7, 5+8, 4+9, respectively) would be resolved in corresponding order. In addition, and as a consequence of this task-oriented activity, the incidence of positive and negative reactions should 'climb' over the life of the group. This would be indicated by a gain in categories 1+2+3, and 10+11+12, respectively. To test this hypothesis, four task-oriented groups were studied over fifteen sessions each group (Matheson, 1971). The four groups were made up of two pairs, two different treatments being applied to these groups.

The fifteen sessions of each group were divided into five equal 'phases' of three sessions each to provide an opportunity for every problem sequence to appear. The percentage values were summed and an average for each problem index calculated for each phase.

In both *self-analytic (SAT) groups the incidence of negative reactions seemed to be unusually high. The nature of the treatment appeared to induce a considerable amount of tension (cat. 11) and negativism (cat. 12)—more so than in more orthodox treatments.

Analysis reveals that the SAT 1 and SAT 2 groups seem to parallel each other very closely. Both groups demonstrate difficulty in problem-solving. They seem to have established their interaction pattern in the very early meetings, they remained quite 'unstable' and non-task-oriented for the remainder of the time. Affective relationships account for the greater part of the interaction, with little time devoted to work. Bales' nested hypothesis is *not* verified in these two groups. It appears as though they might be beginning to get down to work ('the task') towards the very late stages. This could be because of the peculiar nature of the treatment which was quite non-directive in the Tavistock style. It could also be an artifact due to 'premature' termination of the course. For whatever reason, within the allotted fifteen sessions these two groups did not follow the 'nesting' expectations.

The two direct communications training (DCT) groups are more conventional as far as treatment goes. They also seem very much more in line with the 'nesting phase' hypothesis which is almost totally confirmed. The typical nature of the learning situation seems to be the crucial factor in the development of a 'natural' progression of problem-solving.

(2) The *'equilibrium' hypothesis

In the solution of the various group problems it is claimed that an equilibrium is established between the *'task' and the *'socioemotional' problems. An increase in task activity, as shown by attempts towards orientation, evaluation, and control, results in an increase in social–emotional activity. This increase operates to re-establish the social-system balance within the group. It might be demonstrated by a rise in positive and negative reactions as these task problems become of central concern. If the balance between task and social–emotional forces is not established there is an increase in expressive–malintegrative behaviour. This is according to hypothesis.

Various indices can be used to demonstrate the functional relationships between certain group problems and expressive–malintegrative behaviour. These indices are called:

(a) Index of difficulty of communication = Cats. $\dfrac{7}{(7+6)}$

(b) Index of difficulty of evaluation = Cats. $\dfrac{8}{(8+5)}$

(c) Index of difficulty of control over situation = Cats. $\dfrac{9}{(9+4)}$

(d) Index of directiveness of control = Cats. $\dfrac{4}{(4+6)} + \dfrac{5}{(5+6)}$

(e) Overall index = a + b + c + d

(f) Index of expressive–malintegrative behaviour =

$$\text{Cats. } \frac{(10+11+12)}{(10+11+12)+(1+2+3)}$$

To test the hypothesis, the indices a, b, c, d, e and f were calculated for all fifteen sessions of each of the four groups. The overall index e is the best indicator of the instrumental activity of the group and the expressive–malintegrative index f is the best indicator of the affective state of the group.

The results support Bales' contention that the relationship between expressive–malintegrative behaviour and the solutions of problem situations in the group is functionally linear, that is, the relationship is of the form y = ax + b. The best indicator that this is the kind of relationship that exists is the correlation of the expressive–malintegrative index and the overall index. Over sixty sessions, the significant correlation of $r = 0.277$ ($p < .03$) gives strong support to the hypothesis of 'equilibrium' within the treatment groups.

(3) *'Role differentiation' hypothesis

Bales (1951) has developed four other indices which give a quantitative statement of each person's status in the group over any particular period. The index is of course based on the character of the individual's interaction in the twelve categories. These indices are: the index of direct access to resources, of indirect access to resources, an index of attempted control, and a generalised status index made up of the first three. The values of these four indices were calculated for each of the interactions, these were associated with the various phases of the lives of their respective group.

It is obvious that to acquire a value of any magnitude on these status indices, a group member must be an active participant. The most verbal will often receive the highest values. The indices are biased, but in the right direction, since verbal fluency is normally associated with status in small learning groups.

In comparing the status of live participants with the group phase movement, it is clear that particular individuals achieve, maintain and lose status over the life of the group according to the rule that as one problem area disintegrates and another becomes prominent, so the initial influence of some members wanes at the same time as other group leaders emerge. The theory that leadership roles are differentiated in the group, first in terms of 'instrumental *v.* affective' leaders, then in terms of positive and negative affect, then in terms of power, and so on, is verified. The study of the careers of particular individuals during the history of the group process supports the hypothesis of role differentiation. This problem will be taken up again in Chapter 7.

(4) *The overall *phase movement hypothesis*
The concept of three-dimensional 'group space' bears a direct relationship to the functional problems crucial to the life of the learning group. The upward–downward 'power' axis represents the problem of adapting to the external situation. The individual tries to dominate the situation (upward) or he becomes resigned, submissive and yields to it (downward). The positive–negative 'feeling' axis is related to the functional problem of integrating the group in terms of its social and emotional concerns. To contribute in an emotionally positive way is to provide integration: to behave in a negative fashion is to contribute to the disintegration of the achieved social–emotional relationships. The forward–backward axis defines relation to the task—the functional problems of the *instrumental* and *expressive* concerns of the group. To operate in the forward direction is to contribute to completion of the group task. This is therefore an instrumental or goal-directed activity. To operate in a backward direction is to behave as a group deviant, to be non-cooperative, to persist in individually formulated efforts for personal, not group, goals. These relationships are summarised below.

FUNCTIONAL PROBLEMS AND THEIR CORRESPONDING
3-D SPACE DIRECTIONS

Adaptive	Upward (dominating, controlling)
	Downward (submitting, yielding)
Integrative	Positive (arousing pleasant feelings)
	Negative (arousing unpleasant feelings)
Instrumental	Forward (cooperate with authority)
Expressive	Backward (deviant, personal goals)

Concerning the phase hypothesis and this three-dimensional space, the explanation of group dynamics seems acceptable on common-sense grounds and reasonably clear. During the phase of *orientation*, which normally occurs in the early meetings of the learning group, the overall location of the group should be in the upward, positive and forward area, moving towards the downward, forward, positive area as orientation is provided by an acceptable authority (see Figure 5—Phase 1). With the onset of *evaluation* in the medial phase, there

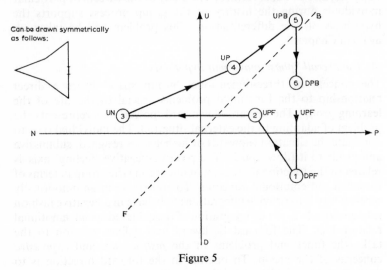

Figure 5

The phase movement in three-dimensional space (ideal model)

The forward dimension can not be shown visually in this diagram, however, and is indicated by the label attached to each phase

will be an increase in opinion-giving, and suggestions will be plentiful. The result is a movement towards the upward (status-seeking) direction and an associated increase in forward (task-directed) activity (Phase 2). As the group enters the *control* phase, to deal with the final 'nested' group problem, there ensues more disagreement, and status-seeking. As a result, there should be movement in the negative direction, but the group maintains its upward, power-oriented activity (Phase 3). As the status issue is resolved, there will be an increase in general agreement and acceptance, and the positive direction of the group is regained. Some individuals have consequently gained in status (Phase 4), therefore the group also rises in the power direction. With the release of tension, as the status issue is resolved, there should be an upsurge of social–emotional, non-task activity: the group moves both upward and backward (Phase 5). This affective behaviour is contagious. The entire group seems to be desirous of terminating without remorse, hard feelings or loss of prestige. Near the close, the direction of movement will be in a downward, positive, backward direction (Phase 6).

The life cycle of the group, in both its phase movements and in 3-D space has actually been observed by research workers, working with Bales (Heinicke & Bales, 1953; Dunphy, 1968). The results of two groups, one led by Bales the other by Dunphy, are shown in graphic form. Alongside are shown our results for four groups (see Figure 6).

Dividing the fifteen sessions of each group into five equal phase periods provided the opportunity to plot the general movement through three-dimensional space for each treatment group. To determine the various locations of each group in this space the method used was to calculate the sum of the total number of directional components accumulated by the overall group membership in each session. The IPA analysis of individual interaction was used as the source of components. Bales' 'simple difference' method was used (Bales, 1968—private communication) to provide a quantitative scale for the three dimensions used in the Figures. Although the groups appear to occupy one particular space, there was directional movement over sessions, within the major group location. For example, the second self-analytic group remained in UNF space but they differed in degree of negativism (or in the forward dimension) during particular phases.

However, there are substantial differences within and across treatment groups. In the case of the two self-analytic groups, there are differences both in the direction and in the degree of movement. This is especially true of the positive–negative dimension. The first SAT group is located *primarily* in UPF space, whereas the second continues to be located in UNF space.

Both groups respond with an initial negative reaction to their group experience. Although they begin by being task-oriented, both groups soon enter a backward phase in which they remain until after the ninth session. The task again becomes a focus for both groups, but this interest is dissipated towards the end of the experience. The issues of power and control are raised very early, they remain on the agenda until the middle sessions. The second group becomes more submissive, and less involved in status disputes than the first, as termination approaches. Both groups end with the task of building status and producing positive reactions.

The sessional movements for the two DCT groups are less comparable. Both begin in UNF space, but go in opposite directions. The first DCT group becomes DNF, while the second becomes PB. Both are anti-task throughout the middle sessions. But their affective directions are reversed. The first group becomes P, the second

C

becomes N. The later sessions see positive feelings rise and the
second group become more task-oriented. The terminal sessions are
negative for both groups, with some concern for control evident in
the first, but not in the second. The reader will observe from Figure
6 that SAT-1 and DCT-2 proceed in a clockwise direction as predicted
by Bales, whereas SAT-2 and DCT-1 fail to confirm his hypothesis
about direction of movement.

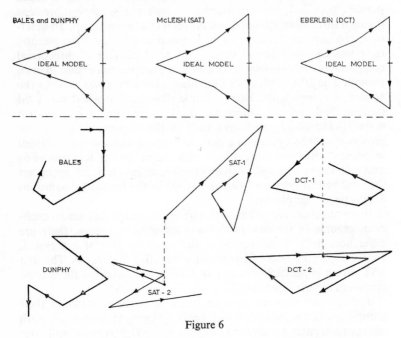

Figure 6

SAT–1 and SAT–2 both begin at the same point in 3D space
DCT–1 and DCT–2 also begin at the same point in 3D space

It may be that the treatments did not last long enough to demonstrate the expected overall phase movements. Whatever the explanation, we must conclude that the overall phase-movement
hypothesis has not been verified.

In summary, it may be concluded that as far as these four experimental groups are concerned, intensive analysis of the interaction
patterns over sixty sessions tends to support certain of the group
development conceptions of Bales and to disconfirm others. The
'nested-phase' hypothesis is confirmed for two of the four groups: in

the case of the other two the discrepancies can plausibly be explained in terms of the nature of the task, and the trainer's role. The equilibrium hypothesis also finds support. There is a tendency for the onset of the task-oriented 'culture' to produce an unbalanced condition in the group which is compensated for by increased social–emotional activity—otherwise dysfunctional, expressive, anti-task deviant behaviour is elicited. The role-differentiation hypothesis is also acceptable as applying to learning groups. When the fluctuations in the status of high interactors is related to the major phase movements, there is an obvious tendency for particularly significant individuals to appear at peak times in the life of the group. The overall phase-movement hypothesis receives less than complete acceptance in these learning groups. There was considerably less movement across three-dimensional space than predicted from the hypothesis. The fact that all four groups started in UNF space may be significant in explaining these failures of prediction.

THE STUDY OF AN INDIVIDUAL CAREER IN A SELF-ANALYTIC GROUP

The Tavistock type of self-analytic group, oriented to the 'here-and-now', manifests unique member–trainer relationships, which appear to be a function of the residuals of unresolved psychosexual conflicts. The trainer who adamantly refuses to engage in open dialogue with group members elevates the anxiety level of the participants by apparently caustic interpretations of the 'on-going' action and 'underlying' dynamics.

The task as given by the trainer may take a variety of forms but is unmistakably clear. In the usual form it is defined as 'to observe behaviour as it happens, and to understand it'. The trainer indicates that he is present in a helping role. Clarity of task definition, and offer of help notwithstanding, the group focuses on its relationship with the trainer, who is ambivalently perceived—sometimes incompetent, sometimes omnipotent in relation to the task, sometimes obstructive, sometimes facilitative. Autistic reactions, in the form of rigidity of interpretation and response in the here-and-now situation, appear to be carried over by the participants from early experiences with authority or love figures (Bennis, 1964). These obstacles to valid communication distort and complicate the group interaction unduly. They operate to block insight into the process and dynamics of the group. The autistic reactions prevent adequate conceptualisation of what is happening in the here-and-now. This in turn activates various self-deceptive mechanisms or group stratagems which, intended to neutralise the anxiety provoked by the trainer, paradoxically lead the participants into a vortex of conflicts which prevent insight into the group experience.

Mann (1967) provides another conceptual foundation and analytic strategies which are particularly directed towards studying the changing relationships between group members and their formal leader. His basic contention is that 'the member–leader relationship is always influencing the member's feelings and behaviour to some extent' (1967, p. 37). He has developed a scoring system which consists of sixteen categories. Eight of these describe the affective relationship of participants to the leader; three categories deal with feelings related to the leader's status in the authority structure of the group; five describe the effect of the leader on the ego state of the participants.

Transcripts of fifteen sessions of a Tavistock training group were coded according to this system. The coded data were analysed by computer in terms of frequency and proportion matrices. In addition, a compilation of each individual's statements in each session was made. The value of processing the verbal content in this way is that the changing perceptions of the trainer, the themes developed by the individual, the strategies he uses, are readily manifest. It appears to be an extremely useful way of understanding the dynamics operative in individuals. By analysing *all* the individual contributions in this way an alternative description of the group dynamic can be built up. The developing interaction with others in various phases of the group life is highlighted. The analysis readily shows changes in perceptions of the trainer, changes in theme and individual strategies over the sessions. These unique perceptions, themes, and strategies are the 'stuff' of which phases or group movements are made. Obviously, the study of an individual career in isolation from the group interaction is a methodological device of great value. Viewing statements in the context of previous contributions by the same individual offers insights into individual functioning which can be obtained in no other way.

The study of Paul's career in the group is based on analysis of the total acts he generates during each session. The description of his performance is arrived at from a content analysis, as well as from a count of his contributions in each of Mann's sixteen categories.

The conceptual framework that underlies individual performance is described by Mann (1967, p. 73):

The first or thematic approach serves as our way of tracing the enormous variety of responses to and about the leader. . . . . Each theme points to a complex of issues, experiences, and residual needs which offer to the member a way of understanding in the new group, a way that permits him to connect the member–leader relationship with important antecedent relationships at both the conscious and unconscious levels.

In general, our procedure is to study the verbal content from the transcript and formulate the member's perception of the trainer (using Mann's factor names). Then we compare this formulation with the frequency counts in each of the sixteen categories. Keeping these facts in mind, Paul's career is outlined in Table 3.

For comparison, we tabulate the 'career' of one of the higher interactors in the same group (see Table 4). When we compare the total interaction initiated by Paul with that of the other members, we are struck immediately by the inconsistency in the amount of his participation in different sessions and by the number of his absences. Examination of his 313 contributions reveals that his initial refusal to accept the implicit demand of the trainer for expression and involvement, and his refusal of the trainer's independent, analytic approach to group life as a model greatly affected his capacity, and willingness, to 'work' in the group situation.

Paul's rejection of the trainer came early (Sessions 1 and 2). After suggesting that the members 'find out the function of the trainer', he listens to their perceptions, quickly rejecting the dependent, distressed climate that emerges at this point.

> 'Suppose we had something specific to work upon . . . we wouldn't even involve the trainer.'

His sarcasm:

> 'Are we showing hostility towards the trainer?'
> 'Yeah, if he (trainer) knows more about it, maybe he should do all the discussing.'

and mistrust:

> 'Yeah, but then, if you do trust a person he may take advantage of you.'

call attention to the fact that he is responding to the trainer, not in terms of his analytic role but that he perceives him as a clever, egocentric manipulator. Paul imagines that the trainer encroaches on his freedom. He offers a display of self-assertion to 'cure' the trainer of any interest he might have in manipulating him:

> *Trainer:* The group continues to attack Professors Matheson and Park whom it feels have deserted them.
> *Paul:* That's news!

Table 3

Paul's 'career' in the group

Session no.	1, 2 (3 absent)	4*	5, 6** (7 absent)	8, 9	10 (11 absent) 12**	13, 14*, 15*
Total interaction initiated	23	23	4	46	1	157
Perception of trainer	Trainer as 'manipulator'	Trainer as 'analyst'	? ⟵	Trainer's effect on ego state	⟶ ?	Trainer as 'audience'
Description of Paul's performance	'Counter-dependent flight'	'Dependent complaining'	? ⟵	Anxiety	⟶ ?	Concern with inner distress
Mann's categories	Counter-dependency	Guilt inducing, showing dependency, moving against	? ⟵	Expressing anxiety, denying anxiety	⟶ ?	Expressing anxiety, expressing depression
Interpersonal theme	Nurturance	Nurturance	? ⟵	Nurturance	⟶ ?	Nurturance control
Strategy used by Paul	Strident theoretic rejection of all influence from above	Pleading for a strong, protective trainer to manifest himself	? ⟵	Self-preservation	⟶ ?	To show how he suffers while advancing the trainer's cause in the group

* Highest initiator of interaction during that session
** Did not initiate any interaction during that session

Table 4

A parallel 'career' in the same group—Peter

Session no.	1, 2	3, 4	5, 6, 7 (absent), 8, 9	10, 11 (absent), 12, 13	14	15
Total interaction initiated	17, 30	21, 77	58, 35, 36, 23	48, 23, 31	19	22
Perception of trainer	As 'manipulator'	As authority figure/manipulator	As 'analyst'	As authority figure	As authority figure	Effect of the trainer on member's ego state
Description of Peter's performance	Counter-dependent flight	Rebellion: counter-dependent flight	Dependent-complaining	Rebellion	Loyalty	Depression
Mann's categories	Counter-dependence	Counter-dependence/moving against/resisting/guilt inducing	Guilt inducing/dependency/moving against	Moving against/counter-dependence/resisting/denying anxiety	Dependency/moving towards/identifying/accepting anxiety	Expressing-depression/denying depression
Interpersonal theme	Nurturance/control	Competence	Nurturance control	Control/nurturance/sexuality	Nurturance/control	Competence
Strategy	Rejection of all affection and influence of the trainer	Seeking a group environment in which their autonomy will be unquestionable	Pleading for the existence of a strong protective trainer	Emphasising the oppressive and autocratic aspects of the leader's role	Assuming the existence of a strong, protective leader	Self-accusation; self-berating and berating of the group

Throughout Paul's counterdependent flight, he works at the theme
that the trainer is trying to stir up the members' dependency needs
in order to meet his own selfish urge to be important. In nurturance
and control terms, Paul fears some kind of magic control by the
trainer, and is bent on mastering his own regressive desires to be
fed something he neither needs nor wants (Mann, 1967, pp. 91–2).

Paul does not attend Session 3. When he returns for Session 4 he
begins by emitting counterdependent behaviour:

> 'Well, I think we all know what poor feelings we have about the
> trainer.'
> 'Do we want him to leave?'
> 'I think it would be a delight to leave him off for one session.'

However, the accepting behaviour of other members in cherishing
the trainer 'rubs off' on Paul. He begins to react differently to the
trainer's silences, to his interpretations, and to his analytic role.

The data on Paul's behaviour during Session 4 shows that he
initiates the most interaction, and that the highest proportion of his
acts are in the categories guilt inducing, dependency, and moving
against the leader (trainer) as contrasted with his earlier counter-
dependence. This reflects a change in his perception of the trainer
(from 'manipulator' to 'analyst'). Concomitantly, there is a change in
strategy. Paul becomes a dependent complainer, expressing frustration
and dissatisfaction with the trainer's analytic role. His dependent
complaining is designed to arouse the guilt of the trainer by reminding
him that he is a 'bad breast' who deliberately deprives the dependent
members of the nurturance they need! By reminding the trainer of
his 'proper' function, Paul hopes that a radically different state of
affairs can be achieved (Mann, 1967, p. 82).

> Exemplars:
> 'The fact that he doesn't smile or anything.' (moving against)
> 'I think after a while we would miss him, because we would miss his
> comments, and we'd really get stuck.' (dependency)
> 'No! No! I think that most of us have decided that we don't want to
> expel him. Except for you . . . you'd like to see him leave.'
> (dependency)
> 'Yeah, what you expect and what you get are two different things.'
> (guilt inducing)
> 'I think he has seen too many horror movies!' (moving against)

Paul's capacity to participate in the work of the group is severely
limited at this point. He still refuses to accept the trainer as a model,
his behaviour reflects a rejection of independence, involvement, and
enactment (Mann, 1967, pp. 138–43).

The data on Paul in Sessions 5 and 6 reveal a significant decrease in the amount of interaction he initiates. In Session 4 he ranks highest; in Session 5 he ranks second lowest; in Session 6 although present he does not participate. He does not attend Session 7 at all!

In Sessions 8 and 9 Paul reveals himself as a vulnerable and threatened person in relation to what he perceives as a judging, dangerous trainer. His non-verbal indications of tension are given a focus by Mike.

> *Mike:* I think the only person in the group—that sort of I'm concerned about, that they should be quiet, is Paul, you know. I feel that Paul is the only person in the group that I can't communicate with. I want to know why he, why he sort of, why I feel like that. So I'm going to, sort of, throw a few balls into Paul's court right now.
> *Paul:* Well, I don't know. Why do you feel that way?
> *Mike:* Well, I don't know. I mean, what, what?
> *Jean:* Answer a question with a question (laughs).
> *Mike:* Why have, why have you been, you know, sort of lacking in participation?
> *Trainer:* The group has decided not to take on the trainer.
> (Group laughter.)
> *Paul:* Saved!
> *Jean:* No, you're not! No, you're not!

This statement of Jean's is the beginning of an attack, led by her, on Paul for his unexplained absences and his spasmodic participation. The barrage ends with Ken saying:

> I guess you're off the hook now.
> *Paul:* Am I, Mike? (He laughs)
> *Mike:* Well, ah, . . . you know . . . I don't even remember what topic we're on.

A few minutes later, when Ken asks what topic the groups should use to 'get going', Paul again becomes the focus of attention.

> (Silence.)
> *Ken:* So what will we use as a topic to get going?
> *Lois:* I knew that was coming.
> *Ken:* I don't know. I always seem to sort of get a . . .
> *Paul:* I think that what we have to do is, you know . . . as Lois was mentioning, is come up with something that is maybe bothering us, or something like this. We can't just talk about a topic.
> *Jean:* Well, that's what we have been wondering. What's bothering you?
> *Paul:* Nothing! I told you what was bothering me. I mean, nothing is bothering me.

Jean: I felt that last session something was bothering you.
Greg: He did tell us in a way what was bothering him. He was . . .
Jean: He said he didn't want to talk about it.

Jean continues to pressure Paul. But this ends quickly with Greg
supporting him, and Mike picking up the action again. The frequency
of interaction initiated by Paul for the rest of the session is higher
than for the first part. However, his contributions take the form of
'right', 'yeah, right', 'yes', 'no'. He appears to be participating, in so
far as he is talking. But he is not actively engaged in the 'work' of
the group.

In Session 10 Paul speaks only once. However, it is a significant
contribution in that he tries to take on the interpretive, intellectual
style of the trainer (enactment) for the very first time. The trainer has
just made three comments in quick succession:

'The group is pressing certain members to declare their loyalty.'
'Who goes with whom? That is the question.'
'And who is the enemy?'

Mike and Greg try to grasp the meaning of these statements and
surprisingly so does Paul:

> *Mike:* With whom, with whom do you sort of have an allegiance with,
> and you know, sort of an intimate relationship with, and those
> that you don't. Those that are the people . . . well, the people you
> have an intimate relationship with are close friends, in the group
> if you like. And those that you don't are, you know, kind of alien
> . . . enemies. I mean, I don't think . . .
> *Greg:* I think what he is trying to say, maybe is that anybody that is
> getting something out of the course readings is a spy or may be a
> spy.
> (Group laughter.)
> *Paul:* From the way Ken is . . . well, maybe he's not . . . but the way
> the trainer interprets it is that Ken is trying to draw out that
> person by presenting all sides.

Unfortunately, the nature of Paul's involvement is ignored by the
group. We observe that he does not attend Session 11, and attends
Session 12 but does not say a word. Early in Session 13, and continuing through Sessions 14 and 15 (during which Paul was the
highest initiator), he continues to express anxiety, but in a way that
is clearly different from his anxiety in Sessions 8 and 9.

In the earlier sessions, Paul's anxiety was based on the expressed
fear of either being abandoned, or attacked, by a malevolent trainer
(Bion, 1961, pp. 29–30). In his efforts to find 'regularity and purpose
amidst chaos' he develops negative perceptions of the trainer—he

sees him as strong, diabolical, dangerous (Sessions 1 and 2) and deliberately depriving (Session 4).

The expressed anxiety in Sessions 13, 14 and 15 are evidence of a changed perception of the trainer. Paul no longer mistrusts the trainer—this mistrust is now displaced and projected on to Mike and the rest of the group. If we interpret his remarks correctly, he seems to be saying that he suffered and failed in this group not because of the trainer but because of the other members.

> *Elaine:* Do you like the group, Paul?
>
> *Paul:* Sure, yeah. But the thing is, after all the apologies we made, away back. Actually, we were back at point one and we never came out of it. And Mike said we were at point one today. We haven't progressed at all.
>
> *Jean:* If you feel that way, and you're a part of the group, don't you think then that may be you should have said something?
>
> *Paul:* I did . . . Mike felt hostile towards me.
>
> *Mike:* I think it's part of your job, if you think the group is not getting anywhere, to come out and say it; and help the group to get along! I mean, it's no use sitting there, scribbling there with a pen! You don't come out to give us advice and help.
>
> *Paul:* I think the only member of the group that has really interacted was Lois. And I think the other members of the group haven't interacted at any time. I think they have said something to say something, but they haven't been themselves.
>
> *Jean:* What about Bonnie?
>
> *Paul:* Bonnie. Well, . . . Bonnie. But not as much as Lois, I think she (Lois) really comes out with what she feels, or how she feels inside . . . I think the majority are not willing to do this. We're not willing to come out with true views . . .
>
> *Mike:* Well, most of what I've said is being how I felt.
>
> *Paul:* You started before, manipulating the group, in saying some sort of things. You've been talking to get people started, to see what they'll say, but I don't know if that's your real true feeling. I don't know you as a person really. In fact, I don't know any of you as a person except Lois . . .

This last statement clearly illustrates the *mechanism of displacement. Paul's hostility towards Mike can readily be seen to be a symbolic attack on the trainer. The hostile and aggressive feelings he experiences towards the trainer (which he is now afraid to express) are displaced on to Mike, and diffused on to other members of the group. Although this displacement serves to relieve anxiety, it impedes Paul's own learning, as well as acting to block the group's awareness of what is going on.

Paul's 'dependency' and 'redemption through suffering' theme is expressed fairly openly at the end of the group; in the total context of his contributions it represents the 'litany' referred to by Mann:

Here one finds the distant God, the faithful who are tormented by all their jealous enemies, and repeated references to the human failings which have contributed to the disaster. The litany is a plea for the all-powerful to work a miracle and save the day; failing that, the next best thing would be to be forgiven for the innumerable consequences of human frailties and sin. . . . The litany expresses the latent hope of many distress performances: to be rescued, to regress, and be rewarded at least for one's efforts, by the compassionate God 'from whom all blessings flow'. (Mann, 1967, pp. 101–2)

Paul initiates most of the interaction in Sessions 14 and 15. He articulates clearly his plea to the trainer, to offer some relief to the 'faithful' who display themselves as bruised and discouraged:

> Well, as I was saying, I had seen this. Maybe I've seen it a little too late, or maybe I should have come out . . . I don't know, as I said, you know, it takes a little while before you notice it.
> Yeah, but don't you feel that if you don't say anything, after a while that it builds up and you don't ah, you can get into one session and they, you . . . it keeps going on until the other session . . . before you know it you haven't said anything for quite a few.
> Well, as I said, when I had started to really become quiet was after the apologies had come up and I couldn't any longer seem to have anything to say, pertinent to say. I don't know why, I just didn't. Ah . . .
> Well, it wasn't even at the beginning but I guess, ah, it's just that, well, you know, as I said. I'd gone through a certain stage in the group. I felt that ah, like I felt there was no progress or anything like this. And ah, I didn't know what to say or what could be expressed, and all these things. You know, and ah, just generally disinterested.
> Somehow I still have to go back to that first session. I don't know why . . . to me, that first session affected me the most. I don't know if it affected anyone else, actually, but it did me.
> Well, the thing is, you feel that you can only spend so much time reacting to the session before, and all of a sudden she's gone down the drain! Everything you've said, you know, has all been for naught. I don't know. That's how I feel.

Mann (1967) describes Paul's disparagement in this termination phrase:

The issue of termination seems also to stir up feelings of failure in the competence area, and members may berate themselves for working and learning less than they should have. (p. 179)

This is reminiscent of Dunphy's 'myth-building', where the group speak of the 'ideal group', the 'ideal leader' or the 'Messiah'—especially as the terminal point of the group is approached.

A SOCIAL SYSTEMS APPROACH TO GROUP PROCESS

It is useful to view the small group as a particular type of open social system. Adopting this frame of reference, it becomes easier to explain certain developmental processes, in particular, the distinctive phase movements. Bales (1950) developed his explanation of small group process and his category system, with theoretical backing from Talcott Parsons. It is Parsons' and Smelser's (1956) model of institutional change which best describes the small learning group as an *open system. This model visualises change as taking place in seven stages, in accordance with scientific law; although, as pointed out by McLeish (1968), the model may be truncated, the sequence may be aborted, certain stages may be acclerated or repeated, etc. These seven stages are associated with and, in a sense, responsible for systemic change. These will be individually presented and examined in an attempt to interpret the relationship between phases and processes of change as they occur in small learning groups.

1st and 2nd stages of system change
  (1) A combination of *dissatisfaction* with productive achievement can be identified in sections of the group, combined with a sense of *opportunity* of the availability of resources for higher achievement.
  (2) These give rise to symptoms of disturbance, in the *form of negative emotional reactions* and *unrealistic aspirations* in certain elements of the group.

The learning groups observed all display these features—dissatisfaction, unjustified negative emotion, and unrealistic aspirations. These characteristics become prominent at a very early stage in the life of each of the learning groups.

Participants enter the group with at least two sets of expectations. The primary expectation is in relation to personal, rather than group-oriented goals. The second set of expectations is oriented towards cooperating in the achievement of an authority-designated objective. If the primary and secondary expectations are found to be incompatible, the attempt will be made to salvage the personal goals at the expense of the others. The authority-designated group objectives will be undermined, usually unconsciously, occasionally with premeditation. The trainer, representative of the authority-designated objectives, becomes the object of various subversive manœuvres. The personal goal expectations of the group members are often unrealistic: at their best, members are quite uncertain about the achievement of these personal goals. If asked to state them, the response is often hackneyed, in terms of clichés. They speak of 'becoming a more self-actualised person' or of 'getting to know myself better'. Further definition or clarification of this terminology reveals merely vacuity and fantasy.

The trainer comes armed with the intention to disclose the task objectives, as he sees them. The fate of this disclosure is often the crucial factor in relation to future group process. If the trainer's disclosure of aim creates a credibility gap between the expectancies of achieving personal *and* group goals, there will be an increase in group anxiety, confliction, and negativism towards the trainer. If the trainer's initial disclosure of aim tends to coincide with personal and group goals positive feelings of resolution, compliance, and initial dependence upon the trainer emerge and are expressed.

It has been mentioned earlier, that the self-analytic treatment lends itself to an initial 'expectancy shock' on the part of participants. The self-analytic trainer does not meet personal goal expectations in an organised way. Consequently, there is an increase, rather than a decrease, in personal anxiety. The expectancy shock also tends to generate overt animosity towards the trainer. The depth and the quality of negativism towards the trainer are out of all proportion to the situation. In terms of the rationale available for interpreting such extensive negative behaviour, its determination is perhaps best examined from a psychoanalytic, rather than a phenomenological point of view.

In contrast to the self-analytic treatment, the direct communications techniques tend to suggest an initial coincidence between personal goals and group task objectives. The resultant feelings are therefore contrary to those of the self-analytic group—at least to begin with. Initially, the direct communications treatment tends to generate contentment, decreased anxiety, and dependency feelings. Such positive reactions do not endure for long. What seems to happen in the direct communications method is that the trainer's task objectives are in initial concert with the personal goals of the group membership, but there follows a period where the participants become aware that *work* is involved. We detect that the expectations of members of these small groups are that they have often come together to *feel*, infrequently to work. They also anticipate a magical, painless, and possibly ecstatic transformation of their personalities and mode of life as a result of the group 'experience'. When the trainer of the direct communications group begins to demonstrate that, regardless of the emotional nature of the material to be covered, there is still a personal risk, involvement, and work, the membership begins to shift emotional gear. The initial feeling of contentment, compliance and trainer-dependence are replaced by the same uncertainties, increased personal anxieties, and trainer-directed hostilities which are prominent earlier in the self-analytic group. What happens is that we see that both methods, extremely divergent in style, in fact generate similar emotional cultures. The basis for the similarity lies in the conflict that develops in group members between the need for emotional *expression* (the personal goal) and the *task* (the group goal). There is a personal goal commitment to emotional expressiveness and a group task requirement for work: these are in conflict. This generates frustration which begets negativism.

A number of authors familiar with group process express a similar view about the early ambivalence between personal and group goals. Kadis *et al.* (1963) interpret the early conflict as a group attempt at *homeostasis*. This involves a number of dichotomies. Decisions must be made by group members on rules about such matters as sensitivity or insensitivity to others; personal aggression or passivity; becoming pro- or anti-task; being for or against change. In a similar vein, Stock and Thelen (1958), borrowing heavily from Bion, conceptualise the group process as a reflection of the shifting balance struck by the group between the forces concerned with expression of emotionality and forces concerned with cooperative work.

From this point on what we see is the need for members to make a number of decisions about their position in the group. This is due to the fact that the group reality has exposed a number of personal goals of some members as unrealistic. Increasingly, the trainer becomes the focus of negative material since he personifies the task, seeking to represent reality and reason in place of personal irrationality and irresponsiblity. Thus the trainer becomes the object of conscious, and unconscious, attempts to thwart progress in achieving the group task. This will come as no surprise to most trainers, nor to group therapists. The existence and nature of negative feelings are expressed through such defence mechanisms as projection and displacement. The unconscious origin of the negative material directed toward the trainer is attested to by the fact that the emotion is largely unjustified, it is beyond all measure, and it is manifestly ambivalent. The members are frequently, and obviously, quite unaware and unconscious of their desires to undermine the trainer. The antagonism they express is described by Foulkes (1964) who sees such behaviour as the result of conflict between the urge to repeat older, infantile patterns and the urge to achieve socially-oriented goals by accepting, combining and cooperating with others in a work-oriented way. In this conflict, now the task, now the expression of emotion takes precedence.

It can be seen that the first two phenomena originating system change become prominent in the initial stages of small learning groups. Symptoms of dissatisfaction, and disturbance, appear in the form of unjustified negative emotional reactions and unrealistic aspirations on the part of group members.

3rd stage of system change

A *covert* process of handling tensions, over-negative emotion and unrealistic aspirations, with the mobilisation of motivational resources to construct new value patterns in the form of new group norms.

The first stages of system change appear in both kinds of small group —warm and structured or cold and unstructured. The third stage also appears, the covert process of 'handling' the emotional tensions resulting from the early meetings of the group. 'Covert' means that the process is out of the awareness of individual participants, and is in this sense unconscious. It is represented by surreptitious and subversive attempts to work out new norms for the group. These unconscious attempts to institute new values in the group are in line with the personal need systems of the membership. These are expressed primarily in attacks directed towards the trainer. The trainer is seen initially as the most influential person in the establishment of group norms: it is not for some time that the members turn to each other as a source of collective power and of new anti-trainer values.

The unconscious attempts to influence the trainer can be grouped under four main heads:

(1) *'Seduction'*. The trainer becomes the object of member patronage, expressed love, attention, and positive 'testimonials'. He is built up as one who can provide help and guidance. The main object of the inflation of the trainer's status is to 'seduce' him into re-structuring the group situation in line with the members' initial expectations. One way of seducing the trainer is to identify with those aspects of work which are in line with personal needs. In the direct communications group, for example, members try to turn the group into an 'encounter' rather than a 'work' group. This desire to become a 'sensitive' encounter group, rather than a more traditional 'learning

group', is based on the expectations for encounter that members bring to the group. The trainer's express plea for personal commitment to the task (learning) is used against him by the 'encounter' members who seek to promote commitment to interpersonal sensitivity. There is normally a short period when the more dependent members adopt a 'work to please' approach to the task assigned by the trainer. Eventually, this leads up to an overture to the trainer for more personal attention and consideration for these members. When the trainer fails to respond, the work ethic is unceremoniously dropped. Wolf (in Rosenbaum and Berger, 1963) has termed this behaviour the 'missionary spirit'. The unconscious mechanism displayed by attempts at seduction is the *positive transference* to the trainer who is perceived as the helpful father.

(2) *'Confrontation'.* To develop new norms for the group in line with member desires, it seems necessary for certain members to confront the trainer as manipulative, or in some way as incompetent. More directly, the trainer-assigned task is treated with disdain, ignored, passed over as irrelevant. Members enter into a confrontive power struggle with the trainer, apparently seeking to promote a re-structuring of the group. Various defence mechanisms can be easily recognised, especially *projection*. All kinds of undesirable qualities are discovered in, or assigned to, the trainer. The intention seems to be to destroy his credibility and that of authority in general.

(3) *'Castration'.* In the display of negative feelings towards the trainer, the exaggerated quality of the negativism can only be accounted for by unconscious dynamics—specifically *negative transference*. The trainer frequently becomes the butt of very poorly disguised jokes, gestures which symbolically reduce him to impotence. For example, his interpretations are treated as gross manifestations of personal prejudice. The explanation of these exaggerated and unreasonable negative feelings which participants sometimes volunteer is the desire to change the group in a direction more favourable to the felt needs of the members. For most members at this stage, the change seems to demand the destruction of the trainer, and what he has come to represent.

The trainer's actual behaviour is hardly at all a justification for the negative hostility he receives. But he is perceived by participants as the evil father who is promoting a 'hard' line—reason, reality and work. For members to achieve their less acceptable, more primordial intentions it is necessary to destroy the 'old man'. In trying to do so, they frequently allow everything to 'hang out'—especially their *negative transference.* The more sophisticated displace their negativism on to a convenient scapegoat. This will normally be a more dependent member who serves as trainer substitute. Other kinds of hostility, of a less sensational form, are reflected in the non-verbal behaviour of certain members. They become sullen, silent and introspective—they behave very much like a child who is in a 'pout' with dad. This may be accompanied by personal distancing in seating arrangements, or in body posture. Actual physical assault has, so far, been rare, although physical threats are not exceptional. It seems merely common sense to view such forms of behaviour as manifestations of an unconscious, negative transference. The reactions described are quite out-of-touch with the realities of the here-and-now group situation.

(4) *'Ambivalence'.* In the eyes of the group, the trainer is responsible for the group task. To influence the trainer it is necessary to adopt a position with regard to this assigned task. In the use of 'seduction' as a strategy it was mentioned that individuals seek to *identify* with positive aspects of the task in line with their personal goals, while deprecating the need for collective action, or extensive work. It is possible also, as we have seen, to resist the task as outlined—the usual forms of resistance being shown in the form of personal *isolation, silence, withdrawal.* Other unconscious task resistances assume more nefarious shapes. Such expressive, non-verbal acts as coming late, missing sessions, leaving early, all carry a latent message of resistance. Various rationalisations are provided which seek to explain away such behaviour. But the intention (conscious or unconscious) is to attract trainer attention to the desire to achieve personal goals, and to set up new and distinctive norms in the group.

Task resistance is also manifested in the sociopathic acting-out and clowning, to which some members resort. All these devices are non-work-oriented, attention-getting devices. The rewards for such behaviours are threefold: (a) the resolution, or at least the expression, of certain personal needs; (b) the undermining of the trainer's influence and the promotion of personal norms; and (c) the destruction of any existing work ethic in the group.

The attempts by individuals to influence the trainer in these ways are usually unsuccessful. It becomes necessary to resort to other individuals to achieve personal anti-task goals in the group. At this point members turn to each other as potential sources of group power. They resort to various manœuvres designed towards influencing the trainer, but using the group as the medium of such influence. These unconscious attempts to influence others and to mobilise motivational resources for new group norms can be grouped under two main headings.

(i) *Achieving personal power through competition for status.* One way to become influential is to overpower the others and force new norms upon the group. In the small learning group it is clear that the highly interactive members are high in group power. Words provide the vehicle for the exercise of influence and control. When the group only meets for a short time, 'air time', i.e. available speaking time, becomes a precious commodity. Those who can monopolise it have access to one of the main resources of power not available to silent members. The verbal monopoliser who, characteristically, uses defensive *intellectualisation*, is frequently the person who seizes and maintains power through verbal control. Those who are more selective and do not monopolise, but who still use 'air time' as a main source of power, are found to be high in *advice-giving, information-giving*, and *suggestions*. (Matheson, 1971). The group is starved for information and direction in its early meetings. It seems that such individuals as the 'monopoliser', 'intellectualiser', 'information- and advice-giver' provide an essential service to the group. But they also tend to undermine many of the learning or work aspects of the group process—this because of their prime concern with their own personal needs. Frequently, their contributions can be objectively designated as a selfish use of group resources for the purpose of personal prestige and status building, rather than as a disinterested service on behalf of the group.

(ii) *Forming cliques.* It appears altruistic, on the surface, to join coalitions to achieve certain group objectives. However, the usual motives behind coalitions are patently selfish. In the case of small learning groups, coalitions are oriented towards altering group norms and achieving personal objectives. The various techniques used in face-to-face groups to develop coalitions are of some interest. One frequently used technique is to relate one's past experience to an attentive group. Normally, a 'mirror reaction' (Foulkes, 1964) will be generated, other members will join in a conscious or unconscious affiliation with the narrator. This is McDougall's principle of contagious generation of emotion. For success, it need not deal with achievements. Sympathetic emotion can arise through the use of fantasy, free association, or dramatisation of group incidents. Another method commonly used in developing allegiances and subgroups is for members to single out the trainer or some other member as a stimulus-object to which all can react with a common emotion. Members of groups find it easier to work in concert than in opposition. The use of the same defensive technique is a way of influencing others. For example, projection of blame for group failure upon the trainer generates a feeling of unity amongst members of the group in conformity with the well-known 'scapegoat' mechanism. Intellectualisations and rationalisations provide similar defensive mechanisms which operate to seduce other members towards affiliative ties. Silence is also a defence: the silent members tend to band together in collusive resistance, signified by withdrawal which is basically and manifestly a withdrawal from the assigned task. Similarly, those who act out, fantasy, or dramatise tend to identify with each other and to form a psychological subgroup.

The appearance of coalitions, which may look promising for the trainer at first sight, is really seldom a good sign. The purpose of cliques and subgroups is to promote certain group values, or norms. These norms will, more often than not, be in contradiction to the values of the majority of the other members, as well as being in opposition to the trainer's learning objectives. This is not to say that subgrouping should be stopped. It is highly unlikely that any trainer would be successful in stopping affiliational trends even if he tried, and any effort towards this objective would be used against him by the subgroupings which would develop in any case. What is more important is that clique-formation be understood in its latent, as well as in its manifest, aspects. It must also be understood as a social system process. The emergence of subgroups is another illustration of the covert process of handling internal group tensions. Subgroups act to mobilise motivational resources: they exist to promote private subgroup norms.

4th stage of system change
    A supportive tolerance for new ideas without any individual member taking responsibility for their implementation.

Up to this point, it has been noted that a combination of unjustified negative emotional reactions, directed mainly toward the trainer, and unrealistic personal aspirations can be expected to generate defensive, unconscious and covert manœuvres from various group members. These defensive reactions are primarily directed towards altering the norms of the group implicitly imposed up to this point by the trainer. The members' reactions are aimed at producing a value structure more in line with their own idiosyncratic, narcissistic goals. The defensive reactions discussed to this point include positive and negative *transference, *identification, *projection, *displacement, *symbolisation, *rationalisation. In addition to these unconscious, covert processes the individual members have turned away from unsuccessful attempts to seduce, confront, antagonise, or resist the trainer and tried, instead, to mobilise the resources of their fellow group members. The intention of acquiring power through coalition and subgroup formation is to alter the existing normative structure of the group and to promote personal goals.

The investment of energy by various members of the group gradually moves away from a single frame of reference (the trainer) to multiple frames of reference (other members). Additionally, the theme of the group alters from competition to cooperation. The change is towards affiliation and shared complicity. A certain supportiveness and cohesion has been building up in the group. To promote various personal values the individual members begin to realise that they need support from others. This means they must support others in turn. A climate of tolerance and compliant listening is seen to be necessary.

The new norm of shared responsibility has several distinct advantages. As new material, in the form of information, suggestion, or ideas, is presented by any one member, he discovers valuable allies in his own subgroup. The responsibility for success or failure is thus shared. The overall success or failure of the group is not yet considered the responsibility of any individual member or subgroup. According to the members' perceptions, it is the responsibility of the trainer to see that the group is successful. Only the introduction of new material, designed to alter the direction of the group towards or away from personal involvement, or towards or away from task investment, is the shared responsibility of the member or subgroup. When the life or death of the group is in question, praise or blame accrues to the trainer.

The process of devolving responsibility to the individual group members seems to be the most difficult task facing the trainer. Not all trainers are prepared to yield their responsibility, especially when the group seems guaranteed success. It is part of the role of the trainer to abdicate authority, and become more and more a member. This means that he must train the group to accept responsibility for their own learnings. If he does not incorporate this as an objective, he does the members a disservice: their learning process will be handicapped because of their continued dependence on him.

The process of change in the group involves a period during which there is supportive tolerance for new ideas without anyone having responsibility for the implementation of these new ideas.

5th stage of system change
    Positive attempts to become committed to the new idea.

This involves continuance of the cooperative, shared-complicity norms which have now been adopted by the group. Materials, or ideas, which have been accepted and which have generated a group consensus, are promoted: materials, or ideas, which do not receive sufficient group consensus are rejected. A member, or subgroup, may promote a particular theme which by virtue of the nature of the material, will find acceptance in the various other group coalitions. The materials, themes or ideas of one faction will be positively reinforced by other factions. If there is a consensus, or majority support for such new material, it becomes adopted. If there is no consensus, then it is dropped for a time, or a quarrel may develop over the contradictions in value, or emotion, represented by this material. In these ways, various themes are promoted over time and the group becomes gradually, but positively, committed to various new ideas.

6th stage of system change
    Responsible implementation by individuals with consequential reward or punishments for their innovations.

The development of responsibility in the group was seen as an initial phase of total absence of individual responsibility and a projection of love, blame, or guilt upon the trainer. At a later point, the development of subgroups and affiliations takes place over a period of shared complicity in the invoking of new material or ideas. At this time, the trainer still bears the greater onus for the success or failure of the group. A major function of the trainer in a small learning group is to move the members out of the responsibility vacuum and into a position of individual responsibility for action, and its learned consequences. It seems necessary for the trainer to become gradually less and less of an authority and more and more an equal member of the group. In the stage of shared complicity individual members do not take individual responsibility for their ideas, but shift the responsibility on to their subgroup. When the material receives group consensus it becomes necessary for certain members, most likely the ones who originally introduced the material, to accept the position of salesmen (or as Parsons and Smelser put it—entrepreneurs) of the new agenda. Individual responsibility now becomes a reality. In this novel role the member must accept the consequences of his individual success or failure. The promotion of the new material, idea, or theme, after adoption as a legitimate agenda, becomes the sole responsibility of the entrepreneur. His success in selling and in changing the values or norms of the group will result in increased status and power. Failure results in the loss of status and power. An alternative agenda will be approved, other members will act as salesmen in the promotion of these agendas.

7th stage of system change
The ultimate stage is represented by routinisation.

The new norms and standards, having been accepted as 'the way of doing things', become institutionalised and remain as part of the group structure until the process of change begins again. The group may become fixated and fail to move from an established position because of this powerful tendency towards routinisation. It may remain, for very long periods of time, in a non-adaptive, non-learning stance—even though this is clearly not to the advantage of the groups in terms of learning objectives. Fear, timidity, lack of intellectual, emotional, or moral resources afflict all groups at some stage or other—in some of the groups we have observed this condition has set in early and has been chronic. The effect of these factors is to inhibit change, progress and learning, sometimes to an absolute degree.

3

SOME NOVEL GROUP METHODS

AIMS AND PURPOSES IN HIGHER EDUCATION

One way of defining the aim of education is in terms of the ideal product. This is the educated man, or woman, professionally trained and competent as engineer, architect, doctor, biologist or teacher. In addition to a body of knowledge and skills relating to his specialism, this person has certain attitudes to knowledge, to society and to professional work. In addition, he should be adaptive and intelligent, with creative 'know-how' in his particular professional field of work since modern technological society demands above all a capacity to change in response to new conditions. There are two different processes in higher education—a training in cognitive and manipulative skills, and an education which involves an orientation towards, and at the same time, a liberation from the here-and-now.

The purposes of training and education are frequently in conflict. Indeed it is often argued that they are incompatible. But, if we accept the aim stated, certain lines of conduct are indicated for the teacher who is interested to ensure that certain essential developments take place in the student. These lie in the direction of transforming relatively irresponsible and immature children into responsible, mature professional individuals. This change is not, of course, the prime responsibility of the teacher. Part of it is the result of growth, part is the result of family and neighbourhood influences, part is due to more personal influences such as books, religious conversion, political movements. But in relation to the educational process five special functions are commonly implied as belonging to the teacher. These are to communicate objective information in a standardised, impersonal form; to develop technical skills in the cognitive and manual fields (e.g. the ability to develop hypotheses, to answer examination questions, to carry out laboratory or studiowork, etc.); to develop social competence in students; to help students in their individual development as personalities (cultivating such qualities as enthusiasm, integrity, courage, commitment); to assist students towards an insight into their own personalities, their own special abilities and weaknesses, and what the future possibilities might hold for them as individuals.

Traditionally, education has concentrated on the first two functions, with some slight attention paid to the third. As far as the average student is concerned this operates to inhibit his powers of creative thinking and performance. The functions of fostering personal acceptability and self-insight have been actualised only in the context of understanding facts, and the relationship between them, within the narrow specialism in which the student is being trained. There is room for a Copernican revolution similar to that which has occurred in primary school education in the past half-century. Under the Ptolemaic regime, everything in the classroom revolves around the teacher who is the centre and source of warmth and light. The Copernican revolution puts the student at the centre of the educational process. Small learning groups in place of large formal lecture encounters come to the forefront.

This involves a revolution in the attitudes and practices of both teacher and students. The spontaneity of the student must be preserved whilst bringing to bear on him in a carefully graduated way the full load of human culture. The first part involves a tolerance of error, immaturity and ambiguity foreign to most teachers. The vast majority operate a work ethic which demands that they direct the student's attention in short order to the 'correct', which means *accepted* answer. Tolerance of ambiguity means that unsolved questions, no less than 'decided' ones, come up for discussion. This implies an ability on the part of the teacher to admit that he doesn't know the answer. Time must be treated as abundant, and expendable, which involves considerable reorganisation of the time-table to cut out what is for most students the deadwood of formal encounters (lectures, routinised laboratory work, routine assignments of one kind or another).

Problems and projects which reflect the students' as well as the teacher's interest replace the attempt at 'comprehensive coverage' so dear to most teachers as an abstract ideal. Information and skills are available in 'banks' (libraries, expert staff, laboratories) to be drawn on at need. Teaching becomes *problem*-oriented rather than *solution*-oriented. It starts from the real needs and interests of the student. Tolerance of error implies four freedoms for the student, and the teacher. First of all, there is freedom to make mistakes and perhaps learn from them (this means non-authoritarian, non-directive teaching). Secondly, he is free to choose from the complex field of knowledge areas which specially interest him and which foster the developments planned for by the school. Freedom to work at his own pace, to learn at his own speed, is recognised. He is given the freedom to develop his own insights and solutions. In the learning group, properly organised, he should discover that freedom is inseparable from responsibility. In large measure, the student is made responsible for his own learnings.

The teacher's role becomes that of 'eye-opener', possibly even 'brain-opener'. His task is to show *connections* between the problems and projects, and the organised body of knowledge. This demands possessing a coherent body of knowledge and skills, together with the capacity to recognise new ways of doing things, and the generosity to applaud new solutions to old problems. If successful, he will draw the student, as if by a magnetic force, towards appropriate criteria and standards. Under the Copernican regime, the teacher's function is to provide a model or exemplar—of objectivity, tolerance, enthusiasm for his special subject and for humane learning.

METHODS OF SMALL GROUP TEACHING

The common element in teaching methods which preserve, or perhaps develop, creativity is a special kind of informality based on fellowship and the essential equality of teachers and learners, partners in a common pursuit. The informality of the method is shown by the fact that the teacher abandons the function of oracle, he relinquishes control of every detail of the didactic situation. The degree to which he abdicates these functions varies from one method to another.

(1) *Free group discussion*

This technique has been used by Barnett (1955) in an attempt to liberalise the science curriculum, and by Abercrombie (1960) in medicine. In each of these areas there is a strong emphasis on content and a prescribed set of technical skills. The method is based on a 'free floating discussion', a group therapeutic technique developed from psychoanalysis. Freud invented the method whereby the therapist (psychiatrist) is trained to listen, and refrain from comment, while the patient, unawares, reveals the source of inner conflict by uninhibited talk. In free discussion the same principle operates. The group meets and is given a brief to the effect that spontaneous talk is invited. A theme may be stated by the 'organiser', 'trainer' or 'promoter'. But this is the extent of the direction supplied to the participating students. Unlike the lecture, or the guided discussion, communications travel in a great number of directions.

In practice, a great number of apparently random exchanges takes place, but an underlying theme soon emerges. This recurs again and again. Eventually, given time, the group may solve the problem. But this is not the real objective of the method. The advantage of this method is that students discover, in the course of discussion, that they each have highly specific, even idiosyncratic reactions to problems, to situations, to individuals; that these reactions often prevent them from learning; that they always slow down their ability to solve problems. An understanding of the nature of knowledge, and self-insight, is given them in a manner no other teaching method can provide. It is first-hand, personal experience of the shifting character of experience, the ambiguity of evidence, the tenuous basis of our most profound convictions. The major disadvantage of the method is the apparently formless nature of the discussion, and the large amount of time necessary whilst the participants adjust to each other, discover where the real problem lies, and assimilate the intended learning outcome. From the point of view of the teacher dominated by the demands of curriculum and time-table, it bears the character of an aimless and interminable discussion. It has the further disadvantage that the learnings are impossible to assess by traditional criteria. But, granted that free discussion has specific objectives, and is not an all-purpose method of teaching, novel criteria of evaluation are essential. This is true of every method of teaching, even the established lecture and examination system. Free group discussion cannot be used half-heartedly; it should not be used without a clear understanding of its limitations and possibilities. The following example shows it in operation.

A group of six volunteers (student teachers), engaged for five hours of free group discussion on the theme, 'How we learn—and what are the blocks to learning?' came up with the following principles. These were not statements culled from textbooks, but were woven out of, and at the same time became part of, the students' living experience.

(a) Events which are bound up with emotion of some kind stay longer in the memory: a certain amount of conflict and anxiety helps learning. Sometimes we recall the emotion rather than the real, complex experience. At the same time, *fear* of conflict and of novelty often prevents learning: we find security in previously acquired knowledge.

(b) Learning patterns differ from one person to another: there are different *styles* in learning. Thus it seems to be impossible to say whether anything in particular is essential to learning—whether it be interest, compulsion, enthusiasm, self-involvement or even self-confidence. Each of these *helps* on occasion, but learning can take place in their absence.

(c) To form one's own opinions and to be able to defend them involves more work than accepting opinions on authority. Enthusiasm is necessary for this. In the last analysis you can only learn from your own personal involvement and experience. The essential thing is to have a 'feeling' about what one has learned as well as remembering it—it is only this kind of knowledge which can be applied.

(d) There are no really 'false' situations (this referred to their own group) although some are more 'contrived' than others. It is possible to learn even in what seems to be a false situation, provided one has both a *goal* and a *method* of learning. The trick is often to define the problem in a form which can lead to a solution.

(e) Our character comes out in the way we present 'facts'. This inevitably produces a *reaction* (sometimes favourable, sometimes unfavourable) which seems to be a reaction to the facts, but is a reaction to the 'instructor'. Thus it is easier to learn from some people than it is from others.

(f) It is possible to learn by analysing one's own experience: books are not necessarily the best instructors. A method of observation and a technique of analysis will make this type of learning more effective and valid.

(g) Learning is a much more complex operation or process than simple rote memory. It involves the emotions and feelings as well as a variety of distinct processes. We are not aware how much our emotions are involved both in learning and in teaching.

(h) Perhaps the most valuable outcome of the series was the sense of inadequacy in confronting a large and undefined problem. Members of the group were enabled to feel 'in their own skins' the emotions of the school child on first going to school, or learning to walk, or indeed learning any new thing. This was an illumination which no other technique of teaching could produce. It would seem to be a vital insight which *all* student-teachers should experience.

(i) Individual members of the group learned about their own mode of learning, the attitudes to novelty and authority which inhibit them, the qualities necessary for success in learning. The group also realised that they had learned more than was possible to verbalise at this stage.

(j) Some members were beginning to see that behaviour of individuals in groups is not arbitrary and random. Some agreed that there may be some significance, for example, in where people sit and how they comport themselves at various points of the discussion. The other recognition of causality in group behaviour was not so readily accepted: that roles are 'picked up' very quickly and that role expectations act as a constraint, as well as giving a certain degree of freedom very quickly.

(k) The main conclusion was that it seemed to be extraordinarily difficult really *to listen* to what others are saying. The discussion could have been more profitable if (even after all these years of class teaching) the group had some knowledge of *how* to listen and had a better method of analysing and remembering what was said.

The students were given no help or guidance at any point. In fact, the termination point was reached when the 'instructor' presented the above summary of insights taken from the taped discussions. It became clear that by accepting the traditional role at this point, the instructor generated a reaction that the students were unwilling, or unable, to develop their own specific insights. They seemed to conclude that the 'instructor' really did know the 'answer' to the questions posed and had been playing a 'game' or confidence trick with them.

(2) *The *Tavistock method*

This is a special adaptation of free group discussion developed by Bion (1961) where the attention of the group is focused on the 'here-and-now' situation with the task of observing and understanding behaviour 'as it happens'. The trainer is a non-participant observer who 'reflects' back into the group the latent messages and group process at irregular, and unpredictable, intervals. By refusing various overtures from members of the group he establishes that his function is to provide analytic interpretations of the on-going dynamics of the group. He attempts by the timing of his interventions to keep the group concerned with process and content, and to retain the here-and-now emphasis. He deals with the defensive styles of group members, but in a fashion which doesn't expose the individual to group criticism. The basis of his interpretation is that everything said and done is done on behalf of the group. He is not supportive, friendly or extraverted, his role is to be a neutral, somewhat ambiguous figure who only speaks to provide an interpretation. In a sense, he acts as a blank screen on which the members of the group can project their images of authority.

'Transference' phenomena appear as a normal reaction of group members to this particular role: these are analysed as part of the on-going group dynamic process. His object is to reflect impressions back to the participants in an objective fashion. Other dynamics which appear within the context of the group are considered in the same manner, their interpretations are provided to the group members in the same objective style. The way in which the group members choose to deal with these interpretations, and with the trainer, is left entirely to them. The only condition imposed by the trainer is that *all* behaviour is subject to analysis.

The Tavistock training is an open-ended exercise where no one, not even those who organise it, can say what the specific outcomes will be for the individual participants. In essence, it is the setting-up of a learning situation where it is hoped that particular insights will be obtained into human behaviour by those participating, behaving at the same time as they are observing others. The method seems to create a considerable amount of anxiety in the individuals and groups participating. A certain level of anxiety is compatible with minimal interference with the learning process, indeed there is an optimal level which promotes motivation and learning. This is known as the Yerkes-Dodson law, in fact. Skilled psychiatric consultancy is usually available to prevent the most extreme reactions which occasionally manifest themselves.

What is learned is probably based on the earlier preoccupations of the participant, whether these be religious, psychoanalytic, psychological, scientific, or whatever. The condition of anxiety generated, and the structure of the learning situation, direct the participant's attention to his own behaviour and his reactions to other members. The opportunity is given to re-examine one's basic attitudes to life, to other people, and to human groups in general.

Extreme forms of behaviour are anticipated where we have groups consisting of different ages and sex, and where we have variations in pace and emphasis arising from the differing backgrounds of experience of participants. In a particular group which contained a large number of professional psychiatrists and psychologists, thoughts naturally turned to the question of therapy in relation to neurosis and insanity. The opportunity presented itself of understanding the nature of mental illness by means of simulated behaviour patterns which were readily taken on, developed, and then abandoned by particular participants. These were regarded by the group as their spokesmen, acting out the particular reactions implicit in the situation.

The particular understandings which individuals develop and

what they may learn are almost certainly bound up with habitual ways of thinking about human behaviour. For example, it is possible to relate what is going on to learning theory. From this standpoint, there appears to be a total disregard of the principle of reinforcement which psychologists tend to assume is how people can be expected to learn. The situation of the group and its dynamics may be understood in terms of Freud's transference theory and the theory of 'insight' propounded by Freud and by the Gestalt psychologists. Or the conceptual model on which understanding is based may be communication and games theory. Group behaviour may be conceptualised in terms of accepting specific rules, and transmitting certain types of communication in symbolic terms. The open-ended nature of the experience means that it can be interpreted from a great variety of theoretical standpoints. Possibly what is actually learned depends on the mental equipment of the individual participant. This is not the whole story, for the learning that is provided for is not so much cognitive in character: the major focus of change is along the affective dimension. Infantile, juvenile and adolescent feelings are resuscitated and projected on to individuals in the group. This makes it possible to understand these relationships and reactions in a non-threatening 'simulated' way.

The insight intended in relation to the function and activities of the trainer in the group is that: (i) it is necessary to listen carefully to what he has to say, as he is normally engaged in spelling out the implications of different kinds of behaviour sponsored by the group: and (ii) that his intention is not to inhibit choice, but to point to the responsible attitude that choice is necessary, that the individuals and the group must act in accordance with a rational decision and take the consequences. This view derives from an existentialist interpretation of group life. This constitutes still another framework within which the group process can be conceptualised.

(3) Synectics: a method of developing creativity

Synectics is a group method developed by Gordon (1961) which uses rather specific techniques designed to develop creative capacity. The difference between synectics and traditional ways of fostering originality is that the inventors of this method claim that the most effective way to *control* creative action is to focus on non-rational, unconscious processes.

The basic theory is drawn from psychoanalysis. Freud defined the pre-conscious as mental content which is not normally available to consciousness, but which can be made so. The unconscious, on the other hand, can reach consciousness only in a heavily disguised and transformed way. In the synectic method it is assumed that human creativity can be markedly increased if people understand these levels of the psychic apparatus and how they operate.

Freud devised this description of our mental functioning to explain dreams and their content. In dreaming, the creative function is, so to speak, disinhibited, and operates more freely than in the waking state. When we are asleep we are most creative. The dream is a wish-fulfilment, charged with emotion. Gordon (1961) emphasises the fact that the emotional component is more important than the intellectual in the creative process. In the first stages of creation at least, the irrational is more important than the rational. This must be understood if we seek to increase the probability of success in devising novel solutions to problems.

The German poet Schiller understood this at the end of the eighteenth century. In a remarkable letter to his friend, the critic Körner, he says:

In the case of a creative mind, it seems to me it is as if the intellect has withdrawn its guards from the gates: ideas rush in pell-mell and only then does it review and examine the multitude. You worthy critics, or whatever you may call yourselves, are ashamed or afraid of the momentary and passing madness found in all real creators. It is the longer or shorter duration of this condition which distinguishes the thinking artist from the dreamer. Hence your complaints of unfruitfulness—you reject too soon and discriminate too severely.

This quotation declares two principles which form the basis for both the method of free association (Freud) and also the synectic method (Gordon). Synectics is very largely the same free association process as Freud used in treating neurosis. The two techniques agree in accepting the 'outlandish' and in breaking down traditional distinctions. Unlike psychoanalysis, however, synectics is organised as a group activity instead of with a single patient. The other main difference is that in synectics, free associations are directed towards a specific purpose, the solution of a clearly defined problem. A quotation from Gordon (1961, p. 158) parallels that from Schiller and points the similarity:

All problems present themselves to the mind as threats of failure. . . . This threat evokes a response in which the superficial solution is clutched frantically as a balm to anxiety. . . . Yet if we are to perceive all the implications and possibilities of the new, we must risk at least temporary ambiguity and disorder. . . . A new viewpoint depends on the capacity to risk and to understand the mechanisms by which the mind can make tolerable the temporary ambiguity implicit in risking.

There is a whole philosophy and psychology of education underlying this paragraph. From this stand-point, education is a *crippling*
process. The total outcome of the teaching process is very like the
outcome of criticism as Schiller sees it—spontaneity is lost and with
it the creative urge. This is because teachers are normally incapable
of tolerating ambiguity and error for any length of time. In Schiller's
words—they are afraid of 'the momentary and passing madness'
found in all real creators and their creations in their early stages.

The synectics group has tried over a long period to discover what
people actually *do* in problem-solving situations. The purpose is to
develop methods which accelerate and improve the solution of
technological problems. The basic purpose of synectic techniques is
to stimulate an attitude which 'makes the strange familiar and the
familiar strange'. Selected individuals are brought together and
trained in methods which it is hoped foster inventiveness. A synectics
group consists of five or six people, from a variety of backgrounds
and training. It is most fruitful to have a variety of personalities,
which tend to complement each other. This seems even more fruitful
than complementary skills. Discussion of the assigned problem is
tape-recorded and analysed to discover how particular concepts
originated and were developed. Essential to the synectic method is
an attempt to implement solutions by constructing models, or
prototypes, to discover whether the concept is really promising.

Three basic assumptions provide the charter for this training
method: first, the creative process can be studied and described concretely to yield a method which can be used to foster creativity;
secondly, the psychological processes underlying invention in the
arts and sciences are basically the same; thirdly, the process of individual creation is closely analogous to that of group creation.

These conclusions break with the commonplace assumptions: (i)
that it is only in pure science, the fine arts, or in poetry that you get
real creativity, and (ii) that the process is a mystery, not open to
scrutiny. By making it mandatory on each participant in a group to
explain his thoughts and feelings, crucial elements of the creative
process are laid bare.

Psychologists before Gordon had discovered a lot from auto-
biographies, and from experiments on problem-solving, about how
novel solutions are achieved. Comparing these materials from
individual psychology with the concepts developed in the course of
synectics exercises, it seems probable that the semi-conscious mental
activity which may take months or years for an individual to run
through can be compressed into a few hours by group work. The
process of creation in human terms seems best described as joining

D

together different, apparently disparate elements. Köhler describes
it as 'insight'. The word synectics is from the Greek, meaning 'to join
together'. Novelty arises by the insightful conjunction of two ideas—
similarly, by bringing together individuals with diverse abilities,
experience and personality in a problem-solving group, new creations
are to be expected.

Synectics, in brief, is an operation involving the conscious use of
pre-conscious psychological mechanisms to foster creative activity.
It can be shown that, when we deliberately function on a non-rational
basis, ideas develop by associative processes to an end-result which
could not be predicted beforehand. It is true that the ideas generated
are of unequal value, the point is that there are many more of them
when we lower our critical standards. Synectics is a group of procedures by which we disinhibit the creative process, casting aside pre-
conceived notions about where the solution to a stated problem is to
be found. Here Schiller's letter to Körner is again apposite. He
continues:

Looked at in isolation a thought may seem very trivial or very fantastic;
but it may be made more important by another thought that comes after it,
and in conjunction with other thoughts that may seem equally absurd, it
may turn out to be a most effective link. . . . When there is a creative mind,
Reason—so it seems to me—relaxes its watch upon the gates, and the ideas
rush in pell-mell, and only then does it look them through and examine
them in a mass. You critics . . . reject too soon and discriminate too
severely.

The ultimate solution must be rational and reality-based; however,
the process of *arriving at the solution* is not necessarily rational. The
process of discovery is not purely intellectual—it does not consist of
a systematic trying out of known solutions until the right key fits the
lock. This would imply that the supply of keys is complete and
comprehensive. On the other hand, synectics insists that to achieve
radical, new solutions we begin by throwing away the existing keys.
Hence, the group should include a diversity of people so that the
problem can be looked at from really novel and differing points of
view. No kind of person, nor specialised training, can be ruled out in
advance. Thus synectics groups can be composed of mixtures of
painters, mathematicians, advertising men, philosophers, actors,
mechanical engineers, architects, sociologists, biologists, musicians,
zoologists . . . What the group does *not* contain is an expert familiar
with the kind of problem being studied. The group can call in such
an expert for advice: the expert will, in any case, be called later into
the group and become a full member of it. But it is a mistake to have

expert opinion too early. A long process of creative communication between members must go on before concepts or solutions are tested in the reality dimension. This interaction, and creative communication, is fostered by specific mechanisms discovered in *successful* problem-solving groups.

In the beginning, Gordon used to give a general instruction to the group, or to a person, to be 'intuitive', to 'play around' with an idea, to 'become involved', 'detached', or 'irrelevant'. Such general instructions are difficult to implement. Individuals become self-conscious and inhibited. Such general instructions encourage them to play a role, instead of being natural and spontaneous. The critical faculty rears its ugly head, the participants wonder whether they are simply making fools of themselves.

Instead of general invitations to be intuitive, or involved, or irrelevant, the synectics method now defines concretely the operational procedure the group should adopt at different phases of the exercise. In the terminology used by synectics, these procedures are designed '*to make the strange familiar, and the familiar strange*'.

The first principle, 'making the strange familiar', is essential at the early stages. The first thing to do is to *understand* the problem, as given. This is the analytical phase. If the group persists too long in this phase the possibility of a novel solution will be excluded. It is not enough to make the strange familiar. We must pass to the next stage, 'making the familiar strange'. Otherwise the problem, confronted initially as a new and intrusive element of experience, will soon be related to previously understood phenomena, forcing it into an acceptable pattern which dispels uncertainty and reduces fear of the unknown. The traditional block to creativity is overlooking the fact that analysis is only a means to an end, a temporary and first stage. The second stage, 'making the familiar strange', is a conscious effort to achieve a new look—to disturb, invert, transpose, disrupt commonly accepted ideas, feelings and every-day way of looking at things. This is what every creative artist, sculptor or poet does in his work. In so doing he induces new experiences and conveys new meanings.

There are four synectic mechanisms or types of analogy which can be arranged in order of increasing detachment from reality.

(a) *The direct analogy*. This involves a direct comparison of parallel facts, knowledge or technology—for example, using the concepts, ideas, assumptions or findings of one branch of science and applying them to another. Brunel discovered the method of under-water construction whilst watching a sea-worm boring a hole in timber. The sea-worm makes a tube for itself into which it moves forward.

This procedure was adapted to under-water construction by the invention of the caisson. Another example is Newton's analogy between sound and light. His experiments on the disperson of light by a prism gave him the idea that 'possibly colour may be distinguished in its principal components red, orange, yellow, green, blue, indigo and deep violet, on the same ground that sound within an eighth is graduated into tones'. This direct analogy between light and sound enabled him to understand the nature of the spectrum.

(b) *Symbolic analogy.* The second kind of metaphor used to elicit pre-conscious and unconscious connections is called symbolic analogy. One synectics group used the Indian rope-trick as a symbolic analogy involving their problem. This was to devise a jacking mechanism which would fit into a box four inches square. The jack must extend to 3 ft and support a load of four tons. The Indian rope-trick was used as a stage leading to a solution. The analogy consists in the fact that the rope is soft to begin with (when shown to the audience) but becomes hard when the Indian begins to climb it. The group solved the problem, devising a jack made of two bicycle chains which emerged from the box back-to-back. Bicycle chains can only bend in one direction, so a rigid lifting mechanism was obtained. It could be stored easily by rewinding the chains separately into the box. Symbolic analogy means finding visual or other images which break away from the verbal mode and illuminate the path to the solution. The Indian rope-trick provides a developing series of images which illuminate how the jacking mechanism will eventually operate.

(c) *Personal analogy.* Personal analogy takes us further away from the reality dimension. This mechanism means identifying oneself with the elements of the problem. For example, useful insights into the nature and directions of stresses in buildings can probably be achieved by carrying a bucket of water at arms-length, pretending that one is (say) a concrete beam supporting a heavy load. Personal analogy means projecting oneself into the situation by identifying with material structures. It has links with an ancient theory in aesthetics, systematised by Theodor Lipps at the end of the nineteenth century in his theory of 'empathy'. Lipps taught that the feelings we experience in response to art, especially architectural works, are due to an unconscious tendency to project ourselves into the art-product. We 'feel ourselves into' the structure, hence the term *Einfühlung*, empathy.

A good illustration of personal analogy was used in solving the problem of converting the variable movement of a shaft into a constant motion. The shaft enters a 'black box' and turns at a speed which varies anywhere between 400 and 4,000 rpm. At the other end is another shaft which should turn at a regular speed of 400 rpm (see Figure 7). The problem is to discover what to put inside the black box to get this effect.

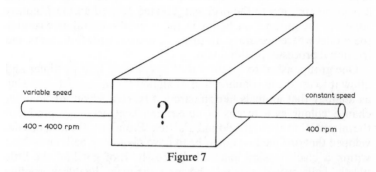

variable speed

400 - 4000 rpm

?

constant speed

400 rpm

Figure 7

In discussing this problem, the group was invited to enter the box metaphorically, and, using only their own bodies, without tools, without gears or any other mechanism, to reduce the speed from 4,000 rpm at one end to 400 rpm at the other. The description of the solution, using personal analogy, is extremely interesting. The group finally decided on a satisfactory solution—a liquid constant speed device. A section of dialogue shows how this answer to the problem was reached:

A. Okay I'm in the damn box. I grab the in-shaft with one hand and grab the out-shaft with the other. I let the in-shaft slip when I think it's going too fast so that the out-shaft will stay constant.

B. I read a watch and count.

C. How do you feel in there?

A. Well, my hands are getting . . . too hot to hold I guess . . . at least one hand, that is . . . the one that's acting like a clutch . . . slipping.

D. Now I'm in the box and I'm trying to be a governor . . . to be a feedback system . . . built in . . . Let's see. If I grab the out-shaft with my hands . . . and let's say there's a plate on the in-shaft so that my feet can press against it. I put my feet way out on the periphery of the plate and . . . what I really would like is for my feet to get smaller as the speed of the in-shaft increases because then the friction would be reduced and I would hold on to the out-shaft for dear life and its speed might remain constant.

(d) *Fantasy analogy.* The fourth synectic mechanism takes us furthest away from reality. Indeed, the easiest way to understand it is to think of the dream, where the reality dimension is abolished altogether. The synectics group may decide to repeal or abolish the well-known laws of science. Imagine what would happen if an anti-gravity device were available, if water flowed uphill instead of down, if burning substances produced cold instead of heat. In this mechanism, conscious self-deceit is advocated. The imagination then presents a possible solution to the problem. Having devised an ideal fantasy solution, the group then builds in the normal constraints changing the model where necessary. In this mechanism, wish-fulfilments and irrational processes predominate.

One group, asked to invent a roof to conserve heat in winter and allow it to escape in summer, first of all tied the problem down using as analogy that animals like the arctic fox, chameleon, or flounder change colour as a means of conserving heat. Zoology produced the information about the flounder's back. From this, the idea was developed that one method might be to have ping-pong balls embedded within a black roofing material. When the roof got hot, the little plastic balls would expand and pop through the black roofing material. The roof would therefore turn white, and reflect the heat of the sun. Given a cold day, the plastic balls would contract and pop back under the dark material. This material would absorb whatever heat was available. It is interesting that in spite of working on false information about the flounder (which changes colour in association with changes in *light* not heat) this group came up with a viable solution to the problem.

Day-dreaming, even megalomania, is encouraged, but only as transitional stages to lead to a reality-based solution. The group reinstates the rules of logic and the laws of nature. But, having disregarded them initially, a new perspective is obtained. Conceivably, too, useful aberrations of the laws may be recognised. Creative scientists who make revolutionary advances (people like Einstein and Darwin) must at some point disregard, disbelieve, forget about, the tight-wrapped science of their day. 'Established knowledge' acts as a constraint which binds the innovator.

The four mechanisms (direct, symbolic, personal and fantasy analogy) are psychological tools in the use of which the group is trained over a period. In solving assigned problems the group is invited to use now one, now the other device. The basic principle of synectics is that, being set a reality-based problem requiring a solution, the group is encouraged to 'play around' with ideas, however irrelevant, manipulating the elements of the problem into strange configurations. Eventually, in the course of mustering their resources of ideas and organising them into numerous patterns, a particular configuration emerges which can be accepted by the group as a step towards the solution. Continuing the discussion, using the same techniques, the complete solution is achieved. At this point the reality-check operates. A model, or prototype, is prepared and shown to work. It may be a new organisation of a work unit, a practical invention such as a new tin-opener—whatever it is, the idea is put to work to discover whether it is more productive, more efficient, *better* in some sense than existing practice.

In concluding this account of the mechanisms, it should be emphasised that synectics doesn't make creative activity any easier. It does introduce group activity which makes possible a continuing discussion, with now one person, now another, taking the lead and putting forward ideas. This induces creative individuals to continue beyond the point where they would normally give up, lacking the group stimulus. It induces people to work harder, in that they work at a high intensity for a longer period of time than normal. This shortens the time taken up by trials-and-errors which are a necessary preliminary to the sudden flash of insight, the perfect solution. The important principle is that the processes leading to the moment of insight are studied and used consciously and deliberately. In fact, people are *trained* to be creative and inventive.

(4) *Case-study method*

This method consists of presenting, in some detail, a problem to which a variety of solutions are appropriate. Case notes are provided for the students for study in advance, when they are expected to prepare their own individual, defensible solution. They meet, under the direction of a tutor, to discuss possible courses of action. As a result, an optimum solution should be reached by the group in the course of discussion. The instructor's task is to answer questions to provide further specific information, to raise doubts about half-way-house solutions, and to facilitate discussion. At the end, he should give a general evaluation.

This method is sometimes used as the sole method of teaching. It seems reasonable to suggest that normally it should be one of a number of techniques used in an integrated course. The case-study method, like other teaching methods, has very specific objectives: this means it is advantageous for some purposes and not for others.

The main advantages, and objectives, of the method are:

(a) It stimulates the students, as no other method does, to see problems as 'wholes' in a total context. It encourages them to synthesise the factual information and general principles of the subject they are studying.

(b) It creates a learning situation from which the student can derive knowledge about social situations, about people and their inter-relationships, thus providing a reality-based training for their future professional roles.

(c) It fosters the development of objectivity by encouraging students to commit themselves to a particular view of the case whilst maintaining an open mind as to the possibility of other solutions. They learn to be tolerant of the views of others and of ambiguity.

(d) It develops the habit of responsibility, since the case will normally call for an identification with some concerned individual who must come to a decision of some kind.

(e) It trains the student in the art of 'listening' and develops a sense of 'timing'.

(f) By constantly plunging students into the same kind of problem situation, the method enables them to 'work through' their irrationalism. It exposes to them their bias in favour of certain types of solution and their tendency to stop at half-way-house solutions. It works to discourage several kinds of academic irresponsibility.

The difficulties and disadvantages of the method are:

(a) It requires considerable experience of the method and the subject to be used successfully. More significantly, it demands a certain sensitivity to other people's points of view (including even that of the most immature student). These qualities develop over a period of time with considerable mental and spiritual travail. They do not come by nature.

(b) The cases must be most carefully selected with a view to:
    (i) the students' actual stage of development, and
    (ii) the particular points which the case illustrates in relation to the general principles of the subject.

(c) It is time-consuming, the discussion often seeming to be totally irrelevant, especially when the case is difficult and the students are unprepared.

(d) Unless the students are fully engaged by an excellent organisation of material, and guided by the necessary combination of permissiveness and leadership, their morale tends to sag sooner or later. This is because of the difficulties confronted in working in the group, and because of the discovered complexity of real, 'live' problems.

(e) There is, as yet, no appropriate method, except intuition, of examining the progress made by students in insight, sensitivity, responsibility, and the other qualities fostered by this method. Indeed, it seems to work against the success of the method when students are conscious of being assessed.

(f) Unless the tutor uses some other techniques (preferably of an indirect kind) students fail to generalise the solutions to particular cases. They concentrate on concrete issues and resist developing abstract concepts of a general character.

(g) Because of the difficulties, there has as yet been no proper evaluation of the case-study method, except in the form of the testimony of those with considerable experience in its use. This is, of course, true of other, including traditional, teaching methods.

(5) *The project*

The project is a means, not an end in itself. Its value is to develop an incentive to learn basic skills in a meaningful context. For the development of creative potential in students, projects need not be tied closely to the reality dimension. In certain cases the more the projects fly off into the empyrean, the better, in terms of the release of the creative imagination. Projects of too precise a nature should not be set, if this is the primary objective. Instead of being encouraged to make a scale model of St Paul's Cathedral, architectural students should be guided towards such problems as: the construction of model theatre sets for a 'technicolored' dream sequence; a summer chalet adapted to the special climatic and atmospheric conditions of the planet Mars, commissioned by a trade union official in the year 2500; a working model of the ideal woman of the same period. The whole thing would be discussed and evaluated in the same way as a normal architectural project. The same general principle applies—that slipshod work is not more acceptable in the realm of the highly imaginative, than in the most humdrum, reality-tied project. Fraternal group criticism, where the student outlines the objectives, the group leader poses certain questions directed to eliciting appropriate criteria to be used, and the student group tries to reach a consensus about whether the objectives have been achieved, is a useful technique ancillary to the free, synectic type of discussion. So long as the principle that there is no final, unique solution can be safeguarded, students can be encouraged to develop their own ideas, and, with them, their powers of original thinking. Knowledge should never be presented as though it were a closed system; feelings and reactions should never be prescribed by the teacher.

An interesting variant of the project method which links it with the objectives of synectics to accelerate creative functions has been devised by Matchett (1968), working in training laboratories in Bristol. It is called *Fundamental Design Method*. This consists of a three-week residential course offered to managers and senior personnel in industry—especially in the engineering and design areas. The

basic principles are of general application. The student is guided in
the choice of a project which would benefit not only himself, but the
sponsoring company. This is done before the course begins, the kinds
of gain anticipated being stated in some detail by the company and
the student. The course itself is organised around the *product* as the
practical outcome, and *system* as the theoretical organising concept.
In the residential part of the course, the student spends a good deal of
time by himself, being visited regularly by a tutor or consultant.
Emphasis is on reflective thinking. Using guidelines provided, the
student is directed towards understanding the nature of the existing
skills which he actually possesses, and how to develop these effectively. The main objective of the training (which consists of graduated
exercises, with continuous evaluation by the student and the trainer)
is to increase the *speed* with which judgements are made, and to
improve their *quality*. The decision process is the main focus on which
the individual concentrates. He himself singles out and analyses the
particular mental skills which are significant for the project and in
his job.

The exercises centre around the development of a series of 'mirrors'
by the student in which he perceives and apprehends the three systems
within which he works. These are the processes and product of his
thinking; aspects of the self which facilitate and inhibit the desired
outcome; aspects of the situation with the complex of needs which
must be satisfied. In constructing these 'mirrors', only those aspects
which have significance for the man and his job are included. The
function of the trainer is to lead the student to an *objective* view of
these three systems. The trainee discovers the nature of the constraints
which operate in these systems binding his powers of spontaneous
action. In this way, he discovers the area of decision open to him and
how to make the appropriate choices.

This description sounds very abstract and divorced from the real
world of industrial design. But, in reality, the student is working
throughout the period on very concrete tasks. Apart from the
project itself, which must be completed in prototype before the end
of the course, he is engaged in such activities as drawing up lists—
thirty jobs he does or is responsible for on his home ground; thirty
critical incidents at work; thirty different activities he is engaged in
during a single day, and so on. From these, an image of the work-
system in which he is involved begins to emerge and to achieve clarity
of definition. Similarly, by graded exercises in reflective thinking
about the design process, a clear image of the mental processes and
abilities necessary for effective functioning in the work situation is
developed. The person's own mental skills are dealt with in the same

way. Models of these various systems are the normal way of reporting. The analysis of progress on the project is carried out when clarity has been attained on the definition of the factors which make for success.

The emphasis here (unlike synectics) is on individual work and tuition—group work is mainly dyadic, although larger group meetings (up to twelve participants) occur. These are cognitively oriented in the sense that they are primarily *evaluative* sessions with the possibility of the group coming up with reality-based suggestions for improvement. The *content* of dyadic instruction has a *systems* orientation—the students on the course are being trained to work more effectively in groups, or rather *teams*, where roles and functions are clearly specified, and the emphasis is on the material product.

The descriptions given are of a few of the *techniques* which are useful for developing certain skills, amongst them creativity, in students. For their proper use, they require a certain *atmosphere* or climate of opinion—a non-authoritarian regime in which there is a real interest in and knowledge of the students as individuals. The methods work best where there is general acceptance of the notion that there is an essential equality of students and teachers, instead of a rigidly defined status hierarchy. The basic assumption is that the educational institution is dedicated to the discovery of truth and knowledge and that all members of the institution, whether students or teachers, share this quest. Therefore, group methods of this open kind can only work if the teachers are not too set in their ideas to consider themselves learners as well as teachers. Their use implies that the learning group is organised as a total educational environment with adequate space, rooms which can be used in a flexible manner, with decent libraries, workshops, studios and laboratories, where individuals can be 'persons within active groups', not 'personally ambitious social isolates'. The relative merits of these novel group methods are compared with more traditional teaching methods in the summaries which follow.

COMPARATIVE ANALYSIS OF GROUP METHODS

(1) LECTURE

Virtues

Coverage of fundamental points
Economical, planned and direct analysis of an area
Provides a general framework

Defects

Does not necessarily engage attention or participation
Inefficient and uneconomic of time when books available
Not adapted to individual needs
Tends to present knowledge as a 'closed' system

(2) GROUP TUTORIAL

Virtues

The interplay of minds stimulates thought
Combines economy of time and direction of effort with two-way
     communication
Permits considerable freedom to pursue interests in depth

Defects

Sometimes may appear to be aimless—therapeutic, not creative
Diffident, shy students may not participate
Tends to move slowly over ground to be covered, coverage inadequate

(3) FREE GROUP DISCUSSION

Virtues

Develops a sense of discipline and responsibility in the student group
Provides opportunity for genuine discussion, discovery and development
Enables instructor really to know students

Defects

May serve merely as an emotional release, but is not really a teaching
     device
Aimless and undisciplined
Often irrelevant to tutor's objectives

(4) SEMINAR

Virtues

Allows everyone to benefit from others' experience in a systematic
     framework
Participants are free to conduct research into their particular problem and
     present the results
Gives diffident members the opportunity to lead in a prepared and
     structured situation

Defects

Students have inadequate knowledge to contribute successfully
Can be ruined by a poor leader or chairman
Some 'sit back' when own interest has been covered

(5) INDIVIDUAL SUPERVISION (or TUTORIAL)

Virtues

Students really work
One-to-one interaction creates understanding and good relationship
  between student and tutor
Individual difficulties can be overcome

Defects

Logistics difficult because of large numbers and limited time
Personal relations between a given tutor and a particular student may not
  be the best
Perhaps intimidating to student

(6) ROLE PLAY

Virtues

Helps with self-expression, lucidity, quick-thinking
Students encouraged to *feel* as well as to think about different aspects
It can be great fun, and acts to improve human relations

Defects

Artificiality results when 'leader' or 'performers' are poor
Over self-conscious to start with: takes time to learn the technique
The 'sophisticated' student finds it difficult to cooperate

(7) LABORATORY

Virtues

Enables pursuit in depth and development of scientific method
It is learning by experience and concrete activity
Stimulates individual work and research attitudes

Defects

Time-consuming for students
Needs other supporting methods and intensive supervision
May be too desiccated and routinised ('school science')

(8) DEMONSTRATION

Virtues

Shows the correct procedure and allows student to analyse it in detail
Teacher's own failures make useful discussion points—criteria of
  excellence are built up
A concrete illustration of a skill is always better than mere talk about it

Defects

It often leads to a pale copy of what was intended, and may prevent the
student finding his own feet
Student may model performance on that of the teacher and thus stifle
initiative
Illustrates only one way of doing a thing

(9) CASE STUDY

Virtues

Draws in students in group interaction and uses their own life experience
Realistic discussion of principles in the concrete instance
Provides for emotional development ('insights') as well as for cognitive
understanding

Defects

Irrelevant material remembered
Over-simplification—abstracted from context may be too concrete
Depends on understanding leadership

(10) PROJECT

Virtues

Personal involvement and commitment in depth gives more thorough
knowledge
Student must use own resources
Demonstrates a number of different approaches to a single problem

Defects

Time-consuming
Needs careful directing, otherwise may achieve little
May prove great strain on the student if task is substantial

4

HOW DO POWER RELATIONSHIPS OPERATE

WITHIN THE GROUPS?

Power is most frequently defined as the ability to influence another person's behaviour (Collins and Guetzkow, 1967; Mishler and Waxler, 1968). The influence of one person on another in a group situation is not easily established. After all, what constitutes influence? Hence what constitutes power? How can we tell when one person is influential in the action, or inaction, of another group member? Where is the behaviour which we can observe and which demonstrates group power in operation? Does an individual have to display such power before we can consider him an influential group member: or can he be just as influential by saying and doing very little? How is power distributed among the membership of a group? What are the sources of variance which operate to redistribute available power? Having located any sources of power how can we measure them? This chapter attempts to provide answers to these questions.

WHAT CONSTITUTES POWER?

One outstanding way in which one person can influence another is through talking. Talking is a resource which can be used strategically by any group member. Antithetically he can also find his talking working dysfunctionally. Verbal behaviour is a source of both positive and negative influence. The greater the degree of sophistication within the group membership the more valuable is the resource of talking. What is meant is that in college groups, in contrast to groups of labourers or to groups in a tavern, the ability to talk intelligently and rationally generally makes it easier to win friends

and influence people. In the latter groups the ability to react emotionally, or physically, rather than verbally may be the more accepted
means of influence. Physical prowess is also a source of influence.

In our everyday life we become heavily influenced by monetary
rewards. It gets us what we most frequently want and it often in-
gratiates us with those who have less. Money is power! Also falling
into this sort of everyday category are such material goods as
expensive clothes, snappy automobiles, and classy women. In
each instance these are resources through which others are
influenced.

Within the small face-to-face laboratory group valuable resources
may become considerably more defined. If your group membership
is constituted from college students, then you can become even more
definitive. In such a situation perhaps the most prized possession is
the verbal fluency which was mentioned earlier. Following closely
behind may be various personality qualities such as a warm, non-
negative approach to people, and ability to withstand criticism. In
experiences with small groups it seems that if you can put on this
particular facilitative 'front' even though you may not mean it
entirely, it will stand you in very good stead. You may not learn anything about yourself, or about what is going on around you, but you
won't make any enemies either.

Another powerful resource in face-to-face groups is *time*. The
individual in the group who can recognise and act on the basis that
there is only one hour or less to accomplish whatever his personal
objectives may be is like a shark in a school of mackerel. This
individual can adopt a strategy to make use of time to his advantage.
If he is a verbally fluent individual as well, he is very strategically
advantaged in the interactive life of the group, especially in its early
life.

We say early life of the group because what frequently occurs is
that early influence is redistributed as time goes on, and the personal
qualities of interaction then become more primary resources. The
high interactor, with a definite programme and the knowledge of
the timed group meetings, starts off with a lead in the race for power.
But he may find that it requires more than these two particular
advantages to maintain power.

WHAT ARE THE BEHAVIOURAL CORRELATES OF POWER?

Power, then, is constructed from the ability to make use of various
resources. Each individual in the group has an agreed amount of
resources; or at least the opportunity to have access to such resources.

The distribution of power in the group, over and above the acknowledged personality inputs of each member, will depend upon the
utilisation of these same group resources. The strategies, or behavioural techniques, used to maximise the use of available resources,
either within the individual, or free floating in the task and affective
concerns of the group, brings about the power and role distributions
within the group. The longer the life of the group the more opportunities there will be to gain or lose power; the more frequently will
occur shifts in the balance of power and the availability of needed
resources to individuals and to the group.

This brings us to the need to inquire about behavioural strategies
used to corner available resources. Mishler and Waxler (1968) have
divided such strategies into two basic approaches: (1) the *attention-
control strategy* and (2) the *person-control strategy*. While Mishler
and Waxler were most concerned with the analysis of family groups
rather than face-to-face heterogeneous (mixed) groups their analysis
of these two particular styles of interaction overlaps considerably
with small group behaviour in general. The unique feature of the
attention-control strategy is that it makes use of verbal techniques
to achieve power. In association with the time limit under which
most groups operate, the controlling technique of high talking rate
is very powerful. The power comes from (a) preventing others from
'having the floor' to use their particular strategy; and (b) maintaining
group attention so as to avail yourself of other control techniques
(Mishler and Waxler, 1968, p. 121).

The person-control strategy consists mainly of asking questions
and interrupting others who have the floor. By interrupting others
the individual can forestall the full exercising of competitive power
strategies. Asking questions has the same effect, but is less direct. It
does have the effect of controlling the content and direction of the
interaction. Some individuals in the group can use both attention-
control and person-control strategies in association. It is the contention of Mishler and Waxler that the use of attention-control is an
interaction device preliminary to and generally necessary for the
other power techniques.

Another strategy with which power is exercised, in a more subversive fashion, is through the use of silence. If a person can establish
his position as a frequent initiator who can be relied upon to relieve
the monotony whenever it sets in, he can then choose to work both
sides of the street. Future high participation achieves power through
attention control. Correspondingly, silence achieves power though
the attention is received from other members who desire to know
why the initiator has suddenly stopped interacting. Sooner or later,

the member who has remained silent throughout becomes a pre-occupation of the other group members: the individual who is an unknown quantity attracts attention and appears to be a threat to the group.

THE DISTRIBUTION OF POWER

The dispersion of 'power' among the membership of groups is the result of nebulous and ill-defined factors. It seems dependent upon many sources of variability which almost defy experimental control. Through research with various types of groups (self-analytic, the direct communications training, leaderless, and task-oriented groups) it is possible to account to some extent for this fluctuation in the sources of 'power' in the group.

When the group is first convened the members have particular expectations about what might happen. There may be a considerable difference between what their personal expectations are and the expectations of the trainer of the group. Regardless of the magnitude in the discrepancy of expectations, it becomes the responsibility of the trainer to communicate as explicitly as is possible in the circumstances (since he must also be concerned with not violating or hampering the expected learning outcomes) what can realistically be expected to happen in their time together. If the kind of group which convenes is special, as in a therapeutic setting, the personality structure of the membership may defy closure of this 'expectancy gap' between leader and member. The way in which the trainer defines his expectations can also become a crucial variable and serve as a further handicap to closing this 'expectancy gap'. We have in mind the unstructured group experience. In this type of group the members (perhaps unaware to this point), come face to face with the issues of authority, lack of closure, ambiguity and normlessness. If the trainer provides some special personal warmth, expectation of closure, or provides 'norms for behaviour' in his opening comments, then certain learning outcomes for these members may have been violated. In fact, such trainer behaviour could later serve as a source of antagonism since he has provided conditions under which the particular anticipated learning structure for the group cannot be established. There cannot be ambiguity about the 'task' if it becomes explicitly defined. There cannot be an authority vacuum if the trainer immediately assumes responsibility in his opening remarks.

In other group situations, such as the structured didactic training, or more common 'sensitivity training', concerns which are prominent in the unstructured experience do not seem so important. The training 'outcomes' for the didactic group are very different. The trainer becomes a model for the sorts of conditions he is trying to bring out in the other members. The members are provided with very concrete learning anchorages by means of *books, exercises, role-playing, practice sessions.* Behaviour is somewhat ordered through modelling the trainer. In addition, early trainer-initiated comments as 'we are here to help each other and to provide constructive criticism about how we are doing' or 'each of us will take a turn in the spotlight and we have to share the responsibility for learning among ourselves' or 'we will use the feedback from each other as a help to learning these particular communication skills', provide conditions designed to build in cohesion, affection and task-oriented activity. This is in contrast to the self-analytic unstructured group where warmth, cohesion and task-activity may develop in small subgroups, usually hostile to each other, but only rarely and spasmodically in the group as a whole. This returns us to our initial question: How does this affect the dispersion of 'power' among the group membership?

One would expect that the more the trainer of the group succeeds in satisfying the initial expectations of the members the more will be the power he retains and the less will be the dispersion of power in the group. In this regard it could be anticipated that the self-analytic experience leaves more room for control struggles, unsatisfactory affective experiences and non-task-oriented behaviour among the group membership. The group is left purposely in a control vacuum; the focus of responsibility for satisfying the briefly outlined task is almost entirely in their hands. To achieve, at least to some extent, the understanding of what goes on around them the members must structure their surroundings in such a way as to facilitate this. Their *feelings* about the situation, however, frequently get in their way. In fact, their feelings dominate over ideas about working towards the authority-assigned task. Most often the membership becomes somewhat divided on an affective-instrumental plane. Burke (1967) has defined this situation as one in which high task participation is not legitimised by the affective circumstances. It is not easy for any member to engage in task participation to any great extent because the trainer has failed in fulfilling his expected obligations; emotions run high. There is a prevailing agenda, that the trainer should provide more information and soothe some feelings before the members move another step. Under such conditions of low task legitimation, role differentiation of the group becomes operative to help provide structure in what is perceived as a very ambiguous situation. This is in line with the initial prediction made somewhat earlier in the chapter. The dispersion of power should be greater in the unstructured group situation.

THE THREE ISSUES OF POWER RELATIONSHIPS

It seems generally agreed that individual performance within a group necessitates an involvement with three distinct issues. These issues are *control, affection,* and *task.* Corresponding to these issues, various roles are assumed by group members to provide closure, or at least a framework for present and future interactions. From the standpoint of abstract analysis the issues of control, affection, and task, and their corresponding role demands, seem as separate as their labels imply. In reality, they are closely and intricately related in a spidery web of confusion. This is especially so when the group is a temporary, normless, deliberately ambiguous, and highly anxiety-inducing one, such as the self-analytic group. The more structure and skeleton one can install in group activities, either through a helpful leader or a highly defined task, the less difficult it is to untangle the overlapping performances as they occur in connection with the issues of control, affection, and task.

To help decipher the tangled triple 'code' of the group; and to help isolate the roles which individuals are performing within the code, various research workers have come to the rescue. Primary amongst these are the names of Bales (1970); Benne and Sheats (1948); Couch and Carter (1960); Dunphy (1968); Moreno (1934); and Slater (1955). Other workers have provided critical clues to the group interaction code (which is certainly not deciphered) but these individuals seem the most prominent. A quick review of relevant research might be in order at this point.

The first question might be 'Why are there three issues? Why not one or two? Why not five or six?' To find out what constitutes individual performance in the small group Couch and Carter (1960) used a factor analytic approach. They collected data on a number of small groups of various sizes and tasks. Simultaneously they collected trained observers' ratings of each of the group member's performances. Throwing all the data together in the mix-master of factor analysis they arrived at a three-factor description of individual performance. The three factors were: an individual prominence factor (control); a factor of group sociability (affection); and a factor of goal facilitation (task). This appears to be a general finding. Schutz (1958) developed his description of group involvement around the same dimensions of control, affection and inclusion (task). Other group theorists and personality experts, working independently, arrived at similar conclusions. Since Couch and Carter's three factors were orthogonal, that is at right angles to one another, this meant they enclosed a three-dimensional space. Bales (1970) saw the value of this particular model, and developed a comprehensive personality typology, to provide a detailed picture of member performances on the three dimensions or issues of control, affection or task. For simplicity, Bales labelled these dimensions upward–downward (for greater versus less control), positive–negative (for good versus bad inter-personal relationships), forward–backward (for cooperative group task work versus uncooperative individual work). Using Euclidean space as a model, and six possible locations U,D; P,N; F,B; Bales' system provides twenty-seven different personality descriptions, or social psychological directions, for group performance. This typology represents a major contribution to group process analysis. It is part of a considerable effort made by Bales, and his associates at Harvard, to help describe the group process. Benne and Sheats (1948), working mostly within the framework of *National Training Laboratory or NTL groups, also provide descriptions of role performance on three particular continua: *Individual roles* such as (i) aggressor; (ii) recognition seeker; *Group building and maintenance roles* such as (iii) information-initiator. The correspondence between these three dimensions and those of Couch and Carter, and Bales, can hardly be considered an accident. It would seem that the three issues are undoubtedly there: they exist for individuals in groups to confront. The roles which appear clearly are designed to deal with these issues confronted as group problems; both the roles and the problems can be recognised as existing objectively.

When a member adopts a particular stance, or role, within the group, he is establishing his position on each of these fundamental dimensions. For example, a UPF personality type will be perceived as somewhat controlling (U), as likeable (P), and cooperative in helping with the task (F). Contrary to Benne and Sheats' description of role typologies, where an individual is performing only on one dimension, Bales' typology provides a more complex explanation and description of the role. He has developed questionnaires which help locate individual agents in this three-dimensional space. Each question corresponds to one of twenty-six social–psychological directions (see Table 5). If each member completes the questionnaire for every other individual in the group, it is possible to establish the group consensus of where each member is with respect to every other member. It is also possible to perform this operation using the results of Interaction Process Analysis. Thus, one can compare the objective reality of the individual's interaction in the group with the member's perception of it. Once the members of the group have been located in social–psychological space, the personality descriptions which correspond to these locations can be studied to provide a comprehensive description of the individual. The scores arrived at using Bales' Questionnaire locates each individual on the dimensions of control (U–D), affection (P–N), and task (F–B). The number of ratings for each individual, assigned him by other members, gives a measure of the importance to be attached to a particular dimension. Suppose that in a group of twelve individuals Person A received an UPF rating from seven others, a UP rating from three others, and a PF rating from one other. He may have assessed himself as P. The group perception of him is then 10U, 12P, 8F, obtained by summing

Table 5

Interpersonal ratings, Form A

	S.p.d.
1. Does he (or she) seem to *receive a lot of interaction* from others?	U
2. Does he seem *personally involved in the group*?	UP
3. Does he seem *valuable for a logical task*?	UPF
4. Does he *assume responsibility for task leadership*?	UF
5. Does he *speak like an autocratic authority*?	UNF
6. Does he seem *dominating*?	UN
7. Does he seem to *demand pleasure and gratification*?	UNB
8. Does he seem to *think of himself as entertaining*?	UB
9. Does he seem *warm and personal*?	UPB
10. Does he *arouse your admiration*?	P
11. Does he seem especially to be *addressed when others have serious opinions* about which they want confirmation?	PF
12. Does he seem to stand for the most *conservative ideas and beliefs of the group*?	F
13. Does he always seem to try to speak *objectively*?	NF
14. Does he seem to feel that his *individual independence* is very important?	N
15. Does he seem to *feel that others are generally too conforming* to conventional social expectations?	NB
16. Does he seem to *reject religious belief generally*?	B
17. Do you feel *liking* for him or her?	PB
18. Does he seem to *make others feel he admires them*?	DP
19. Does he seem to believe that *equality and humanitarian concern* for others are important?	DPF
20. Does he seem very *introverted*, serious, shy, introspective?	DF
21. Does he seem to believe that it is necessary to *sacrifice the self* for higher values?	DNF
22. Does he seem *resentful*?	DN
23. Does he seem to accept *failure and withdrawal* for himself?	DNB
24. Does he seem to *withhold cooperation passively*?	DB
25. Does he seem to *identify with some group of underprivileged persons*?	DPB
26. Does he tend to *devaluate himself*?	D

the 'votes' he has received on each dimension. The interpretation of this average, or consensus, is that this particular person is perceived as exercising considerable control in the group, as a great positive influence over other individuals as judged by their liking of him, as well as a considerable influence in pushing for the achievement of the group task. This person (10U, 12P, 8F) is a *'powerful'* individual in his group, his power coming from his ability to control the more submissive members, to exert a persuasive influence by means of the positive affect he generates and by his cooperative instead of individually oriented behaviour.

The use of the concept of group space can be illustrated from the result of using Bales' Questionnaire, Form A (Table 5) on three occasions in the lifetime of a particular group—these sessions provide a good cross-section of the overall structure and development of this group. The questionnaire was completed by each member for himself or herself, for all other participants, and the trainer. The average

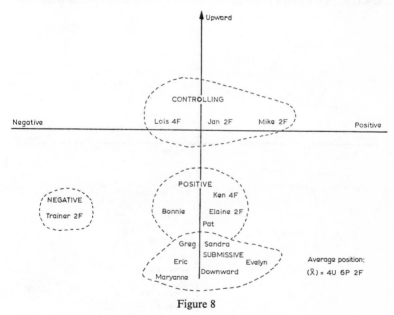

Figure 8

Member locations for SAT group after Session 2 (based upon
  Bales' questionnaire)

Individual locations on the forward dimension are written in beside
  the person's name
Power-blocks appear early in the group

social–psychological direction for each person was then calculated. From these, plots were made from which certain trends can be made out. In almost every case an UPF tendency can be detected. After Session 2, the group average is 4U, 6P 2F (see Figure 8). Similarly, the average score for Sessions 7 and 15 are (4U 4P 3F) and (4U 6P 2F), respectively (see Figures 9 and 10). We can plot the group structure and movement on paper, filling in the scores for the third dimension (F–B) beside each individual's coordinate position in two dimensions.

It is possible to discern some interesting features, using this visual aid. In Session 2, for example, it would appear that subgroups, or power blocks, have already formed. There is a cluster of individuals in a relatively downward position (Ken, Bonnie, Elaine, Pat, Greg, Sandra). (Bales' questionnaire has a tendency to be biased in the UP direction.) These individuals are not distinguishable in P–N space but seem slightly dispersed in F–B space. Another subgroup (Eric, Evelyn, Maryanne) is more downward, being also spread over P–N

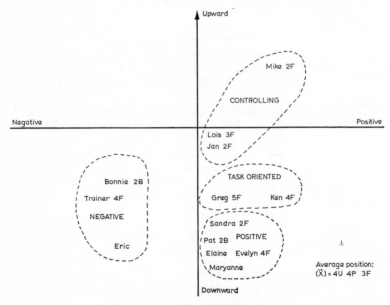

Figure 9

Member locations for SAT group after Session 7 (based upon Bales' questionnaire)

Power-blocks are stabilised but functions alter

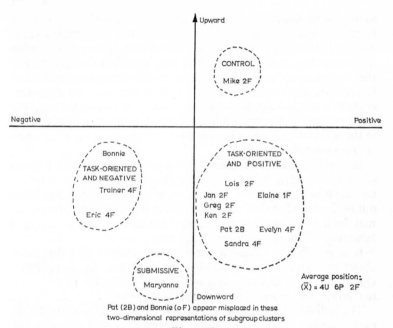

Upward

CONTROL
Mike 2F

Negative   Positive

Bonnie
TASK-ORIENTED
AND NEGATIVE
Trainer 4F

Eric 4F

TASK-ORIENTED
AND POSITIVE

Lois 2F
Jan 2F   Elaine 1F
Greg 2F
Ken 2F
Pat 2B   Evelyn 4F
Sandra 4F

SUBMISSIVE
Maryanne

Average position:
$(\bar{X}) = 4U\ 6P\ 2F$

Downward

Pat (2B) and Bonnie (o F) appear misplaced in these
two-dimensional representations of subgroup clusters

Figure 10

Member locations for SAT group after Session 15 (based upon
  Bales' questionnaire)

Power-blocks continue to differentiate and coalesce

space like the first. The trainer is an 'isolate', being very much at the
negative pole. A third subgroup, with more leadership control, is
located at the upward end of the power axis. The individuals in this
coalition are separated by a range of four positive votes (Mike and
Lois). The group, as a whole, after Session 2, can be described as
existing in an 'affective vacuum'. No single individual seems able to
attract positive feeling: most members seem to be engaged in 'feeling-
out' the others and giving each other the benefit of any doubts. This
is not so for the trainer. He is seen as very negative, with no control
(U), and not clearly oriented towards the task (2F). Subgroups band
together, perhaps for support, perhaps for a control struggle, perhaps
as scapegoated silent members. The trainer has been singled out as
the recipient of negative affect: this can perhaps be explained in
terms of his complete lack of association with other members.

In Session 7 certain changes can be perceived. The group as a
whole is more dispersed. It seems as though the members are now

more discriminating in their choices. The trainer's position has improved, the position of other members has deteriorated (Eric, Bonnie). The groups which banded for support in the earlier session now seem less cohesive. Greg and Ken maintain their neutrality. Pat, Sandra and Elaine join Maryanne and Evelyn amongst the more submissive, non-influential members. Mike has acquired maximum control. Lois and Jan have slipped somewhat in comparison. The trainer is seen as having assumed some task leadership, although not to the point where he exercises any overall influence in the work which the group is doing.

In the last session (Session 15), Mike has become the popular controlling leader. Bonnie, Eric and the trainer continue to collect the negative feeling from other members, and Lois too has fallen out of favour. There is a very large cluster in the neutral roles (which may be a function of termination). Maryanne is seen as the most submissive of the non-influential members.

It is possible to obtain a considerable amount of information about the issues of control, affection, and task by using Bales' Questionnaire in this way. It is possible, in particular, to determine the 'power' which attaches to each of the members.

The individual responses on Form A of Bales' Questionnaire for each member tell us even more. However, instead of using this material we will look at another way of arriving at an index of 'power' through the sociogram, a technique devised by Moreno (1934). The members are asked to choose other members in relation to specific tasks. In this case, the individuals were asked six questions to select the group members with whom they agreed, disagreed, felt were major spokesmen, felt closest to, and felt farthest from. The questions used indicate the locus of *control* ('major spokesman'); *affection* ('closest to'); ('farthest from'); and *task* ('agreed with'); ('disagreed with'). We can determine the sociometric structure of the group and relate this to the structure given by Bales' questionnaire. The sociometric structure cannot be expected to be identical with the structure in social–psychological space, since we are concerned with drawing vectors for mutual choices and discovering the cliques, or isolates, from these choices.

There is definite information which can be arrived at from the sociograms, not so readily through Bales' Questionnaire. We can clearly see subgroups forming, we can also see how each individual in the group develops his allegiances. It is in our interest to discover a way to make sense of the power relationships by combining these two methods. First we tally the choices for each person on each question of the sociogram. These questions are clearly on the U–D,

P–N, F–B continua. Questions 1, 2, 3 are F–B, question 4 is U; question 5 is P, and question 6 is N. We can, therefore, locate the individuals in 3-D group space from the sociogram alone. Second: we join up the vectors corresponding to the individuals who made the choices. Third: we now interpret the results. We know who are the powerful individuals. We know who gave them their power. If we do this over a number of sessions we can discover how they gain and lose power, how they gain and lose the affection of the group, and how their orientation to the task waxes and wanes.

We have chosen Session 2 for the comparison of these two methods of obtaining the power distribution of the group. Examining the sociogram analysis of Session 2 it can be seen that Mike is uppermost on the issue of control (see Figure 11). He has received five votes from various other members of the group in response to the 'major spokesman' question. The individuals who chose Mike as the major spokesman can be recognised by the vectors leading towards him. In this case they are Ken, Bonnie, Eric and Lois.

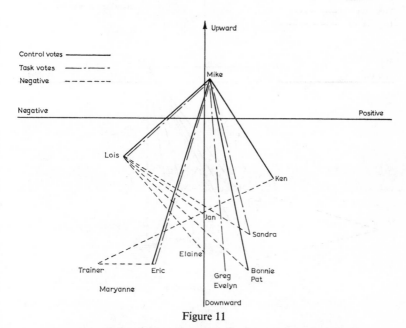

Figure 11

Member locations for SAT group after Session 2 (based upon sociogram)

Sociograms confirm questionnaire power-blocks

Interestingly enough, Mike has voted for himself on this question, this makes the fifth vote on this particular issue. On the issue of affection there is no overwhelming positive personage at this point in the group. Lois is seen as somewhat negative, as is the trainer. They are located in the downward–negative portion of the group space. Lois received her votes as the person 'I felt farthest from' from Jean, Bonnie, Pat and Elaine. The trainer received his votes from Ken and Eric. In each of these cases the vectors are drawn to show this situation. On the issue of the group task we again find Mike as the individual first chosen by Lois, Evelyn and Sandra. He is also the second choice of two other members, Eric and Elaine. Arbitrarily setting a value of 2 for a first choice and 1 for a second choice on this issue would give Mike a total of 8, he is therefore the major task

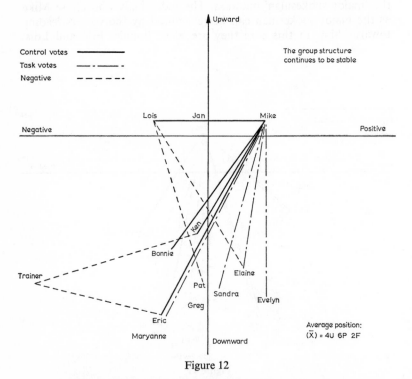

Figure 12

Member locations for SAT group after Session 7 (based upon Bales' questionnaire)

The group structure continues to be stable

leader, followed by Lois with 7, Ken with 6, and Jan with 6 'votes'. Actually this voting situation is a very close one and it might be said that Mike's superiority on this particular issue seems quite tenuous.

Examining the power distribution as given by the questionnaire it seems basically the same as the results of the sociogram (see Figure 12). Slight changes show Mike as less controlling than the sociogram structure initially indicated. He seems locked in a power struggle with Lois and Jan. The trainer is viewed more negatively here than in the sociogram. The voting structures, although not perfectly synchronised, are similar.

5

FEELINGS—IMPLICIT AND EXPRESSED

The emphasis within this book has been on individual learning in the small group. In the previous literature much has been made of group emotion and the influence of personal feelings on group behaviour and consequential learning. Our view is that, although feelings are important, for understanding what happens they may be of lesser import than other dynamic factors in group development. At least the affective concerns of members should be examined in association with other basic processes, and not as though they were autonomous and all-persuasive.

VERBAL INTERACTION AS A KEY TO FEELINGS

The examination of verbal interaction in the small group has been approached, in theory and practice, from a number of different points of view. It would be meaningful to look closely at a few of these approaches.

Bion (1948) considered the verbal behaviour of the group members to be a continual reflection of the moment-by-moment balance struck in the group between free-flowing emotion and deliberate task-oriented work. Accepting this premise Stock and Thelen (1958) conducted an extensive research operation. Their results supported Bion's contention that the language of the group fluctuates from non-purposive, instinctual and unconscious emotional material to more deliberate, reality-bound, goal-seeking discussions. Individuals would make characteristic disclosures on this emotion-work continuum depending upon their valence (preference for a certain group emotional culture) and the particular characteristics of the group.

The past experience of the group member seemed to be the important factor which dictated his earliest responses in the group situation and such member verbalisations could be considered to represent a preference for one of three dominant group cultures of dependency, pairing, or fight-flight.

There seems an overlap between the positions of Bion, Stock and Thelen, and the understandings of verbal behaviour in the group which are reflected in the writings of Foulkes (1964). Perhaps the fact that Foulkes was a colleague of Bion's at the Tavistock Clinic may help to explain these similarities. In any case, Foulkes has expanded upon the original ideas of Bion and is deserving of a singular credit. Foulkes takes the view that the group has a number of bipolar conflicts. These conflicts are expressed through the relationship established at any time between emotional release and task-centred work. There is a personal 'antagonism' (1964, p. 89) between the desire to repeat older neurotic and disruptive patterns in the group (which have their basis in the primordial, infantile and authority-dependent nature of the individual's past) and an opposing desire to accept, combine and cooperate with others in a more constructive, socially accepted way. This socially desirable pattern represents emotional maturity, a reality orientation and a premeditated planning of performance. In the former behavioural pattern there are more latent, unconscious elements, while in the latter patterns there are more manifest and conscious elements. Foulkes therefore recognises two sources of emotional conflict: (1) the neurotic destructive versus socially constructive behavioural patterns, and (2) the latent versus the manifest elements of behavioural expression. Another bipolarity which Foulkes considers to exist in the group, and which finds expression in the verbal interaction of the group members, differentiates between the trainer and the other members (1964, p. 57). Foulkes makes the point that the trainer represents (3) the dimension of reality, reason, tolerance, understanding, insight, honesty, conscientiousness and so on, while the members frequently represent the antitheses of these dimensions, irrationality, spontaneity, lack of control, narcissistic goals, intolerance, resentfulness, competition, aggressiveness, and sexuality. The verbal dialogue can be seen to express these two opposing tendencies. The bipolarities are expressed in behaviour—the trainer trying to promote the task and the members promoting various themes which revolve more centrally around task-avoidance and emotional expressiveness.

Mann (1966) promotes the idea of special relationships existing between the trainer and various other group members, indeed this is the theme of his book *Interpersonal Style and Group Development*.

Mann presents the view that everything verbalised in the small self-analytic group situation, whether directly to the trainer or between other members, contains material which implicitly or explicitly provides a special message to the trainer. It may seem to be an innocuous comment which is spoken rather 'off the cuff' between two participants. But, according to Mann's theory, there are elements in the verbalisation which pertain directly to the trainer, and to the relationship which exists between the speaker and the trainer. Mann has developed a sixteen-category interaction coding system which breaks down verbal interaction in terms of direct or indirect messages to the trainer. Stages of group development are explored through this categorical analysis of verbal interaction (cf. pp. 70–1). It is not surprising to find that both the stages of development and the verbal themes revolve around the trainer as centre and are expressed by such descriptions as 'trainer as dependency figure', 'trainer as incompetent', 'trainer as manipulator'. Such themes are a kind of nucleus around which the verbalisations of the group and the on-going group development are revolving.

Powdermaker and Frank (1953, pp. 141–61) describe verbal interaction in the therapeutic group as representing a number of group themes. In their case, however, the trainer does not establish himself with as much prominence as with Mann. The themes which are depicted by Powdermaker and Frank are presented below. The list is not necessarily representative of the order of appearance in the group dialogue.

    (a) Ambivalent feelings about the group and the task
    (b) Hostility, distrust, and fear of others
    (c) Feelings of inferiority
    (d) Negative attitudes towards the trainer
    (e) Desires for achievement
    (f) Concern over handling emotions or remaining emotionally dependent
    (g) Blaming others or accepting responsibility

Eric Berne (1963) has developed a system for group examination which is described as 'transactional analysis'. The verbal behaviour of the group is not viewed, in Berne's system, as a reaction to emotional-work stress (Bion); nor as the product of a number of antagonistic relationships (Foulkes); nor as a series of progressive themes which involve the trainer (Mann) involving other members (Powdermaker and Frank). Berne, instead, considers the verbal behaviour of each member within the group as a reflection of the equilibrium established between three possible individual ego states

These ego states are called exteropsyche (parent); neopsyche (adult); and archeopsyche (child). In analytic terminology these so-called ego states are somewhat equivalent to the Freudian superego, ego and id. Any analysis of the verbal interaction between, or among, group members can be described as interaction across these three ego states. The patterns of interaction which are frequently displayed in the group are repetitions of fixed, older patterns of dealing with individuals. Members reincarnate these patterns in their behaviour in the group. The analysis of these patterns is accomplished by Berne in the form of *Games people play* (1963, p. 146).

Another and very promising approach to the examination of verbal interaction is that of the 'General Inquirer'. Developed by Stone *et al.* (1964), the General Inquirer System is a computer approach to verbal interaction analysis. The dialogue of a group is punched on computer cards which are fed into a computer which has been previously provided with a special dictionary, the words in which are classified to represent themes related to the variables of concern to the researcher. The computer analyses these variables by means of a tagging system. The number of times various words appear can be added and compared. This provides an estimate of the strength of certain group concerns given by the number under each of the 'tags'. Dunphy (1964) examined group process through the General Inquirer System and was able to make a considerable contribution in support of previous authors such as Couch (1960) and Bales (1950). In addition he was able to throw light upon the phases of the group and the mythologies which become reflected in group dialogue. The unique advantage of this particular approach is that it attempts to combine statistical and clinical material rather than to rely entirely upon impressions and intuitions.

The General Inquirer System has a distinct appeal to the authors of this book for reasons just previously stated. Verbal interaction can be examined from a number of different vantage points, using more than one kind of analysis. We have found it beneficial to combine information about the group dialogue obtained through computerised Interaction Process Analysis, with data provided through personal diaries, group transcripts, sociograms, questionnaires and first-hand observations through a one-way screen. The composite pattern which emerges from such a combination provides a credible picture of the group reality, since it is based on more information than could be obtained by only one form of analysis. Using these materials we will proceed to outline, as systematically as possible, the kinds of feelings which manifest themselves in our small learning groups. We are convinced that identical feelings are generated in *all* learning groups,

E

but for various reasons the whole gamut of emotional reactions remains unrecognised. The feelings may be more transient, they may remain unverbalised, the instructor may ignore them, or forget them as 'irrelevant', they may be regarded as unusual, specific and exceptional and so on.

Since it is congenial and also logical, we will attempt to develop an approach which recognises an evolutionary development in the expression of emotions by, and in, the group.

There are a number of influential factors in the determination of the emotional culture of the learning group. The most obvious of these are the initially idiosyncratic member differences. Each group member is a unique person, but when caught up in a role, behaves in a stereotyped fashion! His resultant contribution to the emotional culture of the group will then be peculiar to him. Other factors which less obviously (but more importantly) contribute to the effective state of the group, at any point in time, are (1) the individual's prior and personal expectations about the group; (2) these expectations as they have become influenced by the nature of the assigned task; (3) the trainer's role; (4) the current state of group development, especially the operation of reinforcers, both positive and negative; (5) the social networks (coalitions) which become established in the group and which facilitate or impede the display of certain feelings and impulses. There are, however, common elements which cut across such individual and group manifestations and which can be used to demonstrate the essential emotional characteristics which all learning groups seem to share.

INITIAL PHASE—ORIENTATION AND ADAPTATION TO THE ENVIRONMENT

Although the personality 'input' which each new group member brings to the group situation is important, developing an objective view of such 'input' presents a special difficulty to the other participants. It is hard, if not impossible, to determine the personality characteristics of the other members without relying upon what has actually been said and done in the group, and in one's presence. In this regard individuals emphasise factors such as personal appearance; they judge personality on the basis of stereotyped notions about physiognomy, size, speech, etc. Since the group members are very infrequently pre-group friends, they must rely almost exclusively upon this highly biased within-group knowledge to provide a picture of the personalities of the other group members.

In this sense group members are more concerned with 'placing' other members on a 'grid' relative to themselves—liking–disliking, helpful–unhelpful, dangerous–non-dangerous. Unlike the other participants, the research worker, in pursuit of objectivity, can use systematic methods, e.g. IPA, content analysis, as well as paper-and-pencil tests to try and obtain this personality information. Arguments can be presented about the validity, or reliability of the information acquired by such methods, but at least it is superior to the subjective judgement of participants. Allowing that the personality picture obtained by each member in the group is coloured by subjective experience and depends on the qualities of their interpersonal skills, the combinations of possible group reactions to their perceptions, in in an emotional sense, are abundant. What seems to happen is that we do not find an abundant number of emotional reactions which are generated from the members' initial experiences with each other; instead, what we see is a small manageable number of demonstrable, stereotyped responses. To account for the way in which a theoretically infinite number of possible emotional responses is somehow reduced to a small definite number requires the establishment of an explanatory model. The small social system which is the group must soon incorporate elements of stability which act to reduce these emotional possibilities to a 'common denominator' of manageable ones. The initial reaction is often one of passivity, caution, reserve and quiet observation. While it is possible that a variety of reactions is concealed by the frequently blank faces, the overt behaviour can be described as shyness, and defensiveness. Perhaps the term 'compliance' (Mann, 1966) is the most accurate descriptive term for the overall reaction to the new group situation and the new membership.

Other group theorists have used similar terms in connection with different types of early group experience. Bennis and Shephard (1956), for example, mention 'dependency' as an initial group reaction. Our experience of learning groups seems no different from these other observers. The group seems initially to desire a short period of silent contemplation. It is almost as though the members would like to 'soak up' the full impact of the room, the trainer, and the other members before venturing into any type of interaction. It seems quite natural to go through this 'soaking' procedure in the new environment; and it is not necessarily confined to these small learning groups. Going to a small house party, being inducted into an organisation, or visiting a new office in search of employment, all seem to bring out the emotional reaction of 'soaking up' the situation and draining away present environmental 'shock'. It seems a learned process of adaptation; an attempt to keep the situation from gaining premature control. In these small learning groups the members can be observed to glance furtively around the room, and to and from the other members, as if looking for, and noting, any unusual detail or mannerism. This reaction seems to disappear quickly in most members. The discussion of any really salient detail will eventually replace the previous mental notation of them. Such a reaction which cushions environmental 'shock' helps to explain why groups will often react irrationally to any change of location for meetings. It is necessary in such a change to re-evaluate and come to terms with the environment, to reduce its potential danger, to resolve any personal dissonance. In doing so there is a 'waste' of valuable work time in the group. The group seems to sense that moving to a new location involves unknown risks. It also means a temporary loss of effectiveness while evaluating the new environment; as a result members seem unconsciously to resent this possibility. Beyond the point at which the members might be expected to have completed an unconscious evaluation of the situation in terms of its potential, they may remain for a time in this passive, compliant, or dependent condition. In most cases they remain reserved until the individual in the situation who has the 'action', or present power, makes an opening statement. This present power figure is most frequently the trainer or acknowledged authority.

What has been discussed to this point then is what seems to happen in the very early stages of the small learning group. These activities of environmental evaluation, passivity, and personal compliance represent the 'common denominator' of the large number of initial personal reactions possible in the early group situation. Perhaps this is the introduction of the elements of 'human learning' into an initially ambiguous situation. The emotional consequences of this adapted learning in terms of the group, are reactions wherein a culture of *anxiety* is combined with the expression of feelings of *dependence, apprehension*, and *vulnerability*. This process, as outlined to this point, does not necessarily have any dimensions of time. It may recur more or less frequently in the life of the group. We have seen it endure throughout the life of one group—through fifteen one-hour sessions. The personal reactions of members are not the same: some members will react very quickly to a new situation, while others will proceed with their own evaluations much more slowly and deliberately.

OPENING PHASE—LOOKING TO THE TRAINER
FOR FAMILIAR LEADERSHIP

The reaction of the trainer, or authority figure, at this particularly high emotional point in the group seems quite important. The importance of the trainer can be demonstrated by comparing two different trainer styles and methods of intervention.

(1) If the trainer fails to respond to member expectations, as in the unstructured group, the initial reaction is often surprise and astonishment. Because the trainer in this case does not respond in the expected fashion his interpretations are met with incredulity. The members' evaluations, and subsequent expectations, do not accord with the pronouncements of the leader. These early comments, which are not designed to alleviate anxiety, or to provide any resolution of dependency feelings, increase the apprehensions raised by the novel environment and serve to increase situational 'shock' rather than reduce it to manageable proportions. The reaction to the initial statement of the unstructured group trainer is quite distinguishable from that produced by the designedly anxiety-reducing, dependency-fostering statements of the more conventional group trainer. Although the preliminary conditions of high anxiety, dependence, apprehension and personal vulnerability are present both in the unstructured 'leaderless' group and in the more traditional structured group situations, there is considerably more overt hostility and dependent complaining (Mann, 1966) resulting from the group members' reactions to this unstructured experience.

(2) In the conventional learning group, the trainer's initial comments are designed to reduce interpersonal anxiety, including his own, and to reinforce certain obvious dependency reactions. Even when the objectives of the trainer may include the development of an independent learning environment, early trainer statements will normally generate dependency. However, successfully reducing anxiety and substituting dependence induction, does not get the trainer out of the dynamic woods. The overt hostility and dependent complaining in the 'leaderless' or unstructured group are replaced, in the conventional situation, by subversive hostility and independent complaining. It is a moot question whether one kind of group environment is more conducive to early learning than the other. Is dependent complaining more closely related to personal growth than independent complaining? This very question is the concern of Chapter 7. What remains in both conditions is hostility towards the trainer. In the unstructured group it is overt and confrontational in nature—this seems a more mature reaction. In the more

conventional teaching–learning group it is surreptitious and under-hand.

A look at the early group dialogue will illustrate the emotional condition and the nature of the hostility towards the trainer in the two kinds of group.

UNSTRUCTURED, 'LEADERLESS' GROUP. Selected comments made by different members about the trainer (during the earlier sessions)

(1) Maybe that's one of the quickest ways to get the group together, to have someone to be hostile against. (Session 1)
(2) We resent the trainer's egotism because he thinks we do everything in relation to him. (Session 1)
(3) Suppose we had something specific to work upon . . . We wouldn't even involve the trainer. (Session 1)
(4) The first good plan is that we're supposed to expel him. (Session 4)
(5) It would be a delight to leave him off for one session. (Session 4)

TRADITIONAL, STRUCTURED, DIDACTIC GROUP

(1) I consider myself a good judge of character. Now in this group I will not hit it off too well with most of the members. I'm not saying they are bad people, I'm saying they're not my type. (Session 1)
(2) There was no leader and I know we will not have a good leader unless I decide to become one. (Session 2)
(3) I don't think I felt any hostility towards the trainer, but more annoyance at myself and the group for not having made the maximum use of the time. (Session 3)
(4) I enjoyed this session more than any before because the trainer wasn't present for most of the time. (Session 7)

To put this reactive material in perspective, it seems that there is a point in time at which the trainer can intervene to generate a unique emotional culture. To interrupt the prevailing mood of the group and to direct the participants to analysis of their own emotional state and tendencies turns the group towards a culture of dependent com-plaining, which may be followed by a systematic individual re-evaluation. To intervene in the conventional manner, in line with, rather than against the prevailing expectations of the group is to foster a leader nurturance and dependent compliance group culture. Both cultures are permeated with hostility as the excerpts from the transcripts show, but this hostility takes different forms. The situation of the group does not remain stable, at least not for long, but with these two leadership styles the reactions in terms of expressed and latent feelings are quite predictable.

CENTRAL PHASE—MAJOR THEMES

After the earlier trainer interventions, and a preliminary examination of the nature of his role and the members' expectations of him and the assigned task, continual alterations in the emotional mood of the group manifest themselves. There can be major shifts in the emotional emphasis of the whole group (such as through a member loss, or termination), but more frequently these emotional shifts are accounted for by fluctuations in the attitudes and status of certain significant group members including the trainer. The impact of this role differentiation, and variations in the course of the development of the unstructured and traditional group methods is our prime consideration.

As we have seen, during group development a number of prominent role 'types' become manifest. These are particular combinations of behavioural patterns and value dispositions, rooted in, or adopted by, certain group members who act to move the group from one developmental and/or emotional phase to another. This does not mean that the group necessarily moves to a more mature condition, or to a more sophisticated emotional response. It only implies that the group developmental and emotional states are *altered* significantly by the activities and contribution of the particular role 'type'. The understanding that particular 'types' involve identifiable behavioural and value dispositions in the process of group interaction is a major contribution of Bales (1970). The further elaboration of the behavioural patterns and the conditions under which these member 'types' become influential in the group is the work of Wayne Matheson. An understanding of the types, and their group contribution, provide valuable understandings of the emotional fluctuations which occur in the group.

Matheson (1971) has found that amongst the highest interactors in our small learning groups the number of influential role types is limited to eight, described in detail in Chapter 8. For purposes of quick review these eight types are provided below.

A   Manipulative politician
B   Shrewd businessman
C   Resident cynic
D   Party host

E   Disenchanted contender
F   Ascendant extrovert
G   Popular contender
H   Insular deviant

Although a number of different psychometric, as well as impressionistic, approaches were used to locate and describe these eight 'types', one approach seems to demonstrate, quite distinctly, the influence of role differentiation upon the emotional change in the group.

A *sociometric method was used to determine the internal status hierarchy in these groups by counting the number of votes accorded each of these eight 'types' on a number of group indices. These indices measure the individual's positive and negative personal attraction (questions 3, 4); his value for the group task (question 1); his personal power (question 2).

THE GROUP *SOCIOGRAM
(1) (a) In this meeting I agreed most with ————.
    (b) I also agreed with ————.
(2)   I agreed least with ————.
(3)   The major spokesman for the group today was ————.
(4)   I felt closest to ————.
(5)   I felt farthest from ————.

When these votes are considered over all fifteen sessions of the group life, a number of patterns become discernible. It is possible, of course, for any member to receive a large number of votes at all times. This was quite unusual, but it did happen. More commonly, certain 'types' (defined from IPA and other data) accumulate votes on particular dimensions at peak times during the fifteen sessions. Frequently the pattern of votes on the five questions is distinctive for each type. Four patterns were uncovered: these are presented in Table 6 with the role 'type' which most frequently appeared in association with each pattern.

Theme (1) What to do with the trainer and the group—ambivalence
THE EARLY ROLE DEVELOPMENTS
(1) Manipulative politician
(2) Party host
(3) Resident cynic
These three roles, which are common to all the groups and methods observed, serve as a catalyst upon the disparate emotional situations

Table 6

Voting patterns and role-types

LARGE POLL (Attracts a number of votes over all sessions; the votes may be favourable or unfavourable)	CHOICES EBB AND FLOW (Fluctuations in status are characteristic)	GRADUAL, CLIMACTIC (Building of allegiances over time)	EARLY HARVEST (Status peaks early then drops)
			Manipulative politician
		Shrewd businessman	
Resident cynic			
			Party host
	Disenchanted contender		
Ascendant extrovert			
	←——Popular	contender——→	
	Insular deviant		

Different participant-styles become a concern to the group at different phases of development.

which result from initial trainer interventions and his delineation of the group task. The different groups have emotional elements which are quite similar. These might be succinctly described as:

(a) A *confusion* over evaluating and adopting the trainer's assigned task or continuing to pursue personal goals.

(b) A *positive–negative ambivalence* over becoming personally involved with others (advocated by party host); cooperating with trainer (advocated by manipulative politician); or viewing the situation with a negative scepticism (advocated by resident cynic).

(c) *Anxiety and fear* because of the confrontational aggressiveness of the resident cynic and the as yet unknown disciplinary resources and powers of the trainer.

(d) *Anger and feelings of impotence* in less verbal members over their apparent lack of influence over the group process.

(e) *Pressure* towards further role differentiation. This is perhaps more applicable to self-analytic groups since the trainer's behaviour creates a 'power vacuum'. In the direct communications group the trainer still assumes a power role, his control being undermined rather than replaced.

Theme (2) Guilt and despondency about initial failures—find the scapegoat!
FURTHER GROUP ROLE DEVELOPMENTS
(4) Disenchanted contender
(5) Shrewd businessman
(6) Ascendant extrovert

As in the previous role developments these three roles are found in both kinds of group: they influence the emotional development of the group in the following ways:

(a) An increase in *negative* feelings about the task and the trainer. This increase in negativism is contributed mainly, as it is signalised directly, by the status rise of the disenchanted contender. *Hostility* is present towards particular group members such as resident cynic and ascendant extrovert. These feelings are compounded by the *loss of positive promotional status by party host and manipulative politician.*

(b) A development of *guilt* over lack of progress and achievement. This guilt inducement is provided by the shrewd businessman. This member frequently uses the impending group termination as a vehicle for stimulating task consciousness. An increased flurry of task activity and a later *re-evaluation of positive–negative feeling* about the trainer may follow from such guilt inducement.

(c) *Frustration* and *anger* over the personal rivalries and individual competitions for attention and power. These rivalries and power struggles demand time from group task work and result in drawing out *negative* feelings. In the direct communications group there seems also to be an exaggerated *disenchantment* with the emphasis of the trainer upon his definition of work at the expense of any resolution of these personal squabbles. The trainer may then be chastised because of this apparent insensitivity to certain more interpersonal group needs.

Theme (3) Impending termination—go it alone!
FINAL ROLE DEVELOPMENTS
(7) Popular contender
(8) Insular deviant

The results of these differentiated roles upon the emotionality of each of the groups studied seems to be:

(a) Feelings of member *consolidation into either positive or negative group factions.* This results from the gradual termination of continual struggles over group influence and control.

(b) A premature *resolution of guilt* over the absence of any concrete evidence for task accomplishment and a replacement of resultant guilt feelings with feelings of (i) attachment to other members through the interventions of popular contender, or (ii) *a defensive displacement of blame* upon the trainer, the insular deviant or the

Table 7

Group emotional development

	Unstructured, leaderless method	Traditional, structured method
(A) *At onset of group*	Dependency Vulnerability Anxiety	Compliance Apprehension Expectancy ⎱ A shared emotional culture
(B) *After initial trainer interventions*	Dependent hostility Negativism through trainer confrontation Expectancy violation with 'shock' Increased anxiety over assigned task Increased feeling of personal vulnerability Individual work 'ethic' promoted and trainer reliance demoted Competition for power in what seems a trainer vacuum	Independent hostility Negativism expressed through trainer subversion Expectancy containment or resolution Decreased anxiety over assigned task Decreased feeling of personal vulnerability Individual work 'ethic' demoted and trainer reliance promoted Ceding of initial control to knowledgeable trainer
(C) *After early role developments*	Confusion over task *v.* personal goals Positive–negative ambivalence Fear and anxiety Anger and impotence Pressure for role differentiation ⎱ A shared emotional culture	
(D) *After further role developments*	Increased negativism towards task and trainer Intermember hostility Guilt about lack of progress Frustration and anger over personal rivalries Disenchantment ⎱ A shared emotional culture	
(E) *After final role developments*	Consolidation into positive–negative factions Resolution of guilt Attachment versus displaced blame ⎱ A shared emotional culture	

resident cynic. Both these latter members may serve as scapegoats for the trainer.

These various themes are initiated, aborted, rehearsed, elaborated, repeated, recapitulated, denied, misunderstood, agreed upon, argued about, etc., etc., throughout the life of the group—this constitutes the group dynamics. The group is wrestling with its emotional problems while ostensibly trying to solve a problem on the cognitive level.

6

THE DYNAMIC STRUCTURE OF
LEARNING GROUPS

In the natural sciences, the words *'structure' and *'function' normally occur together. 'Structure' implies some enduring form made up of various parts which occupy three-dimensional space, and which have some (temporary or permanent) relationship to each other, both spatial and functional. The word 'function' refers to the fact that the form of the object, and the relationship of its parts to each other, are adapted to ensure that some kind of end-result is produced. Changes in the structure normally bring about changes in the function, and vice versa.

When we speak of the 'structure of groups' several ideas are implied. For one thing, there is no immediate intention to describe the way in which the bodies of the members are distributed in Euclidean space—although it is clear that this must have a significant bearing on such matters as communication, psychological relationships, attitudes, interaction. It is these psychological processes with which we are concerned. The structure of the group refers to an abstract conceptual model which simulates, or represents analogically, the ways in which the communication process operates in the group, the relationships of dominance and submission as between the members of which it is composed, the ways in which various psychological processes (especially adaptive processes such as learning) are facilitated or inhibited by these relationships, and many other things as well. In building this conceptual model of the group, the three-dimensional Euclidean space provides a convenient analogue to represent psychological relationships. We must include the fourth dimension of time since particular group structures are transient, changing with the inner dynamics of the group and as the particular functional problems which the group faces arise through time.

At the outset we must make a distinction, since learning groups are of various kinds. The traditional learning group is a highly structured, stable configuration, the central element which dominates all the others being the teacher. Teaching and learning are not identical processes, nor do they necessarily happen together at any particular point in time and space. They are in the best case *complementary*—the teacher's task being to facilitate learning. The relation between them, at any rate, so far as institutionalised instruction and learning are concerned, is shown in the systems-model (Figure 13).

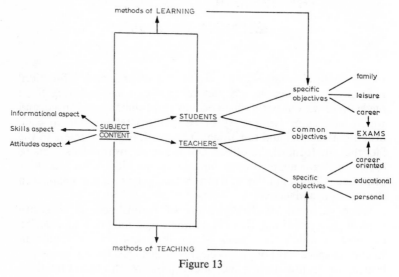

Figure 13

Systems model of the instructional system

At this stage we are particularly interested in the *methods* of teaching and learning —these being closely related to the *objectives* of teacher and learner. The method is, in fact, one of the prime determinants of group structure.

Broadly speaking, teaching involves five different kinds of objectives. These arise from the nature of the subject matter or content which the student has to master. In certain subjects, one or other of these objectives dominates the others. However, the particular objective depends not only on the subject, but, to some extent, the teacher's view of it. The five objectives are (1) transmission of information;

(2) development of technical skills; (3) development of social competence; (4) development of personal acceptability; (5) development of self-insight. These objectives can be classified according to various dichotomies—objective–subjective; impersonal–personal; understandings–behaviour change, etc. The methods appropriate to each of these arise partly from traditional ways, partly from the nature of the end-product desired ('the educated person') and partly from the extent to which the individual teacher is prepared to involve himself with the students as persons. We can tabulate these methods in relation to the teacher's accepted functions as shown:

TEACHING METHODS IN RELATION TO FUNCTION
Objective information
> *Who:* the lecturer, the pedagogue, the tutor.
> *How:* question-and-answer techniques, set assignments from a textbook, teaching-machines, lectures, training in use of reference books, fact-finding research, programmed learning.

Technical skill
> *Who:* the instructor, the coach, the trainer, the tutor.
> *How:* drill, exercises, practical work under supervision, demonstration, analysis, model-building.

Social competence
> *Who:* the tutor, the exemplar.
> *How:* supervised social experience, information about social rules (moral training), parables, case discussion, guided discussion, role-playing.

Personal acceptability
> *Who:* the tutor, the friend, the therapist.
> *How:* informal discussion, the interview, video- and tape-recordings, analysis of experience, psychodrama.

Self-insight
> *Who:* the tutor, the therapist, doctor, priest, guru, 'weirdo'.
> *How:* all of the above, quasi-psychological 'experiments' with drugs, psychedelics, communal living, encounter groups, *Wanderjahren,* etc.

In an earlier section, we classified the various learning groups and teaching methods in terms of two axes—interactive–non-interactive and interpersonal–instrumental. Another kind of classification, which takes more account of structure, would be into formal *v.* informal methods. In the formal methods, the teacher is the centre of the action: the student is expected to be receptive and submissive.

Generally speaking, formal methods are the traditional techniques where emphasis centres on the first two teaching functions—transmission of information and development of skills. Informal methods are used where the emphasis lies on development of social competence, personal acceptability and self-insight. Here the didactic situation is student-centred, normally unstructured, with the student being active.

In the former situation (epitomised by the lecture, controlled discussion, demonstration, group tutorial) the various attitudes and group roles remain unexpressed, abortive and latent. This is the main advantage of the formal method as far as the teacher is concerned—students are expected to suppress their inner reactions, to grapple with the subject and not with the instructor, to play a single inactive, receptive, disciple role. This is what McLeish (1968) has described as the 'oracular' approach to teaching. He has uncovered the different student attitudes and reactions normally masked by this approach (1968, 1970). Students are classified according to their attitudes to the lecture, the seminar and the tutorial methods of teaching. Nine types are recognised as shown in Figure 14. These are accounted for in terms of personality variables and social–political attitudes which have, of course, been developed before the

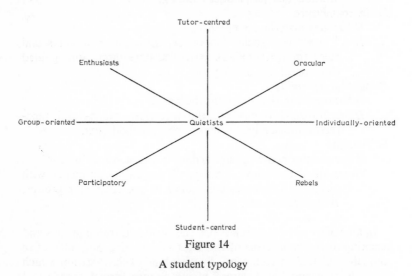

Figure 14

A student typology

Like all scientific typologies, this is neither exclusive nor comprehensive—it is a way of looking at students and trying to account for differences in their reactions to instruction

student actually encounters these methods. It is as though the student were 'pre-sensitised' to accept or reject particular techniques. But in the normal way, no one would be particularly interested in the fact that (say) rather more than ten per cent of a given learning group was completely opposed to any of these three traditional methods, and probably learn very little from face-to-face meetings with the instructor, no matter who he was and what he was trying to teach.

Informal methods, on the other hand (experimental, interactive, group techniques), lend themselves to the expression of feeling, in the course of which various aspects of group structure are revealed. Participants, over a period of time, discover something of the dynamics of the learning group; they align themselves with particular individuals and subgroups; they express both their positive and negative feelings towards the task; they reveal their habitual postures towards people, towards authority, towards various abstract values, such as cooperation, equality, leadership. The small learning group is a kind of microcosm in which we can discover certain kinds of organisation or structure which are written large in the macrocosm of the greater society within which it is embedded and from which, ultimately, it draws its resources—material, abstract norms, cognitive styles, discussion content. We will proceed to explore the structure of such small groups, using materials collected over a period of about five years, during which numerous kinds of learning groups have been observed using standard techniques of recording, coding of behaviour and analysis. These take account of *all* the behaviour of *all* the participants—including not only what they say (verbal), but also what they do (non-verbal behaviour). The actual *content* of the discussion is also used to throw light on the main problem.

There are three major influences which operate to produce structure in such a learning group—*power, orientation to a task,* and *liking–disliking or emotional affiliation.* The distribution of individuals in the group structure can be thought of as the resultant of their relative position along these three dimensions. The total configuration of all the individuals in the group—their spatial relationship to each other, in other words, constitutes the group structure. We should speak about 'movement' along these three dimensions, because the structure of a group is not static. It undergoes change through time. However, the rate of change is not the same in all kinds of learning groups. 'Formal' groups tend to maintain the same structure over many sessions; 'informal' groups may change in structure several times during even one learning session.

How can group structures be elicited? Are there techniques which can readily provide the information from which we can construct a

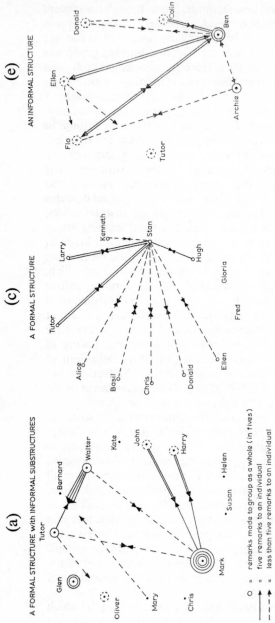

Figures 15a, c and e

Physical distribution of participants

(a) Formal structure with informal substructures

Fifteen minutes of *seminar* on 'the lecture' (Mark is making a presentation and defending it)

(c) A formal structure

Fifteen minutes of *group tutorial*. Stan has just outlined his proposed special study. (NB no group remarks)

(e) An informal structure

Fifteen minutes of *free group discussion*: no overt control on method or content of discussion pairs (Ben–Flo, Ben–Ellen, Ben–Colin)

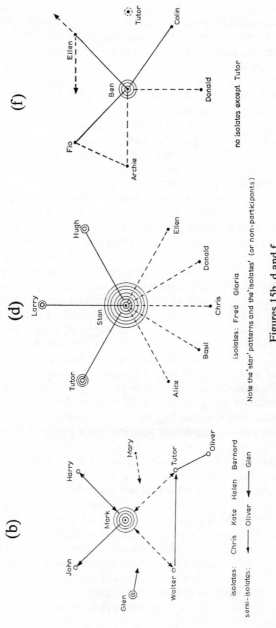

(b)

isolates: Chris Kate Helen Bernard

semi-isolates: ———— Oliver

(d)

isolates: Fred Gloria

Note the 'star' patterns and the 'isolates' (or non-participants)

(f)

no isolates except Tutor

Figures 15b, d and f
Sociometric structure of the same groups

dynamic model of the group? There are several contenders here for recognition. Theoreticians tend to work from various, often conflicting,
assumptions about the nature of group 'life' and the relative significance of the essential processes which can be recognised as belonging
to it. If we accept that *communication* is a primary process in the small
group, a significant pointer to structure is the close study of patterns
of interchange—Who speaks to whom? how often? in what terms?
—and how is the communication received?

Figures 15a, b, and c, each summarise fifteen minutes' talk in three
different kinds of learning group. The patterns of communication
differ enormously. This depends not so much on the nature of
the problem being discussed: rather it reflects the group processes at
work, both manifest and latent. The patterns of communication
point to the power dynamic within the groups. In the first case, Mark
is the most powerful figure (see Figures 15a and b). This is shown,
amongst other things, by the enormous number of remarks he makes
directed to no one in particular. The tutor has withdrawn from the
power struggle which is carried on between John and Mark, and
Harry and Mark. Walter has unfinished business with the tutor from
previous sessions, but the tutor refuses him satisfaction, seeking
instead to elicit support and approval from Oliver and Mark. Chris,
Susan, Helen and Kate take no part, being totally isolated. In the
second group Stan and the tutor are engaged in a power contest
around the task-theme proposed by Stan. In this group, except for
Fred and Gloria, the remaining participants model their behaviour
on the tutor, continuing to harass Stan with questions about his
study (see Figures 15c and d). There are *no* group remarks. Fred
and Gloria remain isolated. In the third case, the tutor adopts a
totally non-directive role (see Figures 15e and f). Pairing takes place
with Ben who assumes the power position in the group abdicated by
the tutor.

Clearly, this analysis of who-speaks-to-whom is an initial breakthrough which throws *some* light on group structure and the changes
which take place in it—provided we use other information. This we
have been doing in an intuitive, or holistic manner. Obviously, the
method we have used is quite inadequate as a scientific technique—
it is merely the beginning of a systematic analysis. However, the
method can be refined if we recognise the nature of the gaps in our
understanding and develop a more comprehensive system of analysis.
For one thing, the summary figures do not tell us who *initiates* the
interchange. It is obvious that a group where Mark is the initiator,
formulating questions which he poses to the others, has a different
kind of group structure from the situation where Mark is the recipient

of the questions. The problem is: What proportion of acts does each participant *initiate* and what proportion does he receive from the other members? We must also make a distinction between the *kind* of interventions people make. For example, are they predominantly concerned with the learning *task* which is in the cognitive area, or are they concerned primarily with the social and *emotional* problems of the group which lie in the affective area. And in relation to the last question: does the individual member *receive* requests for help from the group; does he *offer* help towards the solution of the current group problem; does he *request* help on behalf of the group from some other person?

Figure 16 shows a fourth kind of learning group, where case-workers discuss a problem together for five minutes, in the absence

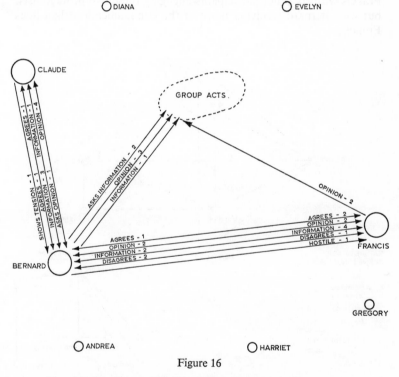

Figure 16

Five minutes of case-study group directed to producing a report

Bernard as 'rapporteur' has the power (only three students' acts
are shown, these are the high interactors)

of the tutor. The group actually contains eight participants but, for simplicity, we have isolated the acts of only the three chief inter-actors. Student Bernard is acting as reporter for the group. From the Figure it is clear that during this short period, the group is working at a specific task; as between these three participants the observer recognises only two acts in the social–emotional area (tension and hostility) in a total of thirty-five acts observed. The configuration of this group over the five-minute period of observation can also be shown in the form of a sociogram which takes account of *all* the interaction (see Figure 17).

The sociogram indicates that this group is an extremely close-knit structure with lines of communication running freely in a great number of directions. The basic foundation of the work in which they are engaged is the continuing dialogue between Bernard and Francis with six other participants engaging these two protagonists, but with Bernard receiving more of the communication than does Francis.

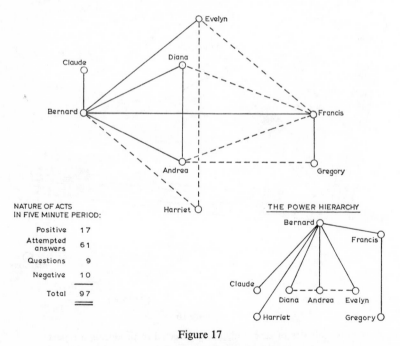

NATURE OF ACTS IN FIVE MINUTE PERIOD:	
Positive	17
Attempted answers	61
Questions	9
Negative	10
Total	97

Figure 17

Complete communication network in previous discussion: sociogram

Verbal output is not, therefore, the only criterion determining one's place and movement in the group structure. Control, decision, evaluation in terms of the on-going group process influence the relative disposition of individuals in relation to the dimension of *dominance–submission*. Identification with the task, as this is perceived by the group, the expression of positive feelings of friendship and agreement, ability to relieve tension in the group by dramatisation of the group emotion or by an appropriate witticism, help to establish the member's position on the *liking* dimension. Acceptance of the group norms as these develop through the discussion process, and active work towards the realisation of the group goals, push the individual member into a position of prominence on the *task-orientation* dimension. This means that a two-dimensional figure, such as we have been employing to this point, does not do justice to the complexity of the group structure. At any instant of the group life the configuration of the plenum of group members can best be represented by a three-dimensional model which captures these three aspects of the individual participant which confer *influence* on him or her. In this regard, the sociogram is too primitive an instrument to accommodate the complexity of group structure.

ROLE DEVELOPMENT AND GROUP STRUCTURE

The problem of group structure and dynamics can also be approached through the study of roles. As we have seen, the changes in the functional problems which the group faces during the establishment, maintenance and dissolution of different phases give rise to a variety of social relationships. Initially, the group is concerned with its assigned or perceived task and with various social–emotional concerns. In consequence, the first 'generation' of social relationships, the earliest roles develop. The most basic of these roles are those of task and social–emotional 'leaders'. As the word is commonly used, leadership is a vague, frequently undefined cliché for behaviour patterns which may include excessive talking, verbal aggression, domineering, controlling and directing behaviour (the 'task-leader') or of helping, soliciting, patronising, scolding (the 'social–emotional' leader). In course of time, usually in short order, more rewarding leaders are 'shaped' by the group, closer to the functional problems and less individualistic and idiosyncratic in character. Then too, with the passage of time, many other roles are broken off and elaborated from these two 'catch-alls'.

This differentiation of second- and third-generation roles can be thought of as a branching structure with its origin in the task and social–emotional problems encountered by the group which were responsible for the earliest roles. The time, and the way, in which these new structures develop also depends upon the equilibrium conditions established in the group life. As problems of group cohesion, learning, use of resources, and sheer expression of feelings become the focus of concern, the group proceeds to 'nominate' individuals who are ready and willing to adopt specific roles which meet the needs of the members at these particular stages. The roles are, so to speak, adopted in response to current particularly pressing problems. As a reward for accepting the responsibility, and the risk associated with active participation in a group role, the member who accepts nomination is granted a certain increase in status and power. He then exercises a specific kind of leadership-role—for a time. As his performance becomes less necessary and less convincing in terms of its usefulness to the group, as the group moves back to equilibrium or into a new phase, the member finds his status deteriorating and his influence waning.

With movement through phases, corresponding to the various functional problems encountered by the group, different individuals figure prominently at one time or another. Depending upon which of the numerous available roles are taken on, and on the number of persons who seek to provide satisfactions for the group needs, a particular group culture manifests itself. For example, the group may be described as more or less formal, more or less permeable to outside ideas, it may bounce from democracy through patronage to autocracy during a single session. This is the significance of the term 'group dynamics'.

The way in which particular roles are performed, and the way in which they are terminated, is crucial to the success or failure of the group. We can recognise with Bales, 'the institutionalisation of a certain indifference, impersonality, impartiality as an explicit obligation in the performance of certain roles' (Bales, 1951, p. 154). The ways in which these 'institutionalised' roles are played, their appearance and their termination, are apparently to be cued by the group as it seeks to maintain the precarious balance between work and pleasure. Any extreme variation in either of these directions for any length of time seems to generate a condition of strain. The strain due to an 'excess' of work (task) tends to bring about a counter-reaction from those more concerned with pleasure (socio-emotional). Similarly, excess 'work' in the social–emotional area brings into being a counter-reaction in favour of the assigned task. This condition of unstable 'equilibrium' seems to operate in favour of a sharing, not to say an equal distribution of status and power throughout the group. There appears to be a consensus that any malfunctioning in the social system is a threat to everybody. As a result there is a continuing zigzag between adaptation to the external situation at the expense of personal feelings, and the pacification of personal feelings at the expense of the achievement of the alloted task. The shifting role-structures of the group provide a commentary on the history of this conflict.

It is possible to chart the progress of individuals, and of the group, using certain quantitative indices devised by Bales (1951). For example, the index of 'indirect access to resources' can be calculated for each member on the basis of the extent to which questions posed in the group are answered. In this way it can be demonstrated, for example, that person A tends to have rather more or rather less access to available resources than do his peers. Similarly, the index of 'direct access to resources' establishes the proportion of acts in the categories of asking for information, opinion and suggestion directed towards each individual. The 'index of attempted control' answers the question: 'to what extent were the attempts of the individual to provide suggestions, opinions or orientation to the group answered positively instead of negatively, compared to other group members?' Finally, the generalised status index gives a composite view of the 'overall' status of any particular group member in relation to other group members by adding the first three indices together and averaging.

The best indicator of leadership in the learning group is the index of generalised status since this subsumes the other three indices. To demonstrate the rise and fall of significant members across the life of their groups, the movement of their status index can be contrasted with the phase movements of their groups.

The relationship between high member interaction and group phase movement verifies that particular group members acquire, maintain, and eventually lose status. It is clear too that the acquisition or loss of status is related to current 'phases' of group development. As one problem area dissolves, another is encountered. Consequentially, those group members who were initially influential become less so, other individuals of lesser status come to the forefront.

Examples of this could be multiplied. For example, in one group the members who were first to attain high status were both task-oriented, positive individuals. They expressed a concern with the initial communication of group norms and the development of cooperation among all of the group participants. They expended considerable effort in trying to organise discussion about the assigned group task. They were a major influence in moving the group from an initial attitude of ambivalence about the task to a stage of task evaluation. The uncomfortable emotional feelings generated through expanded task activity resulted in a gradually increasing status for one of the other members. The person now in question was much less positive in his task outlook, and in his attitude to the group trainer. He soon became spokesman for the more negative group faction, and maintained control of this negative subgroup until challenged in later sessions.

The group then moved from evaluation of the task to a period of conflicted positive and negative emotionality. This had the effect of polarising the group and left the door ajar for a new leadership struggle.

The opportunist in the group then moved up very quickly in status as the influence of the initial group protégés waned in the face of a more vehement opposition. The positive–negative arguments, for which these two had been the major spokesmen, had polarised the group, leaving the negative faction holding the best hand when it came time for the showdown. At this point the opportunist challenged the positive contender for the leadership of the group, and simultaneously used the negative contender as whipping boy. A detailed study of the careers of successive leaders throughout the lives of these learning groups is the basis for the historical description of such groups outlined above.

THE DIFFERENTIATED LEADERSHIP ROLES

A close analysis of the high interactors in different kinds of groups reveals the existence of eight dominant types who occupy various positions in the structure, and who are activated at different stages of the group process (Matheson, 1971). These types can be described in everyday terms, as follows:

Role type	Bales' category
(1) Manipulative politician	UPF
(2) Shrewd businessman	UF
(3) Resident cynic	UNB
(4) Party host	PF
(5) Disenchanted contender	UNF
(6) Ascendent extrovert	U
(7) Popular contender	UP
(8) Insular deviant	NB

Analysis of the performance of these eight major and minor leadership roles reveals the remarkable accuracy with which Bales categorised the activities and value systems of group members located in these positions in social–psychological space. In almost every instance his expectations were corroborated; where discrepancies were found the similarities outweighed the differences.

Three types tend to occur in every task-centred group: these are UPF, UF, UNB. Since they tend to recur, it is suspected that these roles are crucial to this kind of group structure, and to the effective functioning of learning groups in general. Examination of the group performances of these members, using interaction records, sociograms, group dialogue, their diaries, and 'clinical' impressions from observers, reveals the characteristic qualities of these types. Bales (1970) has provided numerous clues about where to look for evidence of specific performances.

(1) *Manipulative politician* (UPF)

(a) *Interaction record.* Usually these are the highest of the high interactors. They initiate many positive statements and receive a considerable number in return. Their total interaction profile shows considerable activity in raising questions and supplying answers. They provide numerous suggestions and opinions. Consequently they are offered a lot of information by others. They also tend to generate a lot of agreement *and* disagreement. Contrary to expectation, the rate of negativism they give out is high as is the reception of negative reactions from others. In spite of this, the role seems to be concerned with overlooking or denying negative feelings, especially when these interfere with the task at hand. This type covers his negative reactions to other members with a veneer of verbal warmth, out of consideration for group achievement. He tends to respond to their negative reactions in the same way.

(b) *Sociogram.* The UPF members are high vote-catchers, especially on questions which refer to the upward dimension. This is probably a direct result of their high participation. They receive a large number of votes on the forward dimension, being viewed by others as identifying with the task.

(c) *Group dialogue.* In the group, communications indicate a positively focused, cooperative, task-oriented but somewhat power-driven behavioural style. There is a marked tendency to speak to the group rather than to individuals, to deny negative feelings, and to promote their own values whenever possible.

(2) *Shrewd businessman* (UF)

(a) *Interaction record.* The interaction pattern of this type demonstrates an average interactor who receives more acts in the emotional areas than he initiates. His role seems to be to remain emotionally neutral: for the most part he seems to succeed in this. Additionally, he initiates suggestions, opinions, and information more than he receives from others. He is the recipient of many questions from others. The total picture is one of emotional blandness coupled with a heavy emphasis on control of the group, especially through control of information. In fact, the role could be described as an attempt to cultivate dependence in others through control of the crucial task resources. Acts are addressed to the group rather than individuals. There is a tendency for initiating acts in the various categories to surpass the number of similar acts received.

(b) *Sociogram.* The voting response of other members to this leadership style is generally restricted. The UF members do not receive many votes on any particular dimension. When votes are awarded them, especially in early sessions, they tend to be in the negative and backward directions. This indicates a lack of initial acceptance by other members. In the early meetings it helps the UF member to pretend to an interest, concern or affection which he may not feel with full sincerity. The emotional neutrality of UF members would probably come over as negative to others at this stage, as the trainer's role tends to do. Later, as the group becomes less emotionally 'hung-up', the UF members acquire more controlling votes. They begin to be seen as 'valuable' for the 'task' by others.

(c) *Group dialogue.* This illustrates the emotional neutrality of UF members and their continuing attempts to work on the intellectual, rational side of the group by the control of information and by the promotion of cooperation towards the task. There is a marked tendency to phrase remarks in a 'collective' fashion.

However, the analysis shows that personal involvement is kept to a minimum. The emphasis is on achievement through group harmony. The UF members act as a kind of 'group conscience', they serve as a living reminder that the task is ever-present and must not be forgotten. They place heavy reliance on techniques of guilt inducement, and this tends to generate dislike, especially in the initial stages.

The group dialogue and diaries show a clear tendency for UF members to speak of the group as 'we', 'us', 'our group'. This promotes cooperation, in this respect they agree with the UPF 'politicians'. Similarly, they confide a conspicuous desire to their diaries to be considered more important persons in the group than they perceive themselves to be. They report this to their diaries, but not to the group members.

(3) *Resident cynic* (UNB)

(a) *Interaction record.* The UNB members are also amongst the highest of the high interactors. Their interaction profiles show that they initiate very few positive statements; they are the highest initiators of negative statements. They receive more positive reactions than they initiate, but they also receive many negative reactions. They do not interact readily in terms of giving suggestion, opinion and information, but receive a considerable number of acts in these categories. Additionally, the output of questions is quite low. This lack of engagement in the task area coupled with the marked tendency for UNB individuals to address the group a great deal testifies to a personal 'agenda' which, more often than not, is anti-task and anti-trainer, and which finds expression through deviance, disagreement and hostility. This tends to generate a high negative reaction in other members. The high scores of UNB members in the 'joking' and 'fantasy' category are explained through their predominant use of these media to express their deviance from trainer-initiated activity. This is reflected, not only in the group dialogue, but to some extent in the diaries.

(b) *Sociogram.* The votes cast for the UNB members agree closely with the IPA interaction profiles. They are considered by their fellow members to be powerful, albeit negative and deviant, participants. The reaction of most participants is to reject them as disruptive and uncooperative elements. The votes recorded show little change over time, the consistency in reaction towards the UNB members reflecting the disenchantment and discomfort other members feel for and with them.

(c) *Group dialogue.* The UNB members are shown in group dialogue to be demanding, high in negative confrontation, posed against authority as this is vested in the trainer, uncooperative and oriented towards their own personal goals.

However, UNB members retain their influence in a very idiosyncratic fashion. They are domineering and overbearing. They submit their personal goals again and again as standards for the group, and very actively work for their adoption. Generally they are negative not only towards the trainer, but they are equally distrustful of others, especially any sort of authority. Much of their time is taken up in seeking to undermine and disenfranchise the task leader.

These UNB members are highly interactive, talkative and prone to flights of fantasy. The lengthy 'ego trips' are characteristic. These fantasy trips are attempts at so enchanting the other members that they will accept the frame of reference offered by the UNB member. If they are rejected, or fail to influence, there is a negative backlash, usually directed at the more positive and task-oriented members.

The other group members commonly succeed in seeing through the UNB 'game plan' and react negatively towards them personally. They are rated as among the persons least agreed with, and persons whom many felt farthest from.

Part of their influence comes from their ability to defy authority without serious consequences to themselves. The diaries and group dialogue demonstrate the omnipotent feelings of many UNB members, and their habitual anti-authority reactions. They appear to generate fear in other members and gain power in the group as a result of this negative influence. There is a close identification with the UNB individual by other more submissive individuals, because of this they continue to receive support for their deviance from these less explosive members. Their scepticism and pessimism about group success, and the value of investing positive affect and energy in the group, find support among those group members who lack a proper work ethic.

The three role types which occur with regularity have been described in some detail. The descriptive titles, 'manipulative politician' (UPF), 'shrewd businessman' (UF) and 'resident cynic' (UNB) were used to provide convenient labels for the respective group performances of these members and the particular kinds of function they serve in the group.

As an additional point, it should be noted that each of our groups seems to accommodate three kinds of leaders. There is a positive (UPF), neutral (UF), and negative (UNB) high interactor in each group. This permits the full emotional range of the group members complete expression. It is also to be noted that both pro-task (forward) and anti-task (backward) role types are represented in each group by these three kinds of leaders. This is an interesting hypothesis, requiring further investigation.

Two other leadership roles occur frequently, although they do not seem to be so crucial to group functioning as the first three types. When they appear they do perform certain particularly vital functions in their respective groups. These are the 'party host' (PF) and the 'disenchanted contender' (UNF).

(4) *The party host* (PF)

(a) *Interaction record*. Not the highest of the interactors, but often above the average in expression of positive feelings, while his rate of negative reactions is only average. In some cases, the rate of emitting positive reactions may be more than double his reception of such acts. While his negativism may be high, it is well below other highly interactive members. There is a tendency to give numerous suggestions, opinions, and information. There is less interaction in the form of asking questions. The high interaction in the task area is in line with the promotion of a positive approach to work and attempts at fostering cooperation.

(b) *Sociogram*. These members do not appear aggressive enough to command serious attention. The votes they do attract are gathered early, probably as a result of their attempts to foster a positive reaction in face of a new experience. Later, this allegiance begins to fade away.

(c) *Group dialogue*. A good example of the undecided, rather soft-hearted, and apologetic nature of the PF role type is the way in which one such proposed to eliminate the trainer:

> 'Well, from our point of view, after having, you know, partaken of these discussions for, what's this, our third or fourth one . . . I'm just wondering if . . . you know, I wouldn't mind seeing how things would go without the trainer here.'

Or again:

> 'You know, I think though, whether or not it was the result of Greg and his, you know, ideas or his readings or what. But I think last week's discussion was about the best we've had, and I think one of the reasons being that, you know, here Greg was, uh, sort of not afraid, if you will, to come out and really speak his mind, you know, cause I mean, thinking about that time and myself, here I am, sitting and, and really, I'm still, you know, a bit well, inhibited about, you know, really coming out with a lot of, uh, things among the group, you know. And seeing Greg last week, ah, you know, as it were, voicing his opinion and then other people, sort of getting back at him, you know, to me, I really felt that, you know, we had things really going. What I'm trying to say is I think that may be this is sort of what we need, is something like this to, uh, I don't know, get us stimulated or something.'

The PF type is characterised by an unfailing faith in affection. Love will conquer if he can only persevere. The function of the PF member is to boost the failing spirits of those members who are about to lose faith in the task, and to promote group cohesion whenever possible. This type has an implicit belief in the goodness of authority. Individuals of this type are agreeable, and somewhat docile in their obvious dependency. They advocate cooperation. Their role can be identified with the analogue of the party host, whose main objective is to get through the evening without incident or embarrassment and who would like, in the last analysis, to be considered a nice person for going through all this inconvenience.

(5) *Disenchanted contender* (UNF)

(a) *Interaction record.* These are the least active of the group of lively participators. The main feature of their interaction profile is an extremely high rate of negative reactions, in one case triple the amount of a comparable interactor. Their activity in the task area is average, or less than average.

(b) *Sociogram.* There seems to be no consistency in the way these leaders are viewed by others. Some are 'late developers' who accumulate power in the terminal phases of the group. Some consistently win favourable mention, while others appear to be very unpredictable, their popularity waxes and wanes. The only common feature seems to be the ability of UNF members to be chosen as major spokesmen for the group at particular times. The control dimension, so defined, is the strongest feature in the sociogram voting pattern of the UNF participant.

(c) *Group dialogue.* The section of dialogue which follows is between two participants, Eric being identified as the 'disenchanted contender' and Mike as the 'manipulative politician'.

> *Eric:* I'm not trying to criticise you, I mean, he does you know, talk and everything, that's fine; but what I'm criticising here then, is that I think he's using other members of the group, to come out and express themselves, and I don't think he's really doing it; fine, you're talking, I don't disagree with that, you're doing a lot of talking . . . involvement, but, as you have mentioned, a lot of involvement but no interaction . . .
>
> *Mike:* You know, I sort of get the impression that you're trying to load all your troubles on to me.
>
> *Eric:* Not really, no. But you see, you've been the only person who has been doing all the talking, the majority of the talking, and I think people have just let you do it; because . . . you've read a lot of things and come up with different topics; but as far as I'm concerned . . .
>
> *Mike:* Yeah, but, you know, I mean, I try to get the group moving off

the ground quite a lot of times, otherwise it would have just been flat . . . with no conversation at all; it's only through conversaiton that this group is going to get off the ground. I mean, it's not one of those sort of groups where you can go around, you know, almost as a sensitivity group.

Eric: Well, I know that the people you ask are the people who always interact; or the people who talk, that would be either Lois, Jean or Ken . . . This is where I noticed . . . (Laughter) yeah, Pat, he'd ask Pat sometimes.

Mike: Why put the onus on me, why not say something your damned self, instead of putting the onus on me all the time?

Eric: No . . . you're the one who seems to be leading the group, now, you've asked me how I felt, this is the way I feel, I'm giving you how I feel.

The UNF role seems the hardest to define. The negativism is mostly latent or manifested in a projection on to outsiders such as the observers of the group, or instructors, or the trainer. The attitude of this kind of leader towards the task often appears very ambivalent. They may begin with an exuberance and excitement, especially in a structured, problem-oriented group, but this turns sour after a number of sessions. The expressed reactions then are that the task is 'too hard', or the learning period 'too short'. They condemn other group members as not trying hard enough. In consequence, the UNF leaders *seem* to be very achievement-oriented, they are prone to invoke their values of work and seriousness in the group situation. They express a desire to be influential, but generally they have difficulty in persuading other members to back them up. The sociogram records show up this inconsistent support. The UNF members react adversely to the overtly positive members, they do so by sarcasm and more veiled forms of negativism. As a rule they seem untrusting, and suspicious of others.

There have been five role types discussed up to this point. As we have seen, three of these occur with considerable regularity in discussion groups, they represent kinds of leadership styles which seem to be congenial to certain individuals, and to the other group members at particular times. The two other roles dealt with so far do not occur with such regularity—the 'party host' and 'disenchanted contender'. It seems possible that the groups we are discussing (learning groups with definite tasks) need certain kinds of leadership more than they need others. In addition, at particular points, some groups develop more specific leadership needs which can be met from group resources. In some cases, the group may not have the necessary

F

resource person who can accept the proferred role and play it successfully. Presumably during the interregnum we have the long silences, or the fantasy trips, and other dysfunctional activities which groups engage in.

(6) *Ascendent extrovert* (U)

(a) *Interaction record.* These are very interactive participants who tend to initiate more than they receive in the task and emotional areas. A qualification is needed, in that this kind of leadership tends to generate a good deal of negative feeling. The domineering, high pressure performance, lacking in positive affect of a genuine quality, common to this type provokes negative reactions from others. The high positive scores assigned to the ascendant extroverts are more than somewhat spurious. This is because these individuals operate a good deal in the category 'fantasy' and 'jokes': this tends to balloon their total 'positive' reactions. It is also typical of the ascendent extrovert that they are the recipients of a lot of questions from others.

(b) *Sociogram.* This leader attracts numerous votes, especially in the areas of dominance and task-avoidance. Others see them as aggressive and controlling, but without real leadership quality. They receive a great number of backward 'agree least with' votes.

(c) *Group dialogue.* A classic example of this type appeared as a verbal, monopolising individual, prone to flights of fantasy with sexual and aggressive themes. Taking up a lot of group time, she came across as extremely exhibitionistic and concerned with her visual prominence in the group. A section of monologue provides a good example of a typical performance.

> 'Prostitutes are sort of funny, perhaps not so much funny . . . I didn't think I was that naive when I was working and now I saw all this going on, and I was really shocked for about a week. I couldn't see how come these nicely dressed gals could sit in a corner, right under a red light. Why didn't she come and sit closer to the bar, and this waitress looked at me as if to say how could you be so stupid, she was there for business and then you could gradually see who are the regular ones, and this hotel is noted for having the professionals, they came from Winnipeg and Vancouver, and they come and stay for a couple of days and you have the ones in the city who stay and wander around, and I guess they're sort of free.
>
> They dressed very smartly, colours are coordinated, you can tell their hair is just done to a tee and I got to know one, she's in the city and she's not really professional, she works in the office in the day time and then . . .

She just sort of wants a male companion, and like the other night she came in and said gee it's dead in town and I've been to all the places and there is no action . . . she says, she reminds me. I don't know, I just think the girls get to know one another and they go along and two of them go together and then a guy approaches their table and they say go away we're not free, so they'll buy the most expensive drinks. When we had the big conventions in May, the professionals stayed away because they're being bothered by detectives and things and so the pimps were bringing in girls off the street, but none of these businessmen would want them, their dress, their appearance wasn't attractive so they just wandered from table to table, never got taken.'

(d) *Diaries*. The diary comments of these participants project the same kind of image—boisterous, unconventional and sexually aggressive. The diary of the ascendant extroverts reflect in many ways the group performance although in a much less free-wheeling, open-ended fashion.

The composite picture of this kind of leader is one of external confidence and internal turmoil. They are highly dramatic, excitable persons with an exhibitionistic flair and a tendency to develop lengthy fantasy themes in the group. Their primary concern seems to be with themselves rather than others. As a result they provoke negative feelings over their selfishness and monopoly of group 'air time'. Their closest group allies are the deviant, backward individuals to whom they appeal by virtue of their spontaneity and careless attitude. The effect of this leadership style on the group is to develop a kind of conversation piece. They are the persons who are subject to question-and-answer barrages. Their power need is evidenced through their unremitting verbal control of the group.

(7) *Popular contender* (UP)

(a) *Interaction record*. These are amongst the highest of the high interactors. Especially is this true of positive reactions. Their interaction in the task areas is only average in amount. The total of negative reactions is, contrary to expectation, very high. They tend to talk in longer statements than most other members: they also speak frequently to the group rather than to individuals. They initiate more negative remarks than they receive from other members; presumably the nature of their role allows them to be critical of others without too many repercussions.

(b) *Sociogram*. This kind of leadership seems to generate votes, but at sporadic intervals. The other members see the UP members as upward and positive, but tend to react to them in an ambivalent way, especially with respect to their attitude to the task.

(c) *Group dialogue.* Characteristics are long and positive statements. Leadership control is exercised by the device of monopolising 'air time' whilst at the same time advocating cooperation. This type tends to make use of laughter, joking and fantasy to prolong their control of the group. It is a kind of filibuster once they have the ear of the group. The negativism of these members is obvious to the non-participating observer, but, since it is sandwiched within the positive veneer surrounding most of the UP speech, it may not come over in quite the same way to the group participants. As an example, take this section of dialogue:

> 'I was thinking, you know, when I was writing this out, about how you (Lois) say that you doubt if you can hate a person. I mean is this what, is this the way you said it. I usually get things all mixed up—if you don't feel you could hate a person, you may dislike them but you couldn't hate them. Alright then you say you love your future husband very much. Now if someone came along and cut him up into little pieces and carted him off, you know, and made a big play for him and took him right out of your life, you wouldn't hate that person or would you just dislike them? I was just wondering (laughs).'

(d) *Diaries.* The diary entries of the popular contender express this negative reaction to other participants rather more than comes across in the group dialogue. There is more written in the diary about the 'lack of progress' of the group and the UP member's concern for a more prominent influence than is expressed openly in the group. For example:

> 'Everyone seemed so phony—as if they were just talking to say something and be heard—it had all been said before and in exactly the same way. I found it very frustrating and a complete waste of time. Before the session started I had decided to keep quiet throughout the session, and just take notes because I didn't feel I was learning much.'

Or again:

> In this lab I felt frustrated and disappointed since it is clear we are not achieving anything . . . we have not been able to understand most of the trainer's comments and maybe he is hindering us a bit. We have been very unkind to him, but he seems undaunted by our sarcastic remarks . . . too bad he keeps disappointing us!

In summary, this leadership style suggests a highly positive member within the group, with negative reactions to others confided to the diary or manifested in other out-of-group activities. The main source of influence, besides the use of positive affect, comes from the exploitation of group time to promote a particular platform. This kind of leader is not overtly aggressive, and relies on humour and fantasy to maintain the floor. Other members tend to address remarks to him a great deal because it usually elicits a positive response.

(8) *The insular deviant* (NB)

(a) *Interaction record.* This member is the lowest interactor of those in the significant contribution category. There is little or no positive feeling generated; activity is very low also in the area of the task. Reception of task information is also low. The negative reactions are out of all proportion to the rest of the interaction. Concurrently, there is a marked generation of negative feeling from others as well. The NB member is not addressed except in an attempt to bring him into a more interactive relationship to the group or out of curiosity over his group silence.

(b) *Sociogram.* Very rarely does the NB member get many votes. If so, it is almost invariably in choices which point to the negative and backward direction. On questions which indicate leadership control or positive feeling votes are conspicuously lacking.

(c) *Group dialogue.* Two excerpts express the cynical, unconventional, and often openly hostile approach of this kind of contributor as well as the negative reaction it evokes. Although not highly active, on the few occasions when the NB person does speak it is usually in lengthy, prolonged style. Thus, although interaction may be relatively high, it is also spasmodic, sometimes almost cataclysmic.

> *Len:* Don't you have a reaction to some of these problems?
> *Nora:* My reaction is that, oh, well to begin with my reaction was to the person, what the person said, rather than to the person. And a lot of what people said to begin with irritated me to the point where it just, I didn't, my opinion of the person wasn't good, but there again this is my personal opinion, so OK, I'm not going to say I disagree . . .
> *Peter:* Why? . . .
> *Nora:* Because.
> *Peter:* Are you afraid to express how you feel?
> *Nora:* A lot of times I don't feel it's important enough to argue about, because unless it's significant, unless it means something to me, I really don't think it's worth the effort.

Later, in the same session:

> *Greg:* Why do you feel that you have to contribute only in a superior
> sort of way!
> *Nora:* Is that what you think of me too?
> *Greg:* Well that's what you said, at least that's the impression I got,
> maybe I misunderstood you.
> *Rita:* I think you get the impression when you said that you don't see
> where your comments would be useful to the group, you know,
> giving them, I think that's where we got that impression.
> *Nora:* Well, I don't know, maybe some people in this group talk a lot,
> I have my friends outside this group, and normally I talk a lot.
> When I'm with people I don't know, I don't talk at all no matter
> who they are, whether I think it's the Queen of England or a page,
> I don't care who they are. Because I don't come in and tell all my
> personal problems and go on and on and on, doesn't mean I feel
> superior.

(d) *Diaries.* The diary characterises this kind of person as rather
manipulative, certainly critical of others. Mostly the material is
impersonal, being loaded with intellectualisations, or diagnostic
impressions of group performance. One quotation must serve:

> For weeks during these sessions I've expected Prudence, and maybe
> another to come forth with a comment concerning my silence.
> I felt it has irritated her since day one, but I did expect her to
> speak before now. It probably seems quite silly to say I was quite
> happy (and amused) that she had expressed her thoughts. I think
> more of her for it; but amused how people interpret silence. Much
> to people's dismay it isn't always negative. I don't honestly think
> I felt hurt or even angered—that could be because I'm not at all
> emotionally attached to each or any individual concerned,
> although I do feel somewhat involved in the group.

In summary, this role, probably better described as an anti-role,
characterises a participant who is totally uncooperative, irresponsible
and self-contained. There is no appreciation for others who seek to
work towards group solutions. Instead, there is manifested a resigned
and silent scepticism, coupled with a cynical, private amusement.
Feelings are kept from the group, except when it becomes necessary
to become expressly negative to keep from becoming involved and
to keep others at a distance. This behaviour results in an extreme
curiosity and interest on the part of others who seek to penetrate
'the mystery'. This is the way in which silence can be used as a controlling group mechanism. Considering the actual amount of time

taken up by this individual, the impact on the group is surprising. The use of manipulative silence, and the refusal to allow the other members access to 'hidden resources' is a source of constant irritation to the group. This is the 'leadership' style of the insular deviant.

This completes the comparative analysis of the eight leadership role types we have been able to identify amongst the high interactors in relatively free discussion groups. If *all* the members had been considered there would have been many more 'types', but limitations and space militate against discussion of other kinds of participants. (Locations of types in social–psychological space are shown in Figure 18.)

The fact that there are only eight different roles out of twenty-seven

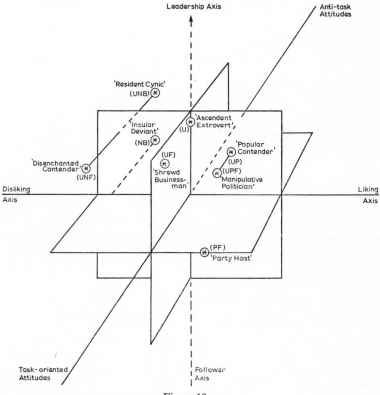

Figure 18

Informal leadership styles in discussion groups: locations in social–psychological space

possibilities (Bales, 1970) among the high interactors is not surprising. It would be remarkable if downward directionality were to appear in the profiles of highly verbal members. The fact of the matter seems to be that there is sufficient variability within the eight types in terms of task and emotional emphases to cover the range needed by the kinds of learning groups we have been considering. Two leadership styles seem to be missing—UN and UB (Bales, 1970, 230–7; 245–51). The qualities of these two leadership styles (i) tough-minded assertiveness, and (ii) value-relativism and expressiveness, respectively, may be uncongenial to these particular groups so that the individuals who might have developed these roles were not allowed by the groups to become high interactors.

7

TEACHING AND LEARNING IN GROUPS

THE TEACHER IN THE LEARNING GROUP

There appears to be no valid measure for identifying or predicting teacher effectiveness. Several hundred research projects have been undertaken since 1900, directed to uncover variables related to teacher and method outcomes, as well as on-the-spot studies of teachers-in-action. No single variable has consistently been identified as related to effective teaching. Indeed, there is no agreement even on how 'effectiveness' should be measured, other than by the traditional intuitive reports or in terms of student 'gain scores' (Gage, 1963). The most comprehensive review (Morsh and Wilder, 1962) concludes that:

No single, specific, observable teacher act has yet been found whose frequency or percent of occurrence is invariably and significantly correlated with student achievement.

There is the strong suggestion, however, that, to the extent that the instructor questions in the areas of student interest and experience rather than assigned subject matter, to the extent that he challenges the students to support ideas, in spontaneous student discussion, effective teaching, measured by student gains, is increased.

Flanders (1970) takes up this point and maintains that the search for teaching acts which are correlated significantly with positive pupil attitudes and content achievement has been more successful since the reviews referred to above. However, he would agree that much more attention must be devoted to studying the subtle processes which take place in teacher–student interactions. It is commonplace that two teachers teaching the same lesson and acting in the same manner, may elicit very different reactions from the two groups. Indeed, one teacher, covering the same material with two different classes, may obtain a totally different effect in terms of response, assimilation, class atmosphere. This can be explained in terms of minute, even subliminal, responses which 'cue' the teacher, and the group differently. It is known that quite subtle, verbal and non-verbal cues shape the behaviour of animals and other recipients of messages. In our experimental studies, we have observed remarkable patterns, in the form of dissonances between the verbal 'message' being communicated and the covert non-verbal cues being emitted without awareness, and picked up, perhaps at an unconscious level by the students. For example, in teaching skills such as empathy, positive regard, sincerity and so on, the verbal content is ostensibly devoted to the exposition of these skills, but other non-verbal behavioural cues emitted by the instructor to the group actively communicate a negative, cold, unempathic unconcern.

Whenever students confront instructors in a didactic situation, specific kinds of individual and group dynamic processes can be observed. These may acclerate or impede instruction. Whatever method be adopted—whether it be lecture, seminar, case discussion, simulated skills training, it is our belief that such dynamics appear. These processes can be identified in terms of the theoretical systems previously discussed—they can be referred, for example, to Bales' system. Certain types of situation tend to magnify the group dynamics, others to minimise these processes. The lecturer who uses a discussion method, for example, can expect to witness the surfacing of a greater amount of hostility than the one who chooses to dominate the group by lecturing, without allowing students to generate feedback. Discussion leaders teaching subjects which readily provide for different opinions (psychology, history) are likely to be more aware of the group process than instructors in formal groups concerned with less easily debatable topics, such as science or mathematics. In highly structured situations, the attack on the personality of the instructor or on other members, is more likely to be deflected and appear as disagreements about topics, rather than between individuals. In settings with less formal structure, the attack may be projected; more commonly it tends to become personal and direct, and centred in the group.

In the discussion of outcomes in learning groups, we must recognise the complexity of the problem. We have to consider a variety of situations, such as the lecture, case study, seminar, training laboratory, lecture–discussion, teacher-centred classes, student-centred classes, and so on. In addition, we must consider the purposes for which such groups might be used; who is teaching and in what manner; who are the students, and so on. Our knowledge of outcomes at this stage can best be termed primitive. We cannot say definitively that a lecture is more or less valuable than a discussion. Some lecturers have the power to 'spell-bind' their audiences. If we can believe reports from the consumers of such magnetic lectures, some learning has occurred. The real question, however, remains: how valuable is the lecture *method* over a sustained period of time when used by the average lecturer? Would it be more valuable to use the time for discussion; would it be better to allow students to verbalise their feelings, to organise their own knowledge about particular topics? Does the institutionalised lecture have any influence in creating independent thinkers or does it work the other way? In a thoughtful book on this subject, Biddle and Ellena (1958) have pointed to several relevant factors which most educators would agree influence the learning and instructional process. These are: (1) the formative experiences of teachers and learners; (2) the teacher's properties, his skills, motives and habits; (3) his actual teaching behaviours; (4) the immediate effect he has on individual pupils; (5) the long-term consequences of the instruction; (6) interactions within the classroom situations; and (7) the community in which the school is set. They go on to suggest that research in these areas must help determine what are the elements important in teacher effectiveness.

Undoubtedly these areas are important. It seems more likely that the problem is actually more complex—that it is a matter of the teacher style by learner style, by group method, by student motivation, by community situation, and so on. It is not a question of single variables to be optimised so that the total sum guarantees a particular level of effectiveness. It is possible too that the association between particular methods and styles may be non-linear in some particular instances. It seems clear that the individual expectations of students, their idiosyncratic attitudes to knowledge, to society, to group cooperation, their specific reactions to persons (including especially the teacher) guarantee that only a particular design of the didactic situation which takes account of these factors can optimise the learning outcomes for the group.

AUTHORITARIAN *v*. DEMOCRATIC CLIMATES

Research has established at least one maxim as true, that it is basically unprofitable to classify classroom behaviour patterns in dichotomous schemes. No classroom is either purely learner-centred or purely teacher-centred. Teachers are usually not pure autocrats or pure democrats. It is a matter of degree. To what extent can a particular classroom be considered 'teacher-centred' or 'learner-centred', autocratic or democratic in climate? And so on. A more refined classification of teacher behaviours, on the basis of a *score* on one or other of independent dimensions, should help unravel the complexities of group learning settings.

The definitive review of studies of 'autocratic *v.* democratic' teaching styles is by Anderson (1959). He concludes that, despite a multitude of studies, the research results have been quite disappointing. In summary he says:

Eleven studies have reported greater learning for learner-centred groups, thirteen have shown no difference, and eight have found teacher-centred methods superior to learner centred.

Anderson also reports that morale is higher in learner-centred groups. This seems to be a general finding. Hare (1959) suggests that democratic leadership seems to be associated with low productivity and high morale, whereas authoritarian leadership is more often associated with high productivity, but lower morale. However, this cannot be taken as definitive. Leaders of democratically oriented groups tend to find that very marked deviant behaviour rarely occurs, due to the power of group sanctions, but some report different experiences. For instance, Eglash (1954) compared a lecture method with a group discussion method in two different classes. He reports that in the discussion class a considerable amount of aggressive behaviour was exhibited. In such cases, it is possible that the teacher may unconsciously be communicating to students a desire to engage in a power struggle, or otherwise to precipitate deviant behaviour. The dynamics underlying such unconscious 'shaping' processes are particularly obscure—they may bear some relation to guilt feelings and self-punitive needs manifested in other situations, in self-inflicted wounds or attempts at suicide, for example.

It seems clear at this date, that the attempt to categorise classrooms as 'autocratic *v.* democratic', whilst a pioneer step leading to numerous investigations of teaching situations 'on the ground', was too simplistic. The discrepancy in the reports of *outcome* as between learner-centred and teacher-centred groups suggests that other dimensions are obtruding into the research design and confounding the results. Dominance–submission may be the most important dimension in a given didactic situation, but it misses the point completely if we do not recognise that some proportion of a given group will *like* a dominant teacher and a structured lesson (and may be unable to learn in the opposite kind of didactic situation). Additionally, the question of task-orientation *v.* non-task-orientation is another significant variable as between autocratic teachers. Does the teacher opportunistically use the situation for the satisfaction of his own paranoid, ego-dominated, inner-directed, self-centred needs, or does he dominate the group in the disinterested service of some higher ideal—the advancement of group understandings, the pursuit of knowledge in which he is merely a guide? These seem to be some of the variables which confound the work done under Anderson's inspiration.

OUTCOMES ASSOCIATED WITH TRADITIONAL METHODS

In an earlier chapter the variety of instructional techniques currently in use in classroom settings was described. Unfortunately, few objective studies have been made to discover the value of these techniques for attaining their intended learning outcomes. Most research projects limit themselves to a comparison of two techniques. In particular, the lecture method has been compared to discussion. Even to the most naive observer, it is clear that more *information* can be passed to students via the lecture method than using a group discussion method. However, McLeish (1969) presents rather strong evidence to suggest that, even in this regard, the lecture method is somewhat suspect. Most students seem to lack certain basic skills in the areas of 'listening', perceiving the structure of the lecture, a sense of relevance, ability to take notes effectively, and so on. The result is that they are unable to derive much benefit from most lectures and lecturers. McLeish suggests that these facts escape most teachers because the independent work which the student carries out (revision of notes, textbook work, 'spotting questions'), coupled with the lack of validity and reliability of examinations confuses the whole issue.

The invention of printing, the greater availability of books, the decline of dramatic skills, the failure by the lecturer to secure good models, and other factors, have probably contributed to a decline in popularity of this particular method. In the light of the foregoing discussion, we suggest that the poor repute of the lecture method has been brought about by a 'shaping' process whereby instructors, no longer reinforced by student audiences, adopt a more pedestrian, examination-oriented delivery, less florid, less dramatic, duller. It is also a fact that the 'media'—films, books, television, today make up-to-date information available to larger audiences. These audiences, in possession of this, are often able to challenge their lecturers on specific issues. This is one of the effects of the democratisation of knowledge. The degree to which group dynamic processes are evident in the classroom depends to some extent on the 'signal/noise' ratio of the particular speaker's message. Psychology tends to have a low signal/noise ratio. The fact that our knowledge of human behaviour is considerably limited soon becomes apparent to most lay audiences. Students in such cases are more ready and able to challenge instructor-power. In subjects which, apparently, have a high signal/noise ratio (for example, physics or chemistry) the speaker will go unchallenged. The group dynamic processes in these classrooms will therefore be less obvious. But as students become capable of understanding that the apparently high signal/noise ratio in subjects such as chemistry is illusory, dynamic forces will tend to manifest themselves more and more, and attempts to wrestle the instructor's power away are likely to become more obvious. Audiences accustomed to speaking out against lecturers in low signal/ noise ratio subjects will begin to argue with lecturers in other subjects, even when they do not truly possess academic ammunition enough. Thus a novel student–lecturer confrontation culture develops with social science students acting as advance guard.

Of the group teaching techniques described earlier, the lecture method has received the most attention from research workers. This technique lends itself to evaluation in so far as specific objectives can be predetermined and the lecture content specifically structured towards meeting those objectives. On the other hand, when the instructor allows students to participate actively in discussion there is considerable room for deviation from the original plan of instruction. In addition, a lecture or series of lectures can be standardised and presented to a variety of audiences, whereas replication of other techniques is considerably more difficult, if not impossible.

McLeish (1968) has presented the most extensive review of the lecture method. A detailed examination of the research presented in that monograph is beyond the scope of the present discussion. However, some of the more pertinent findings are relevant here. It is safe to say that while the lecture is still a central method of university instruction it is strongly disfavoured by students, in general, compared to tutorial or seminar methods of instruction. Expressed attitudes are 2:1 against the lecture in comparison with those other techniques. But this does not imply that all students prefer other techniques before the lecture. Koenig and McKeachie (1959) discovered that women with high achievement-need preferred independent study and small group discussion to the lecture and large group discussion. Women with lower achievement-need preferred the lecture method. McLeish (1971) discovered that conservatives favour the lecture, whereas radicals favour the student-oriented seminar.

The reports of various studies which have compared the lecture method with discussion methods are somewhat equivocal. Reviews by Wallen and Travers (1963) and McKeachie (1963) indicate that most studies which compared lecture and discussion, using subject mastery as the criterion of outcome, have yielded non-significant differences. McKeachie notes that in six experiments where significant differences favoured the discussion method over the lecture, the outcome measures used were other than final examinations which tested knowledge. McLeish's review of the literature indicates similar findings. He reports studies which favour both methods. For example, Beach (1960) found that the lecture method yielded significantly higher results on a sixty-item achievement test than did three other kinds of presentation. Tistaert (1965) found that the discussion method was superior in developing 'reflective thinking' and retention of subject matter. Eyestone (1966) discovered that there was nothing to choose between the lecture, a bulletin, or a film in conveying information about research findings, except that subjects did better when there was no discussion.

Several studies report that independent study is of more benefit than the lecture method. McCullough and van Atta (1966) found that flexible students benefit more from independent study than those with rigid personalities. Weitman and Gruber (1960) have also shown the superior results of independent study in that students show themselves better in making difficult applications of materials learned and in learning new materials.

Unfortunately, many of the studies which compare various educational techniques lack credibility largely because experimenters have usually not paid careful attention to the effects of reading, private study, and discussions with other students during the interval between teaching and the examination which is used to assess learning gains. McLeish has hypothesised that students develop an intuitive awareness of how much work they need to do to make up for the inadequacies of teaching provided so that they perform creditably in the final examination. This suspicion seems to be well founded when we consider the results reported by Parsons *et al.* (1958). He compared students who participated in a regular introductory psychology course with students who were sent home with the syllabus and returned for the final exam. With regard to retention of factual information, the independent study group obtained the best scores.

In an interesting experiment McLeish has compared the lecture with directed reading, controlling the usual confounding variables. Replicating an earlier study of *Students' Retention of Lecture Material* (and introducing a variation suggested by Sir Edward Hale) this experiment was carried out at the Northern Polytechnic, London. As a preliminary step, twenty full-time fourth-year and thirty-nine part-time sixth-year students in the School of Architecture were randomly assigned to three groups. Care was taken that students of foreign origin, and five women students, were not clustered in the same group. Having randomised the students, it was discovered that, by a happy chance, the number of part-time and full-time students in each of the three groups were virtually the same. The 'treatments' were than randomly assigned to each of the three groups as follows:

Group I: 'Motivated reading group'. This group was briefed to the effect that they were to spend an hour studying the verbatim text of a lecture, 'Synectics: a method of developing potential creativity' written by a distinguished authority on the subject. They were told that they would be using this material very soon in synectic-type exercises on the design process.

Group II: 'Motivated lecture group'. This group was briefed exactly the same, except that they were told they would hear a lecture.

Group III: 'Unmotivated lecture group'. These students were directed into the lecture theatre with no prior briefing: they heard the general introduction of the speaker to all three groups by the Head of the School. This mentioned the lecturer's name, place of work and title of the lecture.

As a few students came late, the original groups were slightly depleted. Although late students were allowed to complete the exercises, the results are not included in the analysis. After a short coffee break, the three groups were brought together in the lecture theatre and submitted to a recall test (reproduction, *not* recognition) which attempted to measure the *amount of factual information* retained. This test was scored, without knowing to which of the three groups individual students belonged. The test included a second part which attempted to assess the degree of interest in the subject of the different student groups and their ability to apply the knowledge gained.

By a striking coincidence, the amount retained by the 44 students who participated in the exercise was exactly the same as in the earlier experiment—namely 42 per cent (McLeish, 1968). The average scores were as follows:

Lecture groups

'Reading' Group I	'Motivated' Group II	'Unmotivated' Group III
33·43 49%	26·27 39%	26·25 39%

It is clear from these results that motivation (in the form provided) has no effect on the amount retained by the lecture group. It is also clear that reading the text is more effective than listening to the same lecture, assuming that equal time is available for the 'readers' and that a minimal context of relevance is provided for them.

The other burning questions this study sought to answer were whether the 'living voice' and personality of the lecturer would stimulate students to think more about *possible applications* of what they were learning, and whether their interest would be higher than the reading group. There is evidence to the contrary. The table below contrasts the 'creative thinking' about possible synectic exercises by the three groups.

Group I	Group II	Group III
3·94 78·80%	3·04 60·80%	2·94 48·80%

There is evidence (based on the numbers in the three groups willing to choose partners to carry out hypothetical synectic exercises) that the reading group had the highest degree of interest, the motivated lecture group the next highest, and the unmotivated lecture group the least interest in the subject.

The often quoted reason for using the lecture method is that it is a satisfactory way of transmitting a relatively large number of concepts and factual information in a limited time period. Whether or not the lecture method is an efficient vehicle for this purpose is a matter of some debate. Three earlier studies which shed light on the value of the lecture method have been undertaken by McLeish (1968). The main purpose was to determine precisely how much lecture content students carry away with them, either in their heads or in their notebooks. A variety of groups served as subjects. Students randomly assigned to groups which were required to listen to either 15, 30 or 45 minutes of a lecture, or to read the verbatim text. The general conclusions derived from these carefully controlled studies may be summarised:

(1) In general, students who listen to an uninterrupted discourse carry away something of the order of 40 per cent of the factual data, the theoretical principles and the general applications referred to by the lecturer. It should be noted that these students were tested immediately after hearing the lecture and made maximum use of the notes and blackboard summary taken down under threat of immediate examination.

(2) After one week, approximately half of the material taken away was forgotten.

(3) There were considerable individual differences in retention.

(4) Under the guidance of a keen instructor, groups which read the lecture materials do as well as, or better than, groups which hear the lecture.

These experiments and review of the research literature paint a rather dim picture of the value of the lecture technique, if this is not supplemented by other kinds of input. No evidence has been brought forward to dispel the suspicion that the lecture method tends to do little more than train students to pass examinations. Without the possibility of a real meeting of minds between instructor and students this technique seems likely to develop conformism to declared 'truths', or an accepted text. Even under the most favourable conditions it fails to engage the complete attention and goodwill of the auditors. Furthermore, most lecturers are not able to reinforce immediately whatever learning is taking place. There is usually no immediate means for feedback to assess the extent to which the instructor's messages are being selectively misperceived.

It would, of course, be remiss to suggest that all lecturers generate the effects mentioned here. Some rare individuals possess unique qualities by which they seem to cast a spell over their audiences. This is especially true of single large, well-publicised public lectures to which people go voluntarily. It is not so true of regular, institutionalised, semi-compulsory lectures. Nekrasova (1960) has suggested eight basic rules useful for improving lectures. These are already employed by some of those who are successful with this method. In brief, these rules are:

(1) Finished conclusions should not be presented, but rather problems and rules for solving the problem.

(2) Controversial subjects should be introduced and debated.

(3) Materials should be presented in accordance with established psychological principles bearing on how concepts are actually developed, and their relationships to things.

(4) The living significance of the materials should be made clear by demonstrating the relation between the theory and practice.

(5) Significant questions should be posed by the lecturer either to himself or directly to the audience.

(6) Experiments in support of particular viewpoints should be cited.

(7) Students should be presented with problems which require independent thought for solution.

(8) Students should be actively encouraged to set problems and questions to the lecturer, towards the conclusion of his discourse.

It seems clear in the light of this evidence, that no single lecturer is perceived as being able to walk on water by all people. The occasional great leader whom we hear about, but never see, seems to be the person who is most capable of acting in accordance with the law of effect. That is, he probably spends part of his lecture satisfying different need systems. Literally, he skates back and forth between the task and social–emotional areas. He presents some materials for cognitive digestion, and then relieves developing emotional pressures with humour, simulated annoyance or anger, and so on. Similarly, whether he realises it or not, he is likely to be responding to dominant group needs which are communicated by many means. These are transmitted by the audience and received by the speaker below the level of conscious awareness. Similarly, he is likely to be responding to group forces and dynamics which have been carried over from other encounters either by the students or by himself. Of these dynamics he may remain completely unaware.

Some individuals are more capable of responding to group needs than others. It is conceivable that the most effective lecturers are those who are capable of perceiving, either consciously or subliminally, the 'group pulse'. The stories they tell, the witty little anecdotes which colour the instruction, the expression of feelings, are possibly fantasy reflections of the group state, or of significant aspects of it. Such instructors are likely to be successful in satisfying the more primitive needs of their audiences. It is these with whom the student will identify, and choose to emulate.

This does not mean that he who presents reality the clearest will be the one who is listened to most, or is most respected. On the contrary, it is more likely that he could be the one that is most resented, being perceived as the most threatening; he sees too much, and is too honest. This, at any rate, seems to be the fate of the trainer in the self-analytic group.

OUTCOMES ASSOCIATED WITH SMALL GROUP TEACHING

The problem here is to determine whether or not, or to what extent, small groups are appropriate vehicles for developing certain specified learning outcomes. As with most educational innovations, practice has outraced research in this area. Those who have discussed outcomes have usually been advocates, rather than sceptics. As research workers in this area there is a need for scepticism about the claims made for groups. It cannot be doubted that groups change people in some ways. The question is: are these changes in the same direction? Are they significant? Are they an improvement which is manifested in changed behaviour? Bettleheim (1958) has discussed his experiences in a prisoner-of-war camp and how that system was too powerful to break its hold over his emotional life. Similarly, colleagues who attend weekend encounter groups sometimes return more free and easy, more open, more expressive and so on. Personal reflection, as well as reports in the literature, lead us to conclude that a variety of forces operate in groups which can generate change. Skinner (1961) states that to acquire behaviour a student must behave: by participating in a group one is forced to interact, this must produce behaviour modification depending on the reinforcers operating at the time. Bandura (1969) has emphasised the importance of vicarious learning. By observing the behaviour of others and the kinds of reinforcement they receive, it seems possible that some people might learn. By participating in a group, one is forced to adopt a role: Lieberman (1959) has carried out an impressive research study where he demonstrated how significantly attitudes can change as a result of changing roles. In this experiment shop workers shifted attitudes in opposite directions according to whether they were promoted to either a foreman position or to a union steward position. Asch (1952) has exemplified the power of groups to influence conformity to accepted norms. Proshansky and Seidenberg (1966) review reports which discuss how cohesive groups are likely to have more influence on the individual than less attractive groups. Groups provide the opportunity to verbalise and to examine these verbalisations. Prima facie, it would seem that this must change the individual in some way. It seems common sense to assume that, after a particular group meeting, the subject remembers what he said more clearly than what anyone else said, and continues to reflect on the issues brought to expression. In private moments, he will review his contribution, he worries about whether it should have been worded differently, whether it had the intended impact, whether he lost face, and so on. Thus the time between group meetings which allows for an integration of thoughts, a reassessment of performance, values and roles, may be more important than the group encounter itself. This is surely the specific virtue of a discussion group compared to the most effective formal presentation by an expert—that it tends to generate reflective thinking because of the deeper personal involvement of the student with the views expressed by himself and his peers. Since the weekend encounter group offers very little free time or cognitive material for such personal reflection we seriously wonder about its usefulness as an educational method. This is not to say that the 'encounter' will not generate 'emotional happiness', at least for a while. But, lacking an educational payoff the justification of the encounter group must be on the same footing as any other non-constructive, self-indulgent activity (a seven-course dinner, watching ice-hockey, visiting a prostitute, etc.). These generate the same, or even better, feelings. It is a matter of personal taste: no educational advantage accrues except, perhaps, incidentally and on the side.

In earlier chapters certain outcome effects associated with groups were reviewed. It was concluded that those studies provided evidence that some groups do change some individuals. Group members seemed to become more open-minded, less defensive, more sensitive to others. These changes are observed by others whom they associate with, before and after the group 'experience'. In general, it can be concluded that most reported studies are favourable to groups as learning media. There is little evidence that groups generate negative effects: there is a good deal of evidence that they do generate positive effects. For instance, Gibb (1971), reviewing 106 studies on outcome effects associated with various kinds of group training, found that most of them reported that groups were beneficial. There were gains in the direction of the intended learning outcomes. In a variety of groups, members apparently increased in sensitivity; this was shown by increased awareness of their own feelings, an increased ability to manage their own and others' motivations, more positive self-concepts, a reduction in authoritarian behaviour and prejudice, a gain in problem-solving behaviour, in the ability to work in groups, and so on. Unfortunately, nearly all of these studies have some major flaw in design. Gibb concedes that, in comparison to standards of research in the psychological laboratory, their methodological naivety is distracting. This point is well taken: indeed it is difficult to justify his recommendation that a more widespread use of groups in various learning environments is desirable. The materials from which he generalises to this conclusion would, more fittingly, lead to a verdict of 'not proven'.

It is conceded, on the basis of experience, that it is extraordinarily difficult to do research of a definitive kind in this area. We suspect that most advocates of group training are overawed by these difficulties, not to mention the considerable outlay of time, money and other resources necessary. As a team we have come to the following conclusions:

(1) There is no reason to believe that groups actually increase interpersonal sensitivity to any significant degree.

(2) There are no detectable changes in personality in any predictable direction.

(3) There is no cogent evidence available at this point in time that groups are any more or less psychotherapeutic than other kinds of psychological treatments.

Gibb expresses the opinion that therapists and trainers would be well advised to experiment with new theory and methodology. Such advice can only increase the gap between research and practice. In contrast to Gibb's enthusiasm, we suggest the need to devote considerable energies to provide an honest evaluation of the effects which are actually generated by groups. Outcome criterion instruments with some validity need to be developed. It is necessary to *demonstrate* that 'encounter', 'experiential' or other groups actually do increase sensitivity, leadership skills, or bring about favourable personality changes. It is not enough merely to *assert* this. The use of groups as an educational tool is addictive, it is satisfying, it generates involvement. But, so far, other claims made for them have not been made out.

AN EXPERIMENTAL STUDY OF OUTCOMES

Our own extensive investigation of outcomes is reported in detail elsewhere (see McLeish and Park, in press) but a brief review of that work may be pertinent here. A research project was designed to examine the effects of direct and *vicarious experience in group training. The training methods were those in common use and were designed to develop various 'human relations' skills. We were specifically concerned with determining what, if any, systematic changes in personality, attitudes, behaviour, and understandings would be observed in teacher-trainees who have participated in, or observed, a human relations training group. The question was investigated through two experimental courses in an undergraduate Educational Psychology course. Two kinds of human relations training treatments were compared: a 'self-analytic' treatment and a 'direct communications' treatment. Training groups were observed by trainees who were either attempting to recognise group forces while learning Bales' Interaction Process Analysis, or studying group dynamics while attempting to develop their total understandings.

The study was of an exploratory nature. Therefore a variety of instruments was selected to investigate possible changes in personality and attitudes. In addition, three specially constructed tests were developed for evaluating understanding of (1) group dynamics, and (2) ability to recognise and (3) to generate empathic communication. Subjects were undergraduates enrolled in various teacher education programmes at the University of Alberta. They were volunteers. Prior to enrolling, students were informed in a general way about the nature of the course. Emphasis was laid on its lack of formal content, the behaviours expected of them in terms of regular attendance, punctuality, completion of a battery of psychological tests, a commitment to the course to be shown by a determination to complete the series of meetings.

The course was conducted over a three-and-one-half month period. All the subjects were required to attend four pre-testing and briefing sessions, fifteen laboratory sessions, and four post-testing and course evaluation sessions. These sessions were all fifty minutes in duration. Students were randomly assigned to observer or participant groups of approximately twelve or so students. Two trainers were employed, each to train two participant groups. In the 'self-analytic group' the trainer's function was to interpret in a neutral manner his perceptions of the group process, laying emphasis on 'latent' content. In this role he was generally perceived as being cold, aloof, difficult to communicate with, and unsympathetic. In contrast, the trainer in the direct communications group was to play the role of a warm, loving, kind, empathic person whose goal was to teach, and develop, *empathic understanding in the student participants. While the self-analytic group had no externally imposed structure, each session of the direct communications group was structured by the trainer. Meanwhile, observers, who were in a one-way observation room, were either learning Bales' Interaction Process Analysis, or paying attention to cues or clues to the total action, as described in a chapter on clinical observation by Millon (1969). The Bales' training is analytic in character, the 'clinical' group of observers was encouraged to take a synthetic approach in viewing the group.

Table 8 summarises the results of this study. No changes in personality, attitude, or dogmatism were associated with any of the

Table 8

Summary of changes on personality, attitude and learning measures

Measure	Self-analytic group (SAT)			Direct communication group (DCT)		
	Participants n=23	Bales' Obs. n=12	Clinical Obs. n=12	Participants n=24	Bales' Obs. n=11	Clinical Obs. n=13
16 PF (personality)	0	0	0	0	0	0
Cambridge survey (attitudes)	0	0	0	0	0	0
Dogmatism scale	0	0	0	0	0	0
Carkhuff discrimination scale (empathy)	0	0	0	+	+	+
Park-Matheson HRVT (empathy)						
(1) Free response	++	++	++	++	++	++
(2) Multi-choice	++	++	++	++	++	++
Group process analysis test	0	++	++	+	0	+

0 virtually no change
+ some increase
++ major increase

treatment conditions. With regard to learning outcomes, our criterion measures indicate that the self-analytic group participants, and observers, show slight increases in ability to make empathic responses to videotaped subjects. This outcome was not intended with this group. Subjects in all the direct communications training groups show greater gains on measures of empathic response. This applies to participants and observers. While participants gained the most, they were not significantly higher than the observers. This outcome was planned for, and intended, with regard to increased understanding of group dynamics, the observers watching the self-analytic groups gained significantly more than groups in any other treatment. This learning outcome (gain in understanding group dynamics) was intended. However, the gains noted for *participants* in the self-analytic treatment were virtually nil. Some participants showed large gains while others showed large losses—on average the gain was zero. This was disconcerting at first glance as large gains were expected and intended for this group.

The finding that observers who view self-analytic groups learn most about group dynamics is extremely interesting. It sheds light on why so many trainers think that groups are useful for teaching group dynamics skills. It seems clear from our results that, in most self-analytic groups, the trainer benefits the most. He is most likely to be in the best position to observe; he is also most likely to be steeped in group dynamics literature, and so relating it to what happens in his current groups. Trainers are, more than anyone else, group-wise. They take on styles which reflect this group-wiseness. They have the least work to do in carving out a role in the group. This leaves them with a great opportunity to observe, to study, to think about the action.

Participants are most likely to be somewhat uncomfortable about their roles. They show themselves to be more concerned about discovering how *they* function, rather than how groups in general function. Thus, we hypothesise that the person who establishes a relatively comfortable role in the group, who is least concerned about his personal performance, and instabilities, is most likely to learn by participating. Later, we will discuss the special character of learners and non-learners as identified by standard methods. To summarise, it may be stated:

(1) There is no evidence to indicate the use of groups are any more effective, or less effective, than other types of teaching method, except perhaps for teaching direct communications skills.

(2) By reducing the amount of structure, by including topics of a

controversial or ambiguous nature, that is, increasing the signal/ noise ratio, the appearance of various dynamic processes become more apparent in learning groups.

(3) There is no evidence available which shows any particular forms of group training to be the best, except in so far as direct communications training leads to an improvement in empathy and also in the understanding of group dynamics.

(4) We suspect that it is the interaction: learning style by teaching method by instructor style by student by environmental variables which holds the key to identifying who will learn what in groups.

(5) There is no cogent evidence that small groups can predictably be used to generate attitudinal or personality changes.

(6) There is some evidence that individuals who observe groups learn more about group dynamics than those who participate, while those who participate are in a more advantageous position to receive feedback of a more personal nature about their effect on the group, and on individuals.

(7) There is considerable reason to be suspicious about promises made by advocates of any particular training method.

THOSE WHO TALK *v*. THOSE WHO LEARN

The core questions to which this study was addressed were: 'Who talks? Who learns? Do different people tend to learn different skills—some empathy, some group dynamics?' The varied data collected—IPA analyses, personality test scores, attitude measures, dogmatism, cognitive complexity, as well as pre- and post-treatment scores on four criterion tests enable certain tentative judgements to be arrived at on these basic questions.

The results obtained on the criterion tests indicate that some subjects did indeed profit from the training programme. The question 'Who learns?' is, of course, central in an evaluation of human relations training. We were uniquely placed to tackle this question, as we had a wealth of personality and attitudinal and other data on the subjects of the experiment which could be related to their achievement on the criterion tests. We had also complete records of the group interaction on videotape, as well as an ongoing IPA analysis of the participants over all the sessions.

A 'plot' of gain scores for all subjects indicated that individuals from both kinds of treatment were represented in the highest, middle, and lowest (negative) levels of the group dynamics test. On the other hand, the highest gains on the empathy tests were by subjects in the direct communications training groups: subjects with the lowest gains on empathy were from the self-analytic groups. It was decided that it would be pointless to compare individuals who were high on both tests, or low on both tests, since the difference in treatments would act as a confounding variable. It makes little sense to compare the high, medium, and low learners on empathy, since this would be treating all subjects as though they had all been given the direct training in empathic response. The comparisons were actually made, but, as expected, they indicated that no significant differences between learners and non-learners could be found when the treatments were confounded in this way.

Who learned about group dynamics?

An examination of the personality and attitude scores from subjects in high, medium, and low gain groups on the group dynamics test seemed sensible. First of all, the ninety-four subjects were ranked according to their gain scores on this test. They were then divided into three groups: a high learner group (gain scores between $+20$ and $+70$), a medium learner group (-3 to $+19$) and a low learner group (-4 to -48). The third group, in fact, consisted of persons whose scores *deteriorated* over the treatment period.

Statistical analysis reveals that the higher learner group is somewhat more stable, or 'better adjusted', than the others. The major differences lie between those whose scores increased and those whose scores decreased.

In comparison with those whose understanding seemed actually to decline over the testing period, the high learners are characterised on a standard personality test as being emotionally more stable, more able to face reality, less suspicious, more self-confident, and less frustrated. On another standard instrument, the high learners appear to be less disturbed emotionally and more interested in activities leading to personal improvement than are subjects in the low learner group.

These results strongly suggest that learning group dynamics is facilitated by the possession of a stable personality. Subjects who cannot face reality have difficulty in maintaining objectivity about positive *or* negative group forces. The recognition of such forces in others must ultimately lead to the confession that similar forces govern one's own behaviour. This acceptance of the reality of group processes may be too much of a threat to insecure persons. The discovery of this relationship between personal stability and the possibility of learning group dynamics is considered to be an important breakthrough.

Further analysis, taking account of the nature of the group subjects were in, indicates that the learners in both groups are quite similar. That is to say, in both self-analytic and direct communication groups, subjects who made the most impressive gains in understanding group dynamics were most stable, more self-assured, less suspicious and less frustrated than those who showed no evidence of improvement in their understanding of group dynamics. It was also verified that these differences between learners were not influenced by sex differences: the high learners, whether males or females, were less neurotic, more enthusiastic about their work, less power-oriented, more outgoing and warm-hearted, more emotionally stable, more uninhibited, less suspicious, and less insecure than their peers in the low learner group.

Who learned to communicate empathically?

In both the human relations treatments some learned empathic communication skills better than others. The range of gain scores on the empathy test was quite large (-8 to $+36$) for both groups. While the direct communication subjects' gain scores were normally distributed around a mean of 15·9, the self-analytic subjects' gain scores were skewed with a mean of only 5·6. It was clear that the characteristics of high, medium and low learners must be examined separately for each group.

Subjects in the two treatments were again ranked according to their gain scores on the empathy test. They were classified into six groups; high, medium and low learners in both kinds of treatment group. In the self-analytic group, those who learned empathy skills were significantly more tenderminded and more careless of protocol. They believe more in naturalist spontaneity in dealing with children and less in formal methods of instruction. They are less oriented towards practicality in the school curriculum. In the direct communications group, those who learned most about empathy were less punitive in their attitudes to children, and keener on naturalistic spontaneity. They were also less interested in power and mixing with influential persons.

Characteristics of high scorers

A question related, but not equivalent, to 'Who learned the most?' is 'Who scored the highest on the post-tests?' The group dynamics scores after the conclusion of the training were normally distributed, but the empathy test distribution was bimodal. Self-analytic subjects formed one peak at the low gain end and direct communication subjects at the other. It was decided that achievement groups in those treatments should be examined separately, as well as combining all groups for an examination of the personality and attitude profiles of high, medium, and low scorers.

The same method of analysis was used as before. The scores on the group process test were ranked, and then divided into three equal groups. The analysis established the differences between these groups in terms of personality, attitudes and opinions, as before.

High scorers on the group dynamics test tend to be more intelligent, less interested in acquiring power over others, more certain of their views, and not particularly concerned about helping others in social relationships. On some variables curvilinear relationships were observed. For instance, the medium scoring group is more tender-minded, more helpful in social relationships, and places more value on personal freedom than either high or low scoring groups.

(a) *Group dynamics scores.* The question remains whether the characteristics of high and low scorers depend on which particular treatment group is being looked at. The same procedure was adopted as before—three groups of high, low and medium scorers were chosen in each treatment and the appropriate analysis carried out for all other variables. High scorers on group dynamics in the self-analytic groups were more intelligent, more resourceful, and more interested in a variety of activities than the groups who earned low scores. In some cases the trends were curvilinear. The 'medium' performance group was higher in religiosity, and had a more favourable attitude to 'discipline' than either of the high or low performance groups. High scorers in the group dynamics test in the direct communication groups were significantly more stable, more confident, more interested in individual freedom, and less suspicious than the low performance group. The medium performance group appears to be more committed to values such as freedom, personal responsibility, study and teaching as a career, than the other two groups.

(b) *Empathy scores.* Similar analyses were carried out on the empathy test scores. High, medium, and low groups of subjects were determined for both types of group. The profiles for subjects in the self-analytic groups receiving the highest empathy scores indicate that they are less anxious, less in favour of punishment and formal control of children, more tender-minded, and higher in aesthetic appreciation than the lower groups. The highest empathy scorers in the direct communication groups are less tense, less punitive, more in favour of spontaneous development and of changes in education than the lowest scoring group. An interesting curvilinear trend is noted for the direct communication subjects in that the medium performance group appears as being more frustrated and tense than either the high or low performance group.

High and low interactors

A question of considerable interest to all educators who use a discussion method is whether, other things being equal, those who talk learn more than those who do not participate. The evidence from this experiment is very clear. Those who talk and otherwise interact more than others do *not* learn more than the non-talkers. Our data seem to demonstrate that neither in the self-analytic group nor in the direct communication group do the high interactors have any learning advantage over the low interactors. All distributions could readily arise by chance. This conclusion is already implicit in our findings about vicarious learning. It appears that the 'non-talkers' are in much the same position as the clinical observers on the the other side of the glass. Their lack of direct involvement in the interaction process is compensated for by the facility this provides for studying the task in the DCT group (learning empathy) or the process in the SAT group (understanding group dynamics).

The arbitrary division of participants into two equal groups—high interactors and low interactors, which are then compared with each other and with the two kinds of observers as controls, reveals certain interesting associations between participation and other measured variables. As could have been predicted, the high interactors are more extroverted than the low; they are also more interested in power and social influence; they are significantly more intelligent; they are more assertive, happy-go-lucky and venturesome; they are more imaginative and less calculating. This is the broad picture.

If we make a finer distinction by considering the treatment groups (self-analytic or direct communication) to which the high and low interactors belong, the nature of these differences becomes clearer. For example, it is the low interactors, especially in the direct communication group, but to an extent also in the self-analytic group, who are less than averagely interested in power and social influence *not* the high interactors who are more interested. On the other hand, it appears that the high interactors in the direct communication group are more keenly interested in their personal and professional development and anticipate more satisfaction from teaching than the other three groups. In the self-analytic group they are much less than averagely interested. A similar position exists with regard to stability —the high interactors in the direct communication group are more stable than average, in the self-analytic group they are less stable.

As far as the nature of the interaction is concerned, there are interesting differences between the high and low interactors other than the total quantity of acts initiated in the group. As far as communication to individuals and the group as a whole is concerned, high interactors differ from low interactors in all categories of acts *except* initiating and receiving *agreement*, initiating *disagreement*, and initiating and receiving requests for *opinion*. As far as interaction between *individuals* is concerned, the high and low interactors do not differ in initiating friendly remarks, initiating and receiving agreement, asking for information and opinion, and disagreeing. There are no difierences in the pattern of remarks to the group as between high and low interactors.

Comparison of treatments

To make comparisons of the different treatments as learning experiences at this time would certainly be unfair. The traditional caveat of the need for further research using different subjects, trainers, and environments is in order. However, until this further evidence is available the following tentative comparisons may be made. It would appear that:

(1) Direct communications training is likely to be more beneficial as an aid to teacher-trainees than a self-analytic group treatment. The learning criteria indices employed here show that the self-analytic treatment group participants, in general, learned virtually nothing about group dynamics and increased only slightly in the communication of empathy. From a subjective viewpoint, the SAT groups are considerably more dramatic and interesting to observe; there is also some evidence that one or two participants may make personal changes in their life-style as a result of participating in such a group. But these changes are neither systematic in nature nor are they predictable. It may be that a three-month period is too short to evaluate learnings. At the end of the sessions some members were just beginning to 'face' reality. On the other hand, the participants *and* observers in the direct communications treatment made significant, systematic and predictable gains in the communication of empathy as well as in the understanding of group dynamics. It must be said that the data support Carkhuff's (1969) claim that:

We can do anything in training that we can do in treatment—and more. Training in interpersonal skills strikes at the heart of most difficulties in living. Systematic training in interpersonal skills affords a means of implementing the necessary learning in progressive gradations of experience which insure the success of learning. In making explicit use of all sources of learning—the experiential, the didactic, and the modeling–systematic, group training in interpersonal skills provides the most effective, economical, and efficient means of achieving the individual growth of the largest number of persons. (p. 131)

(2) The various indices employed showed that the direct communications training participants earned superior scores to the observers, in general. With regard to developing understanding of group-dynamics it appears that those who observe self-analytic groups are likely to profit most, whereas participants learn the least. Participants in self-analytic groups are probably well placed to discover about their own personal performance in groups, which may or may not produce changes in behaviour. But as no measure of so-called personal growth (or deterioration) was used it is impossible to do more than record this possibility as a hypothesis.

(3) There appear to be virtually no important differences in the amount learned about empathy and group dynamics as between observers who are working at the skills required for Bales' IPA coding and other observers who are working at developing a clinical intuition skill. However, it is believed that fifteen sessions is not sufficient for undergraduate trainees to acquire even a minimal proficiency in Bales' system. In the fourteenth session a sample of their coding of on-going interaction was taken. It was immediately apparent that several would never be able to master this skill, unaided. The average number of acts coded by each group was less than one-half of the acts coded by the 'expert' Bales' observers (the instructors) in the same period. When the treatments had ended several observers gave indications that they had just begun to appreciate the complexity of the system and the accuracy required in IPA work. In effect, they had just begun to discover the nature of the task as they prepared their final report.

It must be concluded that it was not possible to validate the claim advanced by Bales except in the case of *systematically* trained observers:

Once having learned to observe for a given kind of behavior or type of content—having tried to capture it by a definition, having seen it in many variations, having had to decide definitely whether it is seen at a given point or not, but putting down a score of some kind; after these experiences, one finds that he sees things differently. For better or for worse, he sees and hears things which were comfortably blurred before. (1970, p. 20)

Evaluation of the course

In general, whether they actually learned or not according to the criterion measures, many of the subjects claimed that it was the 'best' course that they had ever taken. Most were able to make several new acquaintances, most found the treatments unique. Anonymous responses to the question 'Would you like to take this course in the second semester if credit could be obtained?' elicited responses as follows: Eighty-five subjects said they would like to take the course again, but had to take other courses for a degree; five subjects said that they would definitely not re-enroll.

Amongst a number of fantasies which develop in courses of this nature, is the predominant wish by subjects in all groups that they could have been in another treatment. Participants fantasised about becoming observers, SAT subjects wanted to be DCT subjects and so on. The 'grass-is-greener' theme was expressed during the earliest sessions. It was indeed interesting to observe that, despite the claims of hardship of being in a particular treatment, and complaints about doing the various tests, so many subjects were keen to return for more. It must be concluded that this type of course appears to satisfy some emotional thirst which is not quenched in other types of course.

With regard to individual changes which were perhaps not detected by the personality and attitude measures used, there was some evidence that powerful effects were being produced on some individuals. For instance, several of the Bales' observers complained half-way through that they appeared to be becoming too sensitive to what was going on in their personal lives. Several DCT participants testified that the course had improved their relationships at home. One participant 'dropped in' several weeks after the termination of treatment to inform the instructors how the course had helped him in his marital relationships. One participant in a self-analytic group said that she realised for the first time in forty years how she had lost her true identity to others who forced various roles on her.

This study assessed the changes in participants over the experimental period. In retrospect it is clear that the trainers should have been tested as well. In particular, the effect of being observed while giving the direct communications treatment seems to place heavy stresses on the interpersonal relationships of the trainers' daily lives. Mackie and Wood (1968) have noted that observers may be perceived by the trainer as hostile critics: certainly the trainers become extremely sensitive to criticism. In the three experiments on which the direct communications treatment has been employed, each trainer has simultaneously encountered difficulty either with colleagues or family. It may well be that in attempting to pass on the values of empathy, honesty, respect and so on, that one begins to be aware of discrepancies in personal behaviour which observers and instructors are also aware of, but which previously had remained unnoticed.

G

8

DYSFUNCTIONAL PATTERNS OF BEHAVIOUR IN LEARNING GROUPS

Most books or articles on group process and development are intended to demonstrate various successful ways through which the authors of the material have handled their small groups. It has been our experience, and very likely every other group leader's experience, that not all groups have successful learning outcomes. If it were true that all groups were successful the rates of failure, in school, mental hospital, and in everyday personal encounter would not be as extensive as we know them to be. This section is intended to convey some understandings about *why small learning groups often fail*.

Within each small group are potentially destructive forces. When these destructive forces become prominent they inhibit learning. A number of these potentially destructive forces, which may inhere in one person, or represent the collective undertaking of the group, are outlined in the following pages. They are not presented in order of importance, however; any one of these patterns in a particular group can do considerable damage to the intended learning outcomes.

*DYSFUNCTIONAL TRAINER STYLE

(a) *Inconsistency*. At the very earliest stages in the life of the group the members rely a great deal upon the trainer, especially to give the group a preliminary structure. It is also at this early stage that they formulate impressions about the trainer which have considerable longevity and are rather impermeable to change. Although certain trainer styles may be more conducive to learning than others, there is a singular need for consistency within the chosen trainer style.

Trainer style involves a built-in variable of group control. The range may be from a trainer-centred, highly controlling style (as in traditional teaching methods); an authority-denying, less controlling style (as in a teachers' staff-room discussion); a group centred, minimally controlling style (as in free group discussion). In the two contrasting styles used in our research on groups, the more successful seemed to be the trainer-centred, highly controlling approach used in the direct communications group. Even though one group method was more successful in outcome than the other, we still consider that consistency of style is crucial. Firstly, the trainer provides, through his behaviour, the norms for communication within the group. In the direct communications group, the communication pattern was established as a one-way, top-to-bottom, question-answer pattern. Less frequently, it might become a three-party exchange. Kadis *et al.* (1963, p. 105) describes such patterns as vertical, or triangular communication, respectively. The self-analytic group communication pattern, on the other hand, was established as circular (Kadis, p. 105). The group quickly accustoms itself to these communication arrangements or styles. It becomes hard to break these patterns, once established. As the communication norms are stabilised, the demands upon work time become understood. If the communication norms are unstable, or fail to become established by virtue of the trainer's inconsistency or insecurity, or because he is seduced by the demands of various factions, there can be a long hiatus before the group gets down to the task. In this sense there is a need for trainer consistency.

In the direct communications group the amount of *work time* was set very high because of (i) the trainer's authority-centred style, and (ii) the fact that communication norms were organised around the trainer himself. In the self-analytic group work time was much lower, because (i) the trainer style was group centred, and (ii) the communication norms were established by the group, the trainer refusing to interact during the establishment of the particular norms. Although the trainer personally devoted all of his interaction to his definition of work, the group did not accept this model. In turn, the trainer did not participate in the group's definition of work.

What we see to this point is the development of the internal structure of each group: the introduction of the trainer's style, the development of the norms for group communication, the acceptance or generation of the definition of work the setting of work time. These developments, regardless of whether they work well in terms of good learning outcomes, are necessary for the group to get off the ground. For the group to reach even this primitive state, the trainer must behave with *consistency*.

(b) *Interactive manner.* Although only part of his overall style, the interactive approach of the trainer has a particular singularity of impact. There are two points of view on the question of trainer style. Arguments are presented, albeit from a therapeutic rather than educational frame of reference, that the trainer should restrict his interaction to the 'here-and-now'. It is demanded of him that he should try to relate whatever learning objectives he may have in mind to the present group situation, and that the material pertaining to the group interaction should be the primary learning medium. Another point of view, espoused by many educators, is that the trainer should come prepared to act as a reservoir of information, disgorging material to a passively awaiting audience. There is always a middle ground. In this case the middle ground might be that the trainer interacts as just another member, offering material as any member would, and with an equalitarian point of view.

In this research, the trainers were briefed to adopt opposing interactive styles. In the direct communication groups the trainer acted as a 'resident genius' on communication skills, and was open to two-way interaction in that he would answer questions and involve others in role playing, practice sessions and other learning games. In the self-analytic group the trainer acted as a non-participant observer who provided a psychoanalytically oriented interpretation of the 'here-and-now' behaviour of the group as a unity.

Within these antithetical interaction styles there were still a considerable number of areas of overlap with potentially destructive elements. The problems the trainers encounter in promoting learning objectives are bound up with:

(i) the level of intervention appropriate in the presentation of material,

(ii) an appreciation of the optimum timing of any intervention,

(iii) consistency within both the timing and the level of intervention and presentation of material,

(iv) the necessity to make any intervention as 'generalisable' to the group membership as possible, or as 'transferable' outside the group, as possible,

(v) the ability to defer interventions,

(vi) the ability of the trainer to withdraw from group interaction and not to become 'ego involved' with certain members or certain themes.

The direct communication groups tended to do better on the post tests of learning outcomes than did the self-analytic groups. This leads one to believe that the potentially destructive elements were more successfully blocked in the direct communication groups. While this may be true, it is still significant that *not everyone learned as much as his neighbour*. Some members in both experiences learned a great deal, others learned virtually nothing. This suggests that there were destructive elements active in both groups. Some destructive forces were more visible than others.

From the point of view of the level of intervention and presentation of material the direct communications trainer had a clear advantage. His primary objective was to have the group members learn certain well defined, personally acceptable, and specific communication skills. He was able to refer to texts and sources of information about these skills and to rely upon outside 'experts' to promote his objectives. In addition, the material which was the subject of his interventions was concrete, if not 'here-and-now'. The self-analytic trainer had no such advantage. His interventions were frequently abstract, indefinite, and subject to serious misinterpretation by any member of the group. The members were being asked to believe that the individuals are governed, in what they say and do, by unconscious forces over which they have little or no control. Such assumptions and objectives of the self-analytic trainer were often in direct contradiction to certain values held by the group membership, and this was frequently pointed out to the trainer. The direct communications group was being trained to behave in a more 'facilitative' fashion, whereas the self-analytic group was being trained towards a built-in scepticism about behavioural intentions and to be less accepting of manifest behaviour at its face-value. The direct communications group had thus certain built-in advantages in terms of member motivation.

Because of this advantage, the trainer in the direct communication group could be somewhat less concerned over the timing of his interventions. He could, in a sense, barge along, with little overt worry about the resistance of individuals. The self-analytic trainer was not in the same position. The timing of his interventions was crucial to member learning. There was considerable individual resistance evident, both as an unconscious defensive reaction towards the trainer's style and a conscious defensiveness about learning this material. The optimum timing of interventions was a continual concern in this training method.

It can be seen that the ability to be sensitive to member needs, and to defer an intervention until the proper time, entails that the trainer be constantly alert to the dynamics of the group. It seems clear that when the material which the trainer contributes is rather concrete, definitive, and with little error possible, there is less need for the trainer to be sensitive about his interventions, or their timing. When the material being introduced by the trainer is abstract, indefinite, subjective, and with room for member misinterpretation, the need for sensitivity over the level and timing of interventions becomes crucial. The ability to defer interventions, and to be consistent in these elements of level, timing, and deferment, is critical. The consequence of error is that individuals fail to learn as much as they might.

The other elements which are potentially destructive in both group training methods are: the generalisability, and transferability, of the material being learned; and the ability of the trainer to withdraw from interaction. With respect to the first point the direct communications group was again at an advantage. In learning these communication skills the member could practise the skills both inside and outside the group. They could thus make the new learning very general, and still quite transferable to another outside situation. In the self-analytic group, the explanation of behaviour as the product of unconscious dynamics, multiple causation of similar behaviours outside the group, and the requirement that members understand behaviour in its context, causes considerable difficulty in either understanding another person's behaviour in the group (generalising) or in relating the trainer's interventions to some other situation outside the group (transferring).

As for the ability of the trainer to withdraw, to avoid ego involvement, or to allow the group to engage in anti-work activity, the advantage was with the self-analytic trainer. Because of the nature of his role he was much more successful in this regard. He was able to accept the defensive ploys and filibustering tactics of group members, and still seek to promote the work ethic. He did so by making use of this member behaviour as material for interpretation to the group. The direct communications trainer, however, could be more readily seduced from the task. He would often become embroiled in the anti-work themes of the group, and would react defensively in face of negative transference or other forms of resistance. In this way, the direct communications trainer failed somewhat in the promotion of learning objectives.

(c) *Personal qualities.* The personal qualities of the trainer bring into play conditions which can facilitate or handicap learning. Carkhuff (1970) claims that the trainer should personify the 'nice guy' when dealing interpersonally. His thesis is that if the trainer can personify, whether in role or in reality, the facilitative dimensions of empathy, respect, concreteness, self-disclosure, and so on, participants will learn more than when the trainer is unempathic, non-supportive, cold, and 'non-facilitative'. This seems obvious and acceptable. Implementing such a role presents a considerable problem to most teachers. The self-analytic trainer behaved quite otherwise to the rubric. His role demanded that he should not behave in a facilitative fashion. This non-supportive approach seems to have increased the level of anxiety of some members to the point where (in accordance with the Yerkes-Dodson law) learning was seriously impeded. The degree of non-supportiveness in this self-analytic approach probably created feelings of insecurity, apprehension, and inferiority in several participants (and observers as well). Such feelings would not be conducive to a task orientation, but would likely lead more to self-consciousness. In a learning situation where awareness about self is not the objective, conditions which promote self-consciousness are very likely to be debilitating. In our self-analytic group treatment, however, learning about self (and others) *is* the stated objective. We cannot therefore simply dismiss self-consciousness as being destructive to learning: it is indeed the medium or matrix within which learning may take place. Where anxiety and other negative emotions are concerned, however, we agree that there comes a point at which the law of diminishing returns becomes operative.

In the direct communications group the trainer tried to promote the facilitative dimensions espoused by Carkhuff—indeed, this was precisely the material the participants were expected to learn. The trainer attempted, without complete success, to be a model of the personal characteristics of empathy, warmth, genuineness, and overall supportiveness. Carkhuff, however, would be the first to declare that one cannot be empathic, warm, genuine, and supportive all the time, or even for some people most of the time; if the trainer is an unsuccessful model of these qualities, then the learning will drop accordingly. This criterion has specific reference to the dimension of genuineness: if the participants detect insincerity in the trainer the learning programme will suffer.

There seems little doubt that supportiveness is an essential characteristic of any trainer. It is the nature and degree of supportiveness necessary for maximum learning which is in question. If the trainer is too accepting, tolerant and supportive, he will come over as weak, and subject to manipulation by the group. Such manipulation would rarely be in the service of the learning objectives of the trainer. Additionally, a climate of over-abundance of support would tend to generate an acquiescence, compliance, and dependence upon the trainer. Such conditions need not be a hindrance to learning, but where the learning is about the self and others, there is often an absence of dissonance or personal discomfort which seems necessary for such learning to take place. Individuals become resistant to change when the environment is too 'comfortable'.

In his position as non-interactive observer, the self-analytic trainer was both willing and able to accept negative affect from the other members. Frequently they were antagonistic, threatening, critical, abusive, and generally nasty. The reaction of the trainer never varied. He unfailingly accepted all materials provided by the group. In terms of personal learning, it seemed necessary for the group to have a person who was able to accept this negative material for it was genuine (although quite often unconscious in genesis). Presumably, if not exploded, it would have held back the learning process. On the other hand, the direct communications trainer was not able to accept these negative feelings. The nature of his role caused many negative reactions to remain underground. This negativism found non-verbal expression and appeared symbolically. There was an increase in displacement, aggression, and scapegoating. Negative feelings were also demonstrated by various kinds of task-resistance, sometimes very open and obvious, sometimes covert and symbolic. It seems clear from a close study of both kinds of groups that there is a need to 'bleed off' *negative*, as well as *positive*, affect. The self-analytic method is more adapted to draining off negativism without the group becoming fixed in an anti-task, anti-learning posture.

THE DYSFUNCTIONAL EFFECTS OF DEFENCE MECHANISMS

The ego defence mechanisms

The significance of unconscious motivations in everyday behaviour was pointed out by Freud. His remarks apply equally to normal as to neurotic, insane and criminal individuals. Their common humanity is attested to by the existence of unconscious processes which, by definition, are infantile, alogical and amoral. According to psycho-analysis, this explains why people who are regarded as intelligent, cultured and well-balanced in their ordinary relations often behave in a stupid, boorish and criminal fashion towards particular people with whom they are intimately related, or towards institutions or persons who substitute symbolically for these. The Freudian explanation emphasises the immature character of such responses, linking them in a causal chain with the infantile relationships of the nursery.

Irrational behaviour, whether in marital, occupational, parental or other relationships, is interpreted in terms of the need to defend the ego against particular threats from the human environment, as well as from self-criticism. When any specific mechanism or mechanisms reach an abnormal development, we are confronted with certain neurotic and psychotic conditions. But it must be re-emphasised that the same mechanisms exist in people adjudged to be normal. Psychoanalysis has recognised about two dozen such mechanisms over a period of approximately sixty-five years. But no attempt has been made successfully to classify them or to delimit the area of their operation. A further complication is introduced by the fact that Freud made a basic assumption that libidinal energy exists in a certain *quantity* in the individual: this unspoken assumption is basic to the understanding of mechanisms. This energy is assumed to be capable of being transformed into various equivalent kinds, so that the original association with the sexual instinct is confused or even obliterated. (Note the derivation: hormé = instinctus = impulse = energy.) The defence mechanisms, in fact, are those very specific processes by which these energy transformations take place so that the unconscious ego cares for, or defends itself, against the overpowering strength of destructive impulses directed against the self or against the environment.

McLeish classifies the defence mechanisms according to the following scheme, observing that although they are most commonly seen in other people's behaviour, they may be identified also at moments of special insight in one's own.

Displacement mechanisms

(a) *Transference.* Within the group the phenomena of transference can take many forms. It can occur as a *positive transference* wherein the trainer, or some other member, receives cathected (concentrated) positive infantile attitudes and reactions from another member. It can also occur as a *negative* transference wherein the trainer or some other member receives cathected negative infantile attitudes and reactions from another member. Kadis *et al.* (1963, pp. 86–9) put forward the view that group transferences are rather unique relationships and may occur in multiple form. In reference to material published by Wolf, these authors contend that the members of the group could respond in a transference reaction to 'the variously provocative characteristics of the multiple personalities in the group, (p. 86). It is also pointed out that certain *prototypical transference mechanisms* are especially visible during the first few group sessions. Such prototypical reactions occur because considerable testing of

G*

the trainer and other group members takes place during these sessions (p. 89).

Regardless of the form in which transference may present itself in the group, it has unconscious derivation in the personal need system of the individual. The origin of transference is narcissistic, primal self-regard: it is just not functional in the service of the group task. This is true of both positive and negative transference.

With positive transference there is frequently a loving reaction to the trainer as good father, rather like 'trainer as Messiah'. The person involved in the reaction, with a male trainer, is very likely a female who develops a 'missionary spirit' about the task (Wolf, from Rosenbaum and Berger, 1963, p. 273) and a desire to defend the trainer at all costs.

The negative transference is in contradiction to any missionary spirit. The trainer is viewed as the bad father who represents punishment and experienced guilt over group failure. The reactions to the trainer in this aspect are those of hatred, hostility, antagonism, confrontation and serious task-resistance. Such resistance is usually expressed through sarcasm and cynicism. The exaggerated quality of the transference reactions are the hall-mark by which the phenomenon can be recognised. Other members may quiz those members involved in transference, about the unrealistic nature of their positive or negative expressed reactions to the trainer. In both positive and negative phases, transference reactions are in the service of personal impulses: they seldom provide fruitful results for individual or group learning. The exception could be when, as in the self-analytic group, the learning objectives are for the group to observe and understand what is happening in the present situation. With such objectives the trainer's references to unconscious transference reactions could provide the information input which promotes a particular aspect of group 'learning'. It is possible for individuals to develop insight into the exaggerated character of their reaction.

(b) *Displacement.* This is the unconscious process of shifting emotionally-charged impulses from an unacceptable object to a more acceptable one. In the group situation the most frequent manifestation of such a reaction is seen in 'scapegoating'. Reactions meant for the trainer are shifted to a more acceptable target. Frequently the scapegoat is the more submissive or silent member. Such members are unconsciously selected because they appear to be among the most defenceless. The trainer, for whom the negative material is really intended, is bypassed as potentially capable of retaliation. The trainer, if perceptive enough, can readily detect such displacement of feelings. The most obvious detection is through the symbolic nature of the disclosures. Other forms of displaced emotional reactions occur in the group through 'sibling rivalry'. It appears as though members are reacting genuinely towards one another, but the 'hidden agenda' of the quarrel is a desire to influence the trainer by appealing for his approval by means of an indirect emotional display. Members will also displace *negative feelings on to the task*. The task represents the trainer, or other authority figures, and the task cannot return any displaced negative feeling. The occasions of displacement drain off group or individual feelings but, as with transference reactions, displacement is not in service of the group task. They are necessary in the sense that it is a requirement of group development that in-hibitory feelings are siphoned off somehow. It is unfortunate that such displacement is without a learning objective. It is impulsive, unconscious and narcissistic.

(c) *Regression*. This is a defensive reaction wherein the member involved falls back on an earlier, more infantile state of personal development. Where there is an uncomfortable experience of personal threat existing in the group, the unconscious reaction to such threat is to revert to unsophisticated, unsocialised, infantile ways. It is as if the adult has temporarily become the child. Instances of such return-ing to childhood are rather common in the group. *Acting-out* displays of loss of temper, and rather infantile *attention-getting behaviours* are the most frequent. In other instances the member will behave childishly by being *exhibitionistic*, *pouting* over some reprimand by the trainer or another member, or engaging in a *stubborn refusal* to co-operate. All of these patterns have a regressive, defensive, and anti-task effect: all have disruptive influences upon individual learning, especially when they are manifested in exaggeration.

Denial mechanisms

(a) *Isolation*. The member who uses isolational defensive man-oeuvres tends to compartmentalise the intellectual, emotional, and doing aspects of an idea. Emotion is drained away from experience, and impressions, experiences and memories are treated in a bland, expressionless, dead fashion. Within the group, the member who adopts a characteristic isolationism may be *withdrawn*, become silent and apparently uninvolved. If approached by another, his involve-ment is expressed as an intellectual interest, or a casual curiosity. Other reactions which are tainted with dysfunctional isolationism are those in which the group member is an active participant in the group, but behaves as a *deviant* in terms of group norms. His behaviour is in contradiction to member expectations and so serves to isolate him from the total experience of the group. Such personal deviance may have obsessional characteristics. A ritualistic seating position near a window or door, or with the back against a wall, or the mechanical use of a particular theme for group discussion are common. The efforts of these isolation mechanisms are to avoid emotional material, and to keep from becoming personally involved in the group or in the task. Isolation is a defensive manoeuvre adopted when the task has a personal relevance of a rather 'pointed' character.

(b) *Denial*. This mechanism operates when the emotional material associated with an idea or concept results in the temporary intellectual incapacity to digest the idea or concept. This mechanism is shown by the member who fails to perceive obvious things, feigns ignorance, or becomes very selective in the information he hears, sees, or incorporates. The member may be highly active and involved in the group, but on his own indefinite terms. When material of 'insight' is presented about an issue which has unconscious emotional associations the member conveniently 'forgets the topic' or 'didn't realise you were talking about me'. If the group is oriented around learning about the self, or others, the members may make use of a 'voyeurism' approach to become 'involved' with others without trying to understand self or transfer any learning from others to self.

(c) *Reaction–formation*. This operates as the use of elaborate, apparently conscious, highly socialised sentiments which are in manifest opposition to the intense, primordial and narcissistic desires of the member who uses such schemes. The member unconsciously may desire, for example, to become intimately involved with the trainer or another member. Suppose the group task is personal learning. In such a case a reaction–formation would be represented by an overwhelming, intellectually based rejection of the task and of any designs toward personal involvement with others. The task of becoming personally involved is unconsciously resisted, since it represents a risk of exposure of what seems to be shameful and disquieting personal intentions.

Identification mechanisms

(a) *Projection*. A process of defence in which the involved member 'projects' his unconscious wishes or ideas upon more suitable targets. In group situations the member may have manipulative and rather shrewd behavioural characteristics. Rather than admit to such characteristics he finds it much more acceptable to blame others, particularly the trainer, for being manipulative and insincere. In other situations the members *project any responsibility for the success or failure of the group* upon the trainer. Any associated anxiety or guilt over personal failure is unacceptable. The failure of acceptance of responsibility for group outcome is a particularly dysfunctional situation. The trainer can find himself spending considerable time trying to persuade the members to become more responsible. Such persuasion is usually in vain, since the source of resistance to accepting responsibility is unconscious.

Conversion mechanisms

(a) *Dramatisation and unconscious fantasy*. These mechanisms are the free association of ideational, unconscious material without the material being bounded by the reality constraints of the group situation. Within the group, the *monopolistic talker* and other such *power-oriented individuals* avoid work and occupy group time through the use of a spontaneous discussion of their personal history. Such personal, usually lengthy anecdotes are frequently designed to disrupt any effort at consistent task behaviour and to promote more irrational, personal impulses.

THE DYSFUNCTIONAL EFFECTS OF GROUP SILENCE

There comes a point at which group silence takes on a non-productive quality, considered in the context of group learning. This is not to say that it is easy to determine at what point group silence is non-productive, and at what point it is pure 'digestion' (Powdermaker and Frank, 1953, p. 277). Anyone who has had the opportunity to chair a meeting, teach a lesson, or generate a discussion remembers how he began to get extremely uncomfortable at the particular point when silence seemed to overextend its 'natural', and rather subjective, limit. It is at this particular point that one becomes aware of the dysfunctional quality of group silence. Within the group there are causative factors for all silences, whether group or individual. It is possible, in most cases, to point an accusative finger at certain group elements and constitutional aspects which may generate these non-productive or disruptive group silences.

(a) *Particular aspects of group development*. There are three distinct group situations which can be used to illustrate the causative factors generating dysfunctional group silence. These are situations where the group exists under the strain of (i) stifling control, or of (ii) power rivalries and competition for status, or (iii) the absence of trust and member acceptance.

In a group situation where there is a usurping of control by one member, or by one subgroup or faction, the resulting member feelings of lack of influence, personal inferiority, non-productiveness, and consequentially decreased task motivation, generate long periods of debilitating group and member silence. Additionally, if the members sense a competitive rivalry for attention, or a competition for within-group status, this can give rise to periods of long non-productive silences since members mostly desire to remain somewhat uninvolved in these internal squabbles.

In the final case the group operates in a situation where there is an absence of interpersonal trust, or of mutual acceptance. Silences will be frequent, and dysfunctional in this event. Therapeutic groups, sensitivity and encounter groups, point to the third non-productive aspect of group development as one of the most difficult early periods of group process. The generation of trust, cohesion and personal commitment to the group are considered, in a therapeutic milieu, to be absolutely essential for member learning and conse-quential attitudinal and behavioural change. Indeed, often the various manuals for group trainers tend to promote the development of feelings of acceptance and trust as one of the primary objectives for the members coming together.

The two previous strains of stifling control and power rivalries are more frequent perhaps in business, organisational, and less therapeutically oriented small learning groups. The destructive potential of such group processes, however, are not less than in those situations where intermember trust is absent.

(b) *Factors associated with group task.* The nature of the authority-assigned task can generate periods of destructive silence in the group, especially, if the task is difficult and oriented around some form of personal learning. In such a case, various defensive reactions appear; silence is one of the most effective of these defensive dis-guises. The task may be perceived as 'too difficult'; members of the group will then react with a silence reflecting *task scepticism*. There are also elements of silence which are produced by personal annoy-ance, and discouragement, with the trainer. This type of silence is also a form of task resistance.

THE DYSFUNCTIONAL EFFECTS OF 'BOGEYMEN'

Each small group develops an internal set of regulatory norms. Within the set of norms which become established are implicit understandings about what can, and cannot, come up for discussion. We are not talking here about the manifest, 'cards on the table' ground-rules, but of the secret, unexpressed agreements which are tacit and made without any public group pronouncement. While the group may take the authority-designed task as the 'occupation'

(Foulkes, 1964, p. 110) there is a covert or 'hidden agenda' which governs the extent to which the group task can be successfully approached. Suppose, for example, that one of the learning objectives of the group has been described as 'understanding more about oneself and others through group involvement, active participation, and honest feedback'. In such a situation, which is not at all rare in human relations groups, the implicit agreements which are quietly established become rather important. It is indeed crucial, in assessing process and outcome, to consider the understandings which have been surreptitiously reached, about what should *not* be talked about. It is these particular unmentionables we call *bogeymen*. Bogeymen are the hidden themes and issues which group members prefer not to become embroiled in. Examples of such bogeymen might be (i) spontaneous interpersonal reactions to other group members, (ii) personal life history and difficulties, (iii) religious or moral values and (iv) sexuality.

When the group is provided with learning objectives which tend to resurrect such 'bogeymen', it is the learning objectives which will very likely fall by the wayside. For example, we have, on a number of occasions, provided a small learning group experience built around the concept that individual behaviour is governed by unconscious forces over which the person involved has little or no control. Such a concept was commonly in opposition to the underlying value-system of some group members. Their reaction to such an idea, within the group, was to avoid acceptance or even *discussion*, of any analytic interpretation which even remotely smelled of the unconscious. Indeed, when our assessments of individual learnings were completed it was realised that those who had reacted with such animosity to this concept of unconscious forces showed a *negative* increment in their understandings of group dynamics—they scored even less than at the beginning of the experience. In other words they had 'unlearned'. We suspect that we had come too close to one of their cherished 'bogeymen' and a counter suggestibility, or reaction–formation, was generated to deal, rather defensively, with this unacceptable theme. The learning objectives were seriously undermined, not to say sabotaged, as a result. The group behaves in such a way that it is clear that there are certain taboo topics and concerns. The objectives of group learning can be affected if members are forced to confront such 'bogeymen'. An undeclared consensus is soon achieved by the learning group that they will 'go along with', or subvert, the declared and implicit objectives of the teacher and that the various threats he presents to the group will be countered by what in other days and other situations was described as 'mute through malice'. The trainer cannot adopt the same procedure as did the Courts of Law, and declare that 'mute through malice' should be recorded as a plea of not guilty, so that the business of determining guilt or innocence could proceed by due process.

BIBLIOGRAPHY

Abercrombie, M. L. J. *The Anatomy of Judgement*, London, Hutchinson, 1960.
Anderson, R. 'Learning in discussions: A résumé of the authoritarian democratic studies', *Harvard Educ. Rec.*, 1959, **29**, 200–15.
Arsenian, S., and Semrad, E. 'Individual and group manifestations', *International Journal of Group Psychotherapy*, 1967, **17**(1), 82–97.
Asch, S. E. *Social psychology*, Englewood Cliffs, Prentice-Hall, 1952.
Bales, R. F. *Interaction process analysis: A Method for the Study of Small Groups*, Cambridge, Mass., Addison-Wesley, 1950.
Bales, R. F. 'A set of categories for the analyses of small group interaction', *American Sociological Review*, 1950, **15**(2), 257–63.
Bales, R. F. 'The equilibrium problem in small groups', in T. Parson, R. F. Bales and E. A. Shils, *Working Papers on the Theory of Action*, Glencoe, Illinois, Free Press, 1953, 111–61.
Bales, R. F. 'Interaction process analysis', *Int. Enc. Soc. Sciences*, 1968 ed. vol. 7, 465–71.
Bales, R. F. *Personality and Interpersonal Behaviour*, New York, Holt, Rinehart and Winston, 1970.
Bales, R. F., and Slater, P. E. 'Role differentiation in small decision-making groups', in T. Parsons and R. F. Bales, *Family, socialisation and interaction process*. London, Routledge and Kegan Paul, 1956, 259–306.
Bales, R. F., and Strodtbeck, F. L. 'Phases in group problem solving', *J. Abnorm. soc. Psychol.*, 1951, **46**, 485–95.
Baller, R. E. *Relationship Between Change in Student Perceptions of Teachers and Sensitivity Training of Teachers*, unpublished doctoral dissertation United States International University, 1968.
Bandura, A. 'Social learning through imitation', in M. R. Jones (Ed.) *Nebraska Symposium on Motivation*, Lincoln, University of Nebraska Press, 1962, 211–69.
Bandura, A. 'Vicarious processes: No trial learning', in L. Berkowitz (Ed.) *Advances in Experimental Social Psychology*, New York, Academic Press, 1965, 1–55.
Bandura, A. *Principles of Behavior Modification*, New York, Holt, Rinehart and Winston, 1969.
Bandura, A., and Walters, R. H. *Social Learning and Personality Development*, New York, Holt, Rinehart and Winston, 1963.

Barnett, S. A. *Free Group Discussion* (personal communication).

Beach, L. P. 'Sociability and academic achievement in various types of learning situations', *J. of Educ. Psychol.*, 1960, **51**, 208–12.

Beier, E. G. *The silent language of psychotherapy*, Chicago, Aldine Publishing Co., 1966.

Belgard, M., Rosenshine, B., and Gage, N. L. *The teacher's ability to explain: Evidence on its generality and correlates,* Research Memorandum No. 10, Stanford Center for Research and Development in Teaching, School of Educ., Stanford, 1967.

Benne, K., and Sheats, P. 'Functional roles of group members', *J. Soc. Issues*, 1948, **4**, 41–9.

Bennis, W. G., and Shepard, H. A. 'A theory of group development', *Human Relations*, 1956, **9**, 415–37.

Berne, E. *The structure and dynamics of organisations and groups*, New York, Grove Press, 1963.

Berne, E. *Games People Play*, New York, Grove Press, 1964.

Bettleheim, B. 'Individual and Mass Behavior in Extreme Situations' in Eleanor G. Maccoby *et al.* (Eds.) *Readings in Social Psychology*, New York, 1958, 300–10.

Biddle, B., and Ellena, W. J. *Contemporary Research on Teacher Effectiveness*, New York, Holt, Rinehart and Winston, 1964.

Bion, W. R. *Experiences in groups*, New York, Basic Books, 1961.

Bloom, B. S. (Ed.) *Taxonomy of educational objectives: Handbook I: Cognitive domain*, New York, David McKay Co., 1956.

Bradford, L. P., Gibb, J. R., and Benne, K. D. (Eds.) *T-Group Theory and Laboratory Method*, New York, Wiley, 1964.

Buchanan, P. C. 'Evaluating the effectiveness of laboratory training in industry', in *Explorations in Human Relations Training and Research*, No. 1, Washington, D.C., National Training Laboratories, 1965.

Bunker, D. R. 'Individual applications of laboratory training', *Journal of Applied Behavioral Science*, 1965, **1**, 131–48.

Bunker, D. R., and Knowles, E. S. 'Comparison of behavioral changes resulting from human relations training laboratories of different lengths', *Journal of Applied Behavioral Science*, 1967, **3**, 505–23.

Burke, P. J. 'Authority relations and disruptive behavior in small discussion groups', *Sociometry*, 1966, **29**, 237–50.

Burke, P. J. 'The development of task and social emotional role differentiation', *Sociometry*, 1967, **30**, 379–92.

Burke, P. J. 'Scapegoating: an alternative to role differentiation', *Sociometry*, 1969, **32**, 159–69.

Burke, R. L., and Bennis, W. G. 'Changes in perception of self and others during human relations training', *Human Relations*, 1961, **14**, 165–82.

Cabianca, W. A. 'The effects of a T-group laboratory experience on self-esteem, needs and attitudes of student teachers', unpublished doctoral dissertation, Washington State University, 1967.

Campbell, J., and Dunnette, M. D. 'Effectiveness of T-group experiences in managerial training and development', *Psych. Bull.*, 1968, **70**, 73–104.

Carkhuff, R. R. *Helping and Human Relations*, Vols. I & II, New York, Holt, Rinehart and Winston, 1969.

Carkhuff, R. R., and Berenson, B. G. *Beyond Counselling and Therapy,* New York, Holt, Rinehart and Winston, 1967.

Carter, L. 'Recording and evaluating the performance of individuals as members of small groups', *Personal Psychology*, 1954, **7**, 471–84.

Cecere, G. J. 'Change in certain personality variables of counsellor education candidates as a function of a T-group', unpublished doctoral dissertation, Rutgers State University, *Dissertation Abstracts Int.*, 1969, 1427–8.

Collins, B. E., and Guetzkow. *A Social Psychology of Group Processes for Decision-Making*, New York, Wiley, 1964.

Couch, A. S. 'Psychological determinants of interpersonal behavior', unpublished doctoral dissertation, Harvard University, Cambridge, Mass., 1960.

Couch, A. S., and Carter, L. S. 'A Factorial study of the rated behavior of group members', paper read at Eastern Psychological Association, March, 1952.

Cronbach, J., and Furby, L. 'How we should measure "change"—or should we'? *Psychological Bulletin*, 1970, **74**, 68–80.

Devereux, E. C., Jr. 'Parsons' sociological theory' in *The Social Theories of Talcott Parsons*, Max Black (Ed.) Englewood Cliffs, Prentice-Hall, 1961.

Dollard, J., and Miller, N. E. *Personality and Psychotherapy*, New York, McGraw-Hill, 1950.

Dunphy, D. C. *Social change in self-analytic groups*, unpublished doctoral thesis, Department of Social Relations, Harvard University, 1964.

Dunphy, D., 'Phases, roles and myths in self-analytic groups', *Journal of Applied Behavioral Science*, 1968, **4**(2), 195–223.

Egan, G. *Encounter: Group processes for interpersonal growth*, Belmont, California, Brooks-Cole, 1970.

Eglash, A. 'Group discussion method of teaching psychology', *J. Educ. Psychol.*, 1954, **45**, 257–67.

Fikso, A. 'Vicarious vs. participant group psychotherapy of underachievers', unpublished doctoral dissertation, Illinois Institute of Technology, 1970 (see Dissertation Abstracts Int., 1970 Vol. 3162-B, 912).

Flanders, N., *Analysing Teaching Behavior*, Reading, Mass., Addison-Wesley, 1970.

Fortune, J. C. *The generality of presenting behaviors in teaching preschool children*, Memphis, Tennessee, Memphis State University, 1966.

Fortune, J. C., Gage, N. L., and Shutes, R. E. 'The generality of the ability to explain', paper presented at the meeting of the American Educ. Res. Assoc., Chicago, February 1966.

Foulds, M. L., Wright, J. C., and Guinan, J. F. 'Marathon group: A six-months follow-up', *Journal of College Student Personnel*, 1970, **11**, 426–31.

Foulkes, S. H. *Therapeutic Group Analysis*, New York, International Universities Press, 1965.

Foulkes, S. H., and Anthony, E. J. *Group Psychotherapy: The Psychoanalytic Approach*, Baltimore, Penguin Books, 1957.

Freud, S. *Group Psychology and the Analysis of the Ego*, London, Hogarth Press, 1921.

Friedman, L. J., and Zinberg, N. E. 'Application of group methods in college teaching', *International Journal of Group Psychotherapy*, 1964, **14**, 344–59.

Gage, N. L. (Ed.) *Handbook of Research on Teaching*, Chicago, Rand McNally, 1963.

Gibb, J. R. 'The effects of human relations training', in A. E. Bergin and S. L. Garfield, *Handbook of Psychotherapy and Behavior Change*, New York, Wiley, 1971.

Goldiamond, J. 'Justified and unjustified alarms over behavior control' in Ohmer Milton (Ed.) *Behavior Disorders*, Philadelphia, Kippincott, 1965a, 237–61.

Goldiamond, J. 'Self-control procedures in personal behavior problems', *Psych. Reports*, 1965b, **17**, 851–69.

Goldiamond, J. 'Stuttering and fluency in manipulatable operant response classes' in Ullman and Krasner (Eds.), *Research in Behavior Modification*, New York, Holt, Rinehart and Winston, 1965c, 106–56.

Goldstein, A. P., Haller, K., and Sechrest, L. B. *Psychotherapy and the Psychology of Behavior Change*, New York, Wiley, 1966.

Golembiewski, R. T. *Sensitivity Training and the Laboratory Approach*, Ithaca, Illinois, F. E. Peacock Publ. Inc., 1970.

Gordon, W. J. J. *Synectics*, New York, Harper and Row, 1961.

Haiman, F. S. 'Effects of Training in group processes on open-mindedness', *Journal of Communication*, 1963, **13**, 236–41.

Hall, J., and Williams, M. S. 'Group dynamics training and improved decision-making', *Journal of Applied Behavioral Science*, 1970, **1**, 39–67.

Hampden-Turner, C. M. 'An existential "learning theory" and the integration of T-group research', *Journal of Applied Behav. Sci.*, 1966, **4**(2).

Hare, A. P. *Social interaction: An analysis of behavior in small groups*, New York, 1900.

Harris, C. W. (Ed.) *Problems in Measuring Change*, Madison, University of Wisconsin Press, 1963.

Harris, R. C. 'Group counseling with teachers: An effective in-service education technique', unpublished manuscript, York University, 1970.

Harrison, R., and Lubin, B. 'Personal style, group composition and learning', *Journal of Applied Behavioral Science*, 1965, 294–301.

Heinicke, C., and Bales, R. F. 'Developmental trends in the structure of small groups', *Sociometry*, 1953, 239–53.

Heslin, R., and Dunphy, D. 'Three dimensions of member satisfaction in small groups', *Human Relations*, 1964, 99–112.

Hiller, J. E., Fisher, G., and Kaess, W. *A computer investigation of teacher structuring behavior*, paper presented at the meeting of the American Educ. Res. Assoc., Chicago, February 1962.

Hough, J. B., and Amidon, E. J. 'Behavioral change in pre-service teacher preparation: An experimental study', Temple University, Philadelphia, cited in E. J. Amidon and J. B. Hough (Eds.) *Interaction Analysis: Theory, Research and Application*, Reading, Addison-Wesley, 1967.

Hough, J. B., and Ober, R. 'The effect of training in interaction analysis on the verbal teaching behavior of pre-service teachers', in Amidon, E. J., and Hough, J. B. (Eds.) *Interaction Analysis: Theory, Research and Application*, Reading, Mass., Addison-Wesley, 1967.

House, R. J. 'T-group education and leadership effectiveness: A review of the empirical literature and a critical evaluation', *Personnel Psychology*, 1967, **20**, 1–32.

Jordan, D. L. 'A comparison of the effects of didactic and experimental training on accurate empathy, non-possessive warmth, and genuineness', unpublished doctoral dissertation, University of Colorado, *Dissertation Abstracts*, 3487–B, 1969.

Kadis, A. L., Krasner, J. *et al. A Practicum of Group Pyschotherapy*, New York, Harper and Row, 1963.

Kanfer, F. H., and Phillips, J. S. *Learning Foundations of Behavior Therapy*, New York, Wiley, 1970.

Kaplan, S., and Roman, M. 'Phases of development in an adult therapy group', *International Journal of Group Psychotherapy*, 1963, **13**, 10–26.

Kemp, C. G. 'Comparison of educational groups, group counseling, and group therapy', in C. G. Kemp (Ed.) *Perspectives on the Group Process*, Boston, Houghton Miflin, 1970.

Koenig, K. E., and McKeachie, W. J. 'Personality and independent study', *J. of Educ. Psychol.*, 1959, **50**, 132–4.

Krafft, L. J. 'The influence of human relations laboratory training upon the perceived behavioral changes of secondary school seminar instructors', unpublished doctoral dissertation, Michigan State University, 1967.

Krumboltz, J. S. *Learning and the Educational Process*, Chicago, Rand McNally, 1965.

Lazarus, A. A. 'Group Therapy of Phobic Disorders by Systematic Desensitization', *J. Abn. Soc. Psych.*, 1961, **63**, 504–10.

Leary, T. *Interpersonal Diagnosis of Personality*, New York, The Ronald Press, 1957.

Lieberman, S. 'The effects of changes in roles on the attitudes of role occupants', in H. Proshansky and B. Seidenburg (Eds.) *Basic studies in social psychology*, New York, Holt, Rinehart and Winston, 1966.

Mackie, R., and Wood, J. 'Observations on two sides of a one-way screen', *The International Journal of Group Psychotherapy*, 1968, **18**, 177–85.

McCallough, C., and von Atton, E. L. *Experimental evaluation of teaching programs utilising a block of independent work*, Ohio, Oberlin College, 1966.

McKeachie, W. J. 'Research on teaching at the college and university level', in N. L. Gage (Ed.) *Handbook of research on teaching*, Chicago, Rand McNally, 1963.

McLeish, J. *The Lecture Method*, Cambridge Monograph Series, No. 1, Cambridge Institute of Education, 1968.

McLeish, J. *Students' attitudes and college environments*, Cambridge, Heffer, 1970.

McLeish, J. 'Characteristics of the Edmonton faculty of education intake 1970', *Report to the Dean of Education*, unpublished manuscript, University of Alberta, 1971.

McLeish, J., Knight, M., and Davis, T. 'An experiment in sensitivity training', *Paedogogica Europae*, 1969, **5**, 80–98.

McLeish, J., and Park, J. 'Outcomes of direct, and vicarious training in learning groups: personality changes', *Brit. J. of Soc. and Clin. Psych.*, in press.

Mann, R. D. 'The development of member-trainer relationship in self-analytic groups', *Human Relations*, 1966, **19**, 85–115.

Mann, R. D., with Gibbárd, G. S., and Hartman, J. J. *Interpersonal Styles and Group Development*, New York, Wiley, 1967.

Matchett, J. (Personal communication.)

Matheson, W. E. 'The structure of learning groups', unpublished doctoral dissertation, University of Alberta, 1971.

Miles, M. B. 'Human relations training: Processes and outcomes', *Journal of Counseling Psychology*, 1960, **7**, 301–6.

Miles, M. B., 'Human relations training: Current status', in I. R. Weschler and E. J. Schein (Eds.) *Issues in Training*, Washington, National Training Laboratories, 1962, 3/13.

Miller, E. J., and Rice, A. K. *Systems of Organization*, London, Tavistock Publications, 1967.

Millon, T. *Modern Psychopathology*, Philadelphia, W. B. Saunders, 1969.

Mills, T. M. *Group Transformation, An Analysis of a Learning Group*, Englewood Cliffs, Prentice-Hall, 1964.

Mishler, E. G., and Waxler, N. E. *Interaction in Families: An Experimental Study of Family Processes and Schizophrenia*. New York, Wiley, 1968.

Moreno, J. L. *Who Shall Survive?* Washington, D.C., Nervous and Mental Disease Publ. Co., 1934.

Moreno, J. L. 'The validity of psychodrama', *Group Psychotherapy*, 1968, **21**, 3.

Morsh, J. E., and Wilder, E. W. 'Identifying the effective instructor: a review of quantitative studies, 1900–52', *Research Bulletin,* October 1954, Air Force Personnel and Training Center, San Antonia, Texas (cited by Flanders, 1970).

Moscow, D. 'The influence of interpersonal variables on the transfer of learning from the T-Group to the job situation', *Proceedings of the International Congress of Applied Psychology,* Amsterdam, 1968.

Nadler, E. B., and Fink, S. L. 'Impact of laboratory training on sociopolitical ideology', *Journal of Applied Behavioral Science,* 1970, **6**, 79.

National Training Laboratories. 'Theory and method in laboratory training', in I. R. Weschler, E. J. Schein, *Issues in Training,* Washington, National Training Laboratories, 1962, 14–32.

Nekrasova, K. A. 'On the activation of thinking in students in the process of teaching by lecture' (Russian), *Vop. Psikologii,* 1960, **6**, 166–71.

Olch, D., and Snow, D. L. 'Personality characteristics of sensitivity group volunteers', *Personnel and Guidance Journal,* 1970, **48**, 848–50.

Paley, D. T. 'The effects of human relations training on empathic accuracy and dogmatism', unpublished master's thesis, University of Alberta, 1969.

Park, J. 'The effects of direct and vicarious experience in learning groups', unpublished Doctoral dissertation, University of Alberta, 1971.

Parsons, I. *The Social System,* Glencoe, Illinois, Free Press, 1951.

Parsons, I., and Smelser, N. *Economy and Society,* London, 1956.

Parsons, T. F., Ketcham, W. A., and Beach, L. R. 'Effects of varying degrees of student interaction and student-teacher contact in college courses', paper read at American Sociol. Soc., Seattle, Washington, August, 1958.

Patterson, C. H. *An Introduction to Counseling in the Schools,* New York, Harper and Row, 1971.

Philp, H., and Dunphy, D. 'Developmental trends in the structure of small groups', *Sociometry,* 1953, **16**(1), 7–38.

Powdermaker, J. L., and Frank, J. D. *Group Psychotherapy,* Cambridge, Mass., Harvard University Press, 1963.

Proshansky, H., and Seidenburg, B. (Eds.) *Basic Studies in social psychology,* New York, Holt, Rinehart and Winston, 1966.

Psathas, G. 'Interaction process analysis of two psychotherapy groups', *International Journal of Group Psychotherapy,* 1960, **10**, 430–45.

Ratner, R. 'The use of interaction process analysis in non-directive group psychotherapy', unpublished Ph.D. thesis, Yale University, 1968.

Redding, A. J. 'The relationship between training in verbal interaction analysis and selected counseling process variables', unpublished doctoral dissertation, University of North Dakota, D.A., 3840–A, 1969.

Reddy, W. B. 'The effects of immediate and delayed feedback on the learning of empathy', unpublished doctoral dissertation, University of Cincinnati, D.A., 1849–B, 1968.

Redl, F. 'Group emotion and leadership', *Psychiatry,* 1942, **5**, 573–96.

Rogers, C. R., 'The process of the basic encounter groups', in J. F. T. Bugenthal (Ed.) *Challenges of Humanistic Psychology.* New York, McGraw-Hill, 1967, 261–76.

Rokeach, M. *The Open and Closed Mind: Investigations into the Nature of Belief Systems and Personality Systems,* New York, Basic Books, 1960.

Rosancranz, H. A., and Biddle, B. 'The role approach to teacher competence', in Biddle, B., and Ellena, W. J. (Eds.) *Contemporary Research on Teacher Effectiveness,* New York, Holt, Rinehart and Winston, 1964.

Rosenshine, B. 'To explain: a review of research', *Ed. Leadership,* 1968, 303–9.

Rosenshine, B. 'Objectively measured behaviorial predictors of effectiveness in explaining', a paper presented at the meeting of the American Res. Assoc., Chicago, February 1968.

Rotter, J. B. *Social Learning and Clinical Psychology*, New York, Prentice-Hall, 1954.

Rubin, I. 'The reduction of prejudice through laboratory training', *Journal of Applied Behavioral Science*, 1967, **3**, 29.

Sawatzky, D. D. 'The relationship between open-mindedness and accurate interpersonal perception', unpublished master's thesis, University of Alberta, 1968.

Schein, E. H., and Bennis, W. G. *Personal and organizational change through group methods: the laboratory approach*, New York, Wiley, 1965.

Schmuck, R. A. 'Helping teachers improve classroom group processes', *Journal of Applied Behavioral Science*, 1968, **4**, 401–21.

Schutz, R. *The Interpersonal Underword*, Palo Alto California, Science and Behavior Books, 1966.

Skinner, B. F. *The Behavior of Organisms*, New York, Appleton-Century-Crofts, 1938.

Skinner, B. F. *Science and Human Behavior*, New York, Macmillan, 1953.

Skinner, B. F. *Verbal Behavior*, New York, Appleton-Century-Crofts, 1957

Skinner, B. F. 'Why we need Teaching machines', *Harvard Educ. Review*, 1961, **31**, 377–98.

Skinner, B. F. *The Technology of Teaching*, New York, Appleton-Century-Crofts, 1968.

Slater, P. E. 'Role differentiation in small groups', *American Sociological Review*, 1955, **20**.

Smith, P. B. 'The effects of T-group training', in Whitaker, G. (Ed.) *T-Group Training, Group Dynamics in Management Education*, London, Blackwell, 1965.

Smith, P. B., and Pollack, H. B. 'The participant's learning style as a correlate of T-group learning', *Proceedings of the International Congress of Applied Psychology*, Amsterdam, 1968.

Stock, D. 'A survey of research on T-groups', in L. P. Bradford, J. R. Gibb and K. D. Benne (Eds.) *T-Group Theory and Laboratory Method*, New York, Wiley, 1964, 395–441.

Stock, D., and Thelen, H. *Emotional Dynamics and Group Culture*, Washington, National Training Laboratory, 1958.

Stone, P. J., Dunphy, D. C., Smith, M. S., and Ogilvie, D. M. *The General Inquirer: A Computer Approach to Content Analysis*, Cambridge, Mass., M.I.T. Press, 1966.

Tistaert, G. 'A classroom experiment on lecture and discussions methods', *Paedagogica Europa*, 1965, **1**, 125–37.

Ullman, L. P., and Krasner, L. *A Psychological Approach to Abnormal Behavior*, Englewood Cliffs, Prentice-Hall, 1969.

Valiquet, M. J. 'Individual change in management development program', *J. of Appl. Behav. Science*, 1968, **4**, 313–25.

Verba, S., *Small Groups and Political Behavior*, Princeton, Princeton University Press, 1961, 144–50.

Waller, N. E., and Travers, R. M. W. 'Analysis and investigation of teaching methods', in N. L. Gage (Ed.) *Handbook of Research on Teaching*, Chicago, 1963.

Watson, C. 'What do we know about learning?', *Nat. Educ. Assoc. J.*, 1963, **52**, 20–2.

Weitman, M., and Gruber, H. E. *Experiments in self-directed study: effects on immediate achievement, permanence of achievement and educational values*, University of Colorado, Boulder, 1960, 7.

Whitaker, D. S., and Lieberman, M. A. *Psychotherapy through the Group Process*, New York, Atherton Press, 1964.

Wolfer, J. A. 'Changes in dogmatism scores of high and low dogmatics as a function of instruction', *Psychological Reports*, 1967, **20**, 947–50.

Wolpe, J. *Psychotherapy by Reciprocal Inhibition*, Stanford, Stanford University Press, 1958.

Zimet, C. N., and Fine, H. J. 'Personality changes with a group therapeutic experience in a human relations seminar', *Journal of Abnormal and Social Psychology*, 1955, **51**, 68–73.

NAME INDEX

Abercrombie, M. L. J., 90
Anderson, R., 172, 173
Anthony, E. J., 29
Asch, S. E., 180
Attlee, C., 54

Bales, R. F., 16, 18, 19, 34, 48, 50,
  56–67, 77, 116–19, 129, 135,
  152–5, 168, 170, 183, 192–3
Bandura, A., 45, 180
Barnett, S. A., 90
Beach, L. R., 175
Benne, K., 116–17
Bennis, W. G., 20, 31–4, 39, 67, 131
Berger, M. M., 81, 202
Berne, E., 128, 129
Bettleheim, B., 180
Biddle, B., 171
Bion, W. R., 16–19, 29–34, 38, 74,
  79, 93, 126–8
Brunel, M. I., 99
Burke, P. J., 115

Campbell, J., 22
Carkhuff, R., 19, 191, 198–9
Carter, L. S., 116–17
Collins, B. E., 111
Couch, A. S., 116–17, 129

Darwin, C., 102
de Gaulle, C., 55
Dodson, 94, 199
Dollard, J., 44
Dunnette, M. D., 22
Dunphy, D., 31, 34, 65–6, 77, 116, 129

Eberlein, E. L., 66
Egan, G., 23
Eglash, A., 172
Einstein, A., 102
Ellena, W. J., 171
Eyestone, J., 175

Flanders, N., 19, 169
Foulkes, S. H., 29, 80, 83, 127–8, 207
Frank, J. D., 128, 205
Freud, S., 16, 18, 28–32, 34, 90,
  95–6, 129, 200–1

Gage, N. L., 169
Gibb, J. R., 181–2
Goldiamond, I., 45
Goldstein, A. P., 46
Golembiewski, R. I., 22
Gordon, W. W., 95–7, 99
Gruber, H. E., 175
Guetzkow, H., 111

Hale, S. G., 176
Hampden-Turner, C. M., 25
Hare, A. P., 172
Heinicke, C., 65
Heller, K., 46

Kadis, A. L., 79, 195, 201
Kaplan, S., 34
Kaufer, F. H., 44, 46
Koenig, K. E., 174
Köhler, W., 98
Körner, C. G., 96, 98

SUBJECT INDEX

The italicised page numbers refer to the definition of the term
* Starred items are defined in the Glossary